NEW DIRECTIONS IN HUMAN RIGHTS

NEW DIRECTIONS IN HUMAN RIGHTS

ELLEN L. LUTZ,
HURST HANNUM, and
KATHRYN J. BURKE, *Editors*

upp

UNIVERSITY OF PENNSYLVANIA PRESS *Philadelphia*

Printed in the United States of America

Library of Congress Cataloging-in-Publication Data

New directions in human rights / Ellen L. Lutz, Hurst Hannum, and
Kathryn J. Burke, editors.
p. cm.
Includes bibliographies and index.
ISBN 0-8122-8128-4
1. Human rights. 2. Newman, Frank C. I. Lutz, Ellen L.
II. Hannum, Hurst. III. Burke, Kathryn.
K3240.6.N49 1989
341.4'81—dc19 88-29984
CIP

CONTENTS

DEDICATION

This book is dedicated to Frank C. Newman. Frank's record as a teacher, judge, and scholar would be sufficient to merit a series of articles in his honor, but the present book is not dedicated to those achievements. It is motivated instead by the legal activism and critical approach to international law and procedures which Frank inspires in his students and colleagues. Indeed, the theme of the book—new directions in human rights—reflects Frank's constant concern to use existing legal procedures more effectively and to create innovative new mechanisms for securing human rights domestically and internationally. Each of the contributors to this book has been a student or colleague of Frank's and has been strongly influenced by his work.

At first primarily known as a professor of administrative law, and later as Dean (1961–1966) of the University of California, Berkeley's Boalt Hall School of Law, Frank Newman became seriously involved with international human rights around the time of the military coup in Greece in 1967. He was not interested in examining the theoretical development of international law in this field, but in finding ways, through the United Nations and other international bodies, to bring pressure to bear on human rights violators around the world.

The active path pursued by Frank and others corresponded to a new era of implementation of the international norms developed in the twenty years following adoption of the Universal Declaration of Human Rights in 1948. For example, the two international covenants on human rights were adopted in 1966 and entered into force a decade later; the American Convention on Human Rights was adopted in 1968. Perhaps more importantly to Frank's work, the UN Commission on Human Rights took the first tentative steps toward a more meaningful role in the promotion and protection of human rights in 1967, when Economic and Social Council (ECOSOC) Resolution 1235 enabled the Commission to consider "the violation of human rights and fundamental freedoms in any part of the world." Four years later, the Commission and its Sub-Commission on Prevention of Discrimination and Protection of Minorities were authorized by ECOSOC Resolution 1503 to consider communications from individuals and nongovernmental organizations (NGOs) concerning "situations which appear to reveal a consistent pattern of gross violations of human rights."

The reaction of UN bodies to the 1973 overthrow of the Allende government in Chile set further precedents, enabling NGOs to make increasing use of UN procedures to raise public allegations of human rights violations. Despite criticisms that UN actions and resolutions have no teeth, the energy expended by governments in diplomatic maneuvering designed to avoid negative international action suggests that well-founded public accusations by NGOs and formal condemnation by the international community do have an impact.

In the midst of these developments were Frank Newman and his "Berkeley Mafia" of current and former students. Arriving at sessions of the UN Commission and Sub-Commission in New York and Geneva, this ever-changing group of activist lawyer-lobbyists did much to encourage, if not inspire, progressive action by both bodies and by sympathetic members of the UN Secretariat. Many of the contributors to the present volume joined Frank in Geneva on one or more occasions; two, Theo van Boven and Antonio Cassese, were Sub-Commission members during the 1970s, and the former became Director of the UN's Division of Human Rights in 1977.

On the domestic front, in 1973 the U.S. House of Representatives' Subcommittee on International Organizations and Movements (later renamed the Subcommittee on Human Rights and International Organizations) initiated a series of hearings on human rights and U.S. foreign policy. Frank Newman worked closely with the subcommittee chair and staff, contributing to congressional initiatives which by the late 1970s firmly entrenched human rights concerns as an important component in the formation of U.S. foreign policy. In 1979 Frank co-authored with Professor Richard B. Lillich what became the standard law school text on international human rights, *International Human Rights: Problems of Law and Policy.*

In 1977 Frank Newman was appointed to the Supreme Court of California. During his five years of active service as an Associate Justice, Frank frequently sought guidance from international law concepts when addressing issues of domestic human rights. In opinions on such issues as the rights of the mentally disabled, privacy, and interstate extradition, he showed how international human rights law could add to domestic civil rights protection.

Since returning to teaching in 1983 Frank has continued to concentrate on the interconnection of civil rights and human rights, teaching an annual seminar on that topic. Another major focus of his work in recent years is the long neglected subject of human rights and armed conflict. At the UN Commission on Human Rights and its Sub-Commission, and through his involvement with nationally recognized peace organizations, Frank has worked to draw public attention to the fact that the worst violations of human rights occur during armed conflict, and that the ultimate human rights violation—the destruction of all life—could occur if the threat of nuclear war is not eliminated.

Frank Newman brings not only critical thought and substance to the field of international human rights law, but an enthusiasm and rich appreciation of life that has affected all who know him. From Alpine ski slopes to his Orinda, California, patio, while sipping Calistoga water or one last kirsch aux Armures, Frank's humanity and humor are as much a part of working with him as is his inquiring and innovative intellect.

It is people who matter, and Frank Newman has never lost sight of the ultimate beneficiaries of UN resolutions or congressional hearings. He inspires all those who have worked closely with him, and that inspiration continues to prod those who have contributed to this book. With the exception of the article by Theo van Boven subtitled "the Frank Newman file," the following pages do not look back at Frank Newman or his human rights accomplishments. Consistent with his spirit and example, our tribute to Frank focuses on what we can do now and in the future to realize human rights as "a common standard of achievement for all peoples and all nations."

INTRODUCTION

KATHRYN J. BURKE

A revolution in human rights occurred forty years ago, when the United Nations adopted the initial component of the International Bill of Human Rights,[1] establishing for the first time a coherent body of universal legal standards for the respect of human rights. Two or three decades ago, perhaps only a handful of people called themselves international human rights lawyers or scholars. Today they are many, from all parts of the world. Students now can learn international human rights law in specialized international institutions and in numerous national law schools. International human rights lawyers work in a variety of ways: lobbying in legislatures and international organizations, arguing before domestic and international courts, traveling abroad on fact-finding missions, and even demonstrating in the streets when necessary. They labor in the context of sensitive political conflicts and the urgent needs of individuals they are trying to help.

The outcomes of human rights lawyering are often uncertain and painfully delayed; yet it is indisputable that through international human rights law and procedures lives have been saved and governments have been shamed into abating oppression.

In this book, some of the new human rights lawyers have paused in their work to consider the future of international human rights law and procedures. The result is a collection of thoughtful, practical, and forward-looking pieces on four topics: emerging international human rights norms and procedures; human rights in armed conflict; domestic application of international human rights norms; and redressing past abuses of human rights.

Emerging Norms and Procedures

Some serious human rights problems are only now beginning to receive focused attention from contemporary international law. Minority group rights are an example, according to Hurst Hannum's article. International human rights law today recognizes only minimal minority rights, and yet many gross violations cause, or arise out of, minority groups' rejection of majority political cultures. Hannum urges international lawyers to think creatively about appropriate new legal concepts to help resolve the conflict between minority demands and state power.

Sandra Coliver looks at the rights of women, and asks how effective the United Nations has been in helping women whose human rights have been violated. While noting certain encouraging developments that may strengthen the women's procedures, she also suggests several additional measures, drawn from the experiences of comparable Geneva-based human rights machineries, that are likely to be necessary if the women's procedures are to significantly assist in exposing and halting violations.

The need for institutions to enforce human rights is also the focus of Jon Van Dyke's article on human rights in Asia and the Pacific. Unlike nearly every other region in the world the Asian and Pacific region has not formed an organization devoted to enforcing international human rights norms. Van Dyke offers some explanations for this fact, and he recounts how one subregion of the area nevertheless seems to be on the road to creating its own regional human rights treaty and organization.

Human Rights and Armed Conflict

One problem international human rights lawyers find increasingly troubling is how to protect human rights in times of armed conflict. In his article, David Weissbrodt compares the practices of the International Committee of the Red Cross (ICRC) with those of other human rights organizations. He urges the other organizations to make their efforts more effective in armed conflict situations by learning from the ICRC's extensive experience and by developing a more careful use of humanitarian law.

Antonio Cassese describes the case of Sabra and Shatila as an example of the failure to apply a careful analysis of international law to an armed conflict situation, and points to some lessons for the future. Both authors plead for human rights lawyers to use the full potential of international law to protect the lives and the futures of persons caught in the midst of armed struggles.

Implementing International Human Rights Norms in Domestic Forums

A theme running through many of the proposals in this book is that international human rights must be enforced, ultimately, at the local level. The authors provide some practical perspectives on an idea expressed by Eleanor Roosevelt, one of the drafters of the Universal Declaration of Human Rights:

> Where, after all do universal human rights begin? In small places, close to home—so close and so small that they cannot be seen on any maps of the world. . . . Unless these rights have meaning there, they have little meaning elsewhere.[2]

Two contributors to this book explore how internationally recognized human rights can be made effective close to home in courts and other forums for resolving disputes. In separate articles, Stephen Rosenbaum and Dinah Shelton look respectively at two areas, the rights of the poor, and the rights of political dissidents to protection from extradition. They both show that lawyers and judges in the U.S., as perhaps in most countries, are reluctant to invoke or rely on international human rights law because they are still unfamiliar with it. Nevertheless, the authors argue that the lives of many people could be improved if the norms of international human rights law were enforced in U.S. courts and administrative agencies.

Redressing Past Abuses of Human Rights

Most efforts of human rights lawyers have been aimed at preventing or halting rights violations. Looking forward, two contributors argue that it is necessary also to come to grips with the consequences of human rights violations for the individuals involved. Nigel Rodley addresses the issue in the context of some of the most serious human rights abuses: torture, disappearances, and extra-legal executions. He demonstrates that international law already contains in diffuse form the principle of state responsibility to punish and compensate for those violations, but that a clearer and more cohesive statement of that law is needed. Ellen L. Lutz proposes that a set of international guidelines be created to ensure that victims of human rights abuses are provided with reparation that is fair and humane.

These nine articles are followed by Theo van Boven's recollection of some of the pioneering efforts of noted human rights lawyer Frank C. Newman, to whom this volume is dedicated. Van Boven uses as examples three United Nations procedures where the effects of Newman's early thinking and prodding are still felt today. His account is a reminder that even though progress in enforcing human rights seems—and is—slow, it is only within the last two decades that it has been possible to discuss in concrete terms any implementing procedures. The story of Newman's persistent advocacy vividly shows the difference that can be made by one international human rights lawyer who thinks creatively and cares deeply about his cause.

Thus, the new international human rights lawyers are taking stock. They ask: How pertinent is international human rights law to the conflicts of today and tomorrow? How healthy are the enforcing institutions and procedures? And, most importantly, what new directions must be taken to ensure that people's human rights are truly being helped?

NOTES

1. The International Bill of Human Rights has four parts: The Universal Declaration of Human Rights; The International Covenant on Economic, Social and Cultural Rights; The International Covenant on Civil and Political Rights; and The Optional Protocol to the International Covenant on Civil and Political Rights.

2. *Quoted in* JOSEPH P. LASH, ELEANOR: THE YEARS ALONE 72 (New York: New American Library, 1972).

PART I

EMERGING INTERNATIONAL HUMAN RIGHTS NORMS AND PROCEDURES

1

The Limits of Sovereignty and Majority Rule: Minorities, Indigenous Peoples, and the Right to Autonomy

HURST HANNUM

If international law has been reluctant to recognize the rights of individuals against states, it has been even more wary of recognizing the rights of minorities or groups of people. The selective application of the principles of "self-determination" and minority rights in the period following World War I gave way to the principles of decolonization and individual rights in the post–United Nations period. Throughout the 1950s and 1960s, it was assumed that "nation-building" in newly independent states, assimilation, and enforcement of the human rights of equality and nondiscrimination would eliminate the need for special protection for groups.

A glance at the headlines of the past decade is enough to tell us that the assumption that majoritarian democracy and individual human rights would be sufficient conditions for the peaceful resolution of disputes was incorrect. Basques, Samis, Tamils, Sikhs, Eritreans, Kurds, Maoris, Miskitos, Corsicans, Quebecois, Karens, and scores of other ethnic, religious, or national groups have rejected absorption into the majority political culture. Few demand independence, but most seek a greater degree of group autonomy than would be allowed under traditional standards of minority rights in the areas of religious and linguistic freedom or local control over education.

This chapter will analyze (in a necessarily summary manner) the reemergence of such assertions of group rights in light of contemporary norms of state sovereignty, self-determination, and human rights. The goal will be to consider the international legal context in which political resolutions to disputes over sovereignty and self-determination should be sought, and the conclusion will suggest that more flexible legal doctrines may be needed in order to contribute to such resolutions.

Sovereignty, Statehood, and Nationalism

"Sovereignty" and the accompanying corollary of the equality of states has been termed "the basic constitutional doctrine of the law of nations."[1] It is the cornerstone of international rhetoric about state independence and freedom of action, and the most common response to initiatives which seek to limit a state's activities is that such initiatives constitute an impermissible limitation on that state's sovereignty.

While the international order has now moved to a stage where the sovereign independent state is much more the norm than the exception, it would be a mistake to conclude that there is little to learn from the international mosaic of the nineteenth century. While dependency was almost invariably imposed on, rather than freely chosen by, for example, protected or semisovereign states, the great variety of international entities recognized as having some degree of international personality in the nineteenth century in some respects mirrors the complex web of relationships among independent states, international organizations, and private international actors that characterizes the twentieth century.

International law has long imposed limitations on the permissible scope of the internal and external actions of independent sovereign states.[2] The nature of territorial sovereignty necessarily implies the fundamental limitation that no state has the right to impose its will on the territory of another, except in certain narrow circumstances such as the protection of a state's own nationals. Since 1945, the prohibition against the threat or use of armed force would seem to have emerged as a norm of customary international law (if not *jus cogens*), although debates as to the precise meaning of article 2(4) of the UN Charter continue.

State sovereignty is limited also by general and customary international law relating to the right of innocent passage and freedom of navigation on the high seas and through international waterways. While it may be premature to speak of an international customary "law of the commons," such law seems to be in the process of development with respect to the peaceful uses of outer space and economic exploitation of ocean resources.

Even within their own territories, states have long been limited by international law in a manner that makes any argument in favor of "absolute" sovereignty difficult to maintain. Some of the limitations are related to the protection of other (equal) states, such as when acts wholly within one state cause damage to another state. The equitable use of water resources upon which other states depend is also mandated by international law.

State responsibility for injuries to aliens in general, and the principle of diplomatic immunity in particular, constitute longstanding restrictions on the unfettered use of state power even within a state's own territory.[3] At least some fundamental human rights norms have achieved the status of customary international law or *jus cogens,* including the prohibition against genocide[4] and systematic racial discrimination.[5]

Even more significant today than those limits on state sovereignty which might be imposed by general or customary international law are the self-imposed or *de facto* restrictions which have resulted from the complex economic and political international order of the twentieth century.

A state may by treaty limit its own sphere of action by delegating certain powers to other states, but this does not affect its status as a sovereign state unless the delegation is essentially a cover for foreign control. Agreements for military protection or the stationing of foreign troops in one's territory are common; even reservation of a right of intervention by another state does not necessarily render a state non-sovereign, as demonstrated by the cases of Cyprus and the Federal Republic of Germany (the latter until 1968).

Of particular significance is the growth of multilateral economic and political treaties which seek to regulate a far greater range of issues among states than did earlier bilateral trade or diplomatic treaties, or even earlier political-military alliances. While neither the United Nations nor the European Community has become a world or regional government, their impact on the conduct of international relations has no doubt been greater than that of any preceding international organization. While these and similar bodies emphasize the sovereign equality of the states on which they are founded, there can be little doubt that, while legal equality has largely been maintained, the actual freedom of action of individual members has been reduced.

The recognition for certain purposes of "national liberation movements" as international actors also might be thought to blur the edges of sovereignty, although such recognition represents a political rather than a legal statement. One should also note the fact than many nonstate entities, such as Hong Kong and Greenland, may be admitted to full or associate membership in various international governmental organizations.

Thus far we have discussed only the legal aspects of the sovereign equality of states, yet it is—and always has been—obvious that legal equality of states within the international community is not matched by political, military, or economic equality. The emergence of many former colonies as "micro-states" has made the disparities among states even more evident.

"Nationalism" as a term did not appear in the *Oxford English Dictionary* until 1844, and it is commonly thought of as a phenomenon that did not exist or was not recognized until the nineteenth century. If development of the notion of sovereignty was in part a reaction against the personalization of all temporal and religious authority in a single ruler, the growth of nationalism has been largely a reaction against an all-powerful sovereign state which was unresponsive to the needs of the many communities of which it was composed.[6]

European "nationalism" generally connoted efforts by a linguistic, religious, and/or ethnic group to gain political power in order to respond to the needs of its "nation." Particularly since 1945, however, nationalism has come to be equated with anticolonial movements that may or may not correspond to the paradigm of a "national" community as that concept was developed in the nineteenth century. Common use of the term "nation-state" by lawyers and others serves only to confuse the issue further.

There are few, if any, nation-states in the world whose population reflects an entirely homogeneous ethno-cultural community to the exclusion of all others, and it is perhaps no coincidence that the few that might claim such status are often islands. Recognition that the classic nation-state does not exist in reality is essential to analyzing the appropriate limits on its actions, which necessarily have an impact on both majority and minority populations.

Nevertheless, one cannot deny the impact of the concept of the nation-state on the legal and political order of the world, and to dismiss either component of this increasingly archaic political concept is to ignore reality.

As an artificial legal creation, the state continues to serve a purpose as the primary interlocutor among those who possess organized military power in the world. Other actors, however—whether international organizations, transnational corporations, or individuals asserting rights against all of the above—are also making their influence felt at the international level.

The "intrusion" of such actors into the affairs of the state is as much a fact as the continued viability of the state itself, and the changing nature of state sovereignty in response to this situation is to be welcomed rather than decried. More flexible state structures will not diminish formal sovereign equality at the international level, but it may encourage responsible independence and respect for human rights internally.

Self-Determination

Perhaps no contemporary norm of international law has been so vigorously promoted or widely accepted as the right of all peoples to self-determination. Yet the meaning and content of that right remain for many as vague as they were when enunciated by President Woodrow Wilson and others at Versailles.

The principle of self-determination by "national" groups developed as a natural corollary of developing nationalism in the eighteenth and nineteenth centuries. As components of the Ottoman, Austrian, and Russian empires began to object to integrationist and chauvinist empire policies or took advantage of weakened central authority, initial demands for autonomy and local self-government often escalated to demands for total independence. With the disintegration of the Austro-Hungarian and Ottoman empires during World War I, territory of the former empires required new sovereigns: thus, the principle of self-determination became the obvious vehicle for the redivision of Europe by the victorious powers.

It must be underscored that self-determination in 1919 had little to do with the demands of the peoples concerned, unless those demands were consistent with the geopolitical and strategic interests of the Great Powers. With a few exceptions in frontier regions (and then only if the region was not an overly sensitive one), plebiscites or referenda to determine the wishes of the people affected by the Versailles map-making were not commonly conducted.

Despite its limitations, self-determination did become a reality for some linguistic and ethnic European groups. In addition to its external aspect, self-determination was felt by Wilson and others to include an internal aspect, that of democracy. While the states created in 1919 offered no specific undertakings in this respect (except with regard to the protection of minorities, discussed below), it is clear that the Great Powers held the view (at least in theory) that the legitimacy of the state depended on the will of its citizens, and that participatory democracy was the appropriate manner in which legitimacy should be demonstrated.

In part because of the inconsistent manner in which the principle of self-determination was applied following the First World War, it was not initially recognized as a fundamental principle of the United Nations regime established in 1945. Indeed, the "principle" of self-determination is mentioned only twice in the UN Charter, both times in the context of developing "friendly relations among nations" and in conjunction with the principle of "equal rights . . . of peoples."[7] Self-determination is not mentioned in the 1948 Universal Declaration of Human Rights, even though there is a preambular reference to developing friendly relations between nations.

Before the moral and political imperative of decolonization, however, the vague "principle" of self-determination soon evolved into the "right" to self-determination. This evolution culminated in the adoption by the UN General Assembly in 1960 of the Declaration on the Granting of Independence to Colonial Countries and Peoples.[8] Premised, *inter alia,* on the need for stability, peace, and respect for human rights, the Declaration "[s]olemnly proclaims the necessity of bringing to a speedy and unconditional end colonialism in all its forms and manifestations" and declares that "[a]ll peoples have the right to self-determination; by virtue of that right they freely determine their political status and freely pursue their economic, social and cultural development."

Also significant, though less often cited, was the adoption by the General Assembly three days later of Resolution 1541, which clarifies that a non-self-governing territory under Chapter XI of the Charter can achieve "a full measure of self-government" by emergence as a sovereign independent state, free association with an independent state, or integration with an independent state.[9] While there was a clear preference for independence as the normal result of exercise of the right to self-determination, either of the other two options is acceptable so long as it is based on free and informed consent.

Despite the reference in the Declaration on the Granting of Independence to the self-determination of "all" peoples, in practice the right of self-determination has been limited to colonial situations. This limitation is demonstrated not only in the title of the Declaration itself, but in the fact that there are three references to the principles of national unity and territorial integrity in its seven operative paragraphs. In fact, it is the principle of national unity that has been almost universally followed by the international community—which, after all, is composed of states whose interest is to maintain themselves. With the single exception of Bangladesh, whose independence was due more to the Indian army than to the precepts of international law, no secessionist claim has been accepted by the international community since 1945.[10]

Even in the context of decolonization, the decolonized peoples have not always been granted the right freely to determine their own future. China's annexation of Hong Kong and Macao (with the agreement of the United Kingdom and Portugal, respectively), Indonesia's invasion of West Irian and East Timor, India's invasion of Goa, Ethiopia's absorption of Eritrea, and Morocco's attempted incorporation of Western Sahara have all been based on purportedly pre-existing sovereignty; only in Western Sahara (and, to some extent, East Timor) has there been international recognition of any rights of the local, formerly colonized, population to determine its own status.

It is also clear that the "peoples" referred to in the Declaration are those members of the population who live within former colonial boundaries; no ethnic, linguistic, or "national" connotation has been accepted. While colonies have occasionally been partitioned prior to independence (e.g., Rwanda-Urundi, the British Cameroons, and British India), the decision by the Organization of African Unity to maintain colonial territorial boundaries regardless of ethnic, geographical, or other considerations represents the norm.

Thus, while appeals to the "right of self-determination" are widely heard wherever a minority seeks greater political power, the evidence of UN and state practice since 1960 is that the international community has recognized only a very restricted right, that is, the right to freedom from a former colonial power. The question that remains is whether the concept of self-determination will continue to play a legal as well as a political role in the future.

Minority Rights

All but the smallest and most cohesive of societies include numerically inferior groups which may be distinguished—and which may distinguish themselves—from the majority. No proposed definition of "minority" has yet been widely accepted by international lawyers, but a common-sense definition of a numerically smaller, nondominant group distinguished by particular ethnic, racial, religious, or linguistic attributes will suffice for present purposes.[11]

One can trace the international protection of minorities at least to the Treaty of Westphalia in 1648, under the terms of which the parties agreed to respect the rights of certain (not all) religious minorities within their jurisdictions. Given the congruence of religious and secular authority in this period and before, however, such agreements could as easily be seen to be founded upon a recognition of the power of certain political groups rather than religious rights per se. Religion was certainly the most significant distinction among groups until at least the eighteenth century, and most of the early provisions for the protection of minorities were concerned with what today might be viewed as freedom of religion rather than group rights.

The most conscious and comprehensive attempts to protect ethnic and other minorities through international legal means were the so-called minority treaties adopted at the end of the First World War and subsequently overseen by the League of Nations. Among the protections commonly included in these treaties were the right to equality of treatment and nondiscrimination; the right to citizenship, although a minority group member could opt to retain another citizenship if desired; the right to use one's own language; the right of the minority to establish and control its own charitable, religious, and social institutions; a state obligation to provide "equitable" financial support to minority schools (in which instruction at the primary level would be in the minority language) and other institutions; and recognition of the supremacy of laws protecting minority rights over other statutes.[12]

Extensive critiques of the minority treaties have been written,[13] and there can be little doubt about their ultimate failure. Nevertheless, the result of the Versailles Treaty was a map of Europe that did more closely approach the theoretical goal of a collection of true "nation-states" than did prewar Europe. While approximately half of the population of Europe were "minorities" in 1914, only one-fourth were minorities in 1919.

Albania, Bulgaria, Estonia, Hungary, Latvia, Lithuania, Poland, and Romania had ethnic majorities, while the somewhat more artificial states of Czechoslovakia and Yugoslavia had dominant, if not majority, ethnic groups.[14]

Despite the failures of the League system, the principle of international supervision of treaty obligations relating to minority rights was significant. The life of the League of Nations and the international order it attempted to maintain was so brief that it is unfair to draw many conclusions about the efficacy of international remedies for the protection of minorities from the League precedent.

Irredentist disputes arose almost immediately and continued throughout the short inter-war period. The post-Versailles map of Europe no longer contained great empires to divide, and minorities in avowedly "nationalist" states were perhaps even less welcome than they had been under the empires.

It was primarily in the European arena that concepts of minority rights and nationalism developed in the nineteenth and early twentieth centuries. Colonial empires were notorious for ignoring ethnic, linguistic, or other "national" considerations, leaving such complexities to be dealt with by the independent states that emerged from decolonization. Of even greater long-term significance might have been the consolidation of many different ethnic groups in colonies, subsequently states, of extremely large size and resulting diversity.

The individualistic orientation of Anglophone countries such as Australia, Canada, and the United States left little room for concern with the rights of minority groups, and the American "melting pot" was concerned only (and rarely) with individual equality and nondiscrimination. Indigenous groups certainly were given no recognition in the Western Hemisphere by the majority settler populations.

Neither the concept of protecting the culture and traditions of numerical minorities nor that of conceding statehood to "nationalities" is evident outside the particular geographical setting of European (including the Russian and Ottoman) empires, and the new United Nations had little difficulty in essentially ignoring the preoccupation with minority issues that was the hallmark of its predecessor.

The United Nations Charter contains no provision specifically addressing the issue of minority rights. The existence of German-speaking minorities had provided an excuse for Hitler's aggression, and one heard little about the rights of "national minorities" from the victorious allies after the Second World War. Rather, the emphasis was placed on (individual) human rights and the collective right of all "peoples" to self-determination.

Instead of adopting the League of Nations approach of attempting to resolve the territorial-political problems posed by the existence of minority groups within a state (particularly those which had linguistic or ethnic ties to neighboring states) by boundary adjustments which might more accurately reflect a true nation-state, the drafters of the UN Charter seemed to assume (1) that European and other minorities would be satisfied if their individual rights, particularly those of equality and nondiscrimination, were respected; and (2) that developing self-government would be adequate to resolve the problem of colonialism. Despite the disastrous consequences for the individual victims of, for example, the Greek-Turkish population "exchange" of 1920–22, migration became the preferred solution for post-1945 European minorities; it was largely the people (especially Germans) who were moved, not the boundaries.

There was, however, at least one postwar example of the recognition of the vulnerability of minority groups to majority repression: the International Convention on the Prevention and Punishment of the Crime of Genocide, adopted in 1948, is directed specifically against the destruction of national, racial, ethnic, and religious groups per se, as opposed to violation of the rights of individuals.

The Universal Declaration of Human Rights, adopted by the UN General Assembly in 1948, makes no specific mention of minority rights, but the UN was nevertheless actively involved in minority issues during the 1950s. The UN's Commission on Human Rights soon established a Sub-Commission on Prevention of Discrimination and Protection of Minorities, although (except as noted below) early attempts by the Sub-Commission to address minority issues were rebuffed by the Commission.

Drafting of binding international agreements to implement the Universal Declaration began soon after the Declaration's adoption, and article 27 of the Covenant on Civil and Political Rights does specifically address the issue of minority rights:

> In those States in which ethnic, religious or linguistic minorities exist, persons belonging to such minorities shall not be denied the right, in community with the other members of their group, to enjoy

their own culture, to profess and practise their own religion, or to use their own language.

After several early attempts, which apparently were unappreciated by the Human Rights Commission, the UN Sub-Commission on Prevention of Discrimination and Protection of Minorities was finally able to address the issue of minorities in some depth in the mid-1970s. Its special rapporteur, Francesco Capotorti, prepared what has remained the leading study on discrimination against minorities, which was published in 1978.[15] The Sub-Commission subsequently suggested preparation of a Declaration on the Rights of Minorities, and a draft declaration was submitted to the Commission on Human Rights by Yugoslavia in 1979.[16] A revised Yugoslav draft was put forward in 1981, and the Commission subsequently has considered the draft declaration in an "open-ended" working group which meets during the Commission's annual sessions.

By 1987, the working group had approved a ten-paragraph Preamble and two articles of the declaration itself.[17] It is perhaps worth noting that the Preamble recognizes that protecting minority rights will "contribute to the political and social stability of States in which they live" and, in turn, "contribute to the strengthening of friendship and co-operation among peoples and States."

Among the unresolved issues still facing the Commission's working group are whether the rights of minority groups per se or of their members should be recognized; whether any definition will ultimately be required; whether mention should be made of any political rights that may inhere in minority groups; and whether indigenous peoples should be included within the scope of the proposed declaration.

Another recent UN initiative relevant to developing standards for the protection of minorities is the adoption by the General Assembly in 1982 of a Declaration on the Elimination of Intolerance and Discrimination Based on Religion or Belief;[18] this was followed by appointment of special rapporteurs by the Commission on Human Rights and its Sub-Commission to consider more concrete aspects of religious intolerance and discrimination.[19]

At least four sociopolitical realities have rendered the question of minorities particularly troublesome.

First, the existence of "minorities" does not fit easily within the theoretical paradigm of the state, whether that state is viewed through the individual social-contract theory of Western democracies or the class-based precepts of Marxism. Thus, the concept of minority rights may be seen as contradicting the fundamental basis of society, although the existence of group or community rights and obligations may be more fully developed in traditional African and Asian societies.

Second, the reality of minorities and largely heterogeneous states in the contemporary world is at odds with the theory of the nation-state as it developed in the nineteenth century. While the rhetoric of "one people–one state" has carried over into the concept of self-determination in the post-1945 period, this rhetoric has been conveniently and almost universally ignored as former colonies have accepted without question the boundaries drawn by the colonial powers, despite the fact that those boundaries often bear no relevance to ethnic, religious, or linguistic realities.

Third, there is a fundamental fear on the part of *all* countries, and especially newer states, that the recognition of minority rights will encourage fragmentation or separation and undermine national unity and the requirements of national development.

Finally, one also must recognize the reality of widespread discrimination and intolerance based on religion and ethnicity. Such intolerance is found in all regions of the world and in states at all stages of economic development; it is fanned by dictators and democrats alike to serve narrow political interests. While the violent conflicts that frequently result from such psychological hatreds may well have strong political and economic components, it would be a mistake to conclude (as some analysts would prefer) that ethnic and religious discrimination is not often a major factor.

The difficulties faced by states in recognizing minority rights have their counterpart in increasing fears among minority groups themselves. These fears are in part a reaction to the nonrecognition of minority rights as such since the Second World War, as the concept of minorities has been sacrificed to nation-building despite the fact that ethnicity and/or religion continues to define many internal conflicts. There also has been a cultural resurgence among smaller ethnic or linguistic groups, whose identities are threatened by the dominance of modern (often, though not necessarily, Western) society.

The result of this confrontation between the reassertion of rights by minority groups and the resistance of states to meaningful pluralism has been that many minority groups today seek broader political and economic power than the more limited cultural and linguistic rights traditionally accorded to them.

Indigenous Rights

Genocide has been committed against indigenous, Indian, or tribal peoples in every region of the world, and it is in this context that any discussion of indigenous rights must occur. However, just as concern with "genocide" itself is of relatively recent origin, the consideration of indigenous rights per se by the international community dates primarily from the past threee decades.

As is true for the concepts of "minority" and "people," it has thus far proved impossible to arrive at a commonly accepted definition of "indigenousness." The most comprehensive effort has been a United Nations study completed in 1983, which offered the following definition:

> Indigenous communities, peoples and nations are those which, having a historical continuity with pre-invasion and pre-colonial societies that developed on their territories, consider themselves distinct from other sectors of the societies now prevailing in those territories, or parts of them. They form at present non-dominant sectors of society and are determined to preserve, develop and transmit to future generations their ancestral territories, and their ethnic identity, as the basis of their continued existence as peoples, in accordance with their own cultural patterns, social institutions and legal systems. . . .
>
> On an individual basis, an indigenous person is one who belongs to these indigenous populations through self-identification as indigenous (group consciousness) and is recognized and accepted by these populations as one of its members (acceptance by the group).[20]

The contemporary movement for the international recognition of indigenous rights originated with Indians of the Western Hemisphere, aboriginal peoples of Australia, and northern indigenous groups such as the Inuit (Eskimo) and Sami (Lapps). Although there is some evidence of a "blue water" syndrome in defining pre-invasion indigenous peoples, it seems clear that Asian "hill tribes" such as the Karen and Hmong, and Arab and African nomadic tribes who pursue traditional life-styles, also should be included in a common-sense understanding of "indigenous." Less certain would be the inclusion of survivors of overland invasions, such as the peoples of central or east Asia, Tibet, and Mongolia, and many African peoples.

Most indigenous peoples have not only been attacked militarily but have subsequently seen their ways of life systematically assaulted. The fact that many North American Indian nations entered into treaties with various Canadian, United States, and other governments has made little difference in terms of the discrimination and land seizures to which they have been subjected, nor did their attempted participation in, for example, the League of Nations. While the existence of treaties has had some significant domestic legal effects in recent years, their breach has been of no more concern to the international community than the breach of countless treaties among European states, many of which were created or destroyed by the acts of so-called Great Powers irrespective of treaty obligations.

While indigenous peoples are obvious beneficiaries of treaties such as the Genocide Convention, the only international instrument that formally addresses the rights of indigenous peoples is International Labour Organization Convention No. 107, which was adopted in 1957.[21] This multilateral convention, now in the process of revision, reflected the common view of the time insofar as its primary goals are assimilation/integration and nondiscrimination. Clearly paternalistic, if well-intentioned, it owes as much to the "white man's burden" theoretically assumed by enlightened colonialists in the nineteenth century as to more modern concepts of human rights and equality.

In 1971, the UN Sub-Commission on Prevention of Discrimination and Protection of Minorities appointed a special rapporteur to study the problem of discrimination against indigenous populations; although his voluminous report was not completed until 1983, during its preparation it did serve as a vehicle for increasing involvement by indigenous nongovernmental organizations at the international level.[22] In response to recommendations contained in the study and proposed by international conferences of indigenous representatives, a pre-sessional Working Group on Indigenous Populations of the Sub-Commission began annual meetings in 1982; its mandate extends to the review of developments concerning the protection of the human rights of indigenous populations and to the developing of international standards for indigenous rights.[23]

Indigenous peoples generally insist that they should be considered separately from minorities, although all the consequences of that distinction are not yet entirely clear. The Human Rights Committee has found that indigenous persons have at least the rights set forth in article 27 of the Covenant on Civil and Political Rights, in the context of a claim brought by a Canadian Indian for the right to reside on an Indian reserve.[24] The Committee on the Elimination of All Forms of Racial Discrimination also has considered the situation of indigenous peoples within the scope of its work.

In addition to creating conditions under which indigenous peoples can protect themselves from exploitation and be secure from gross violations of "traditional" human rights such as the right to life, due process, and nondiscrimination, future international attention is likely to focus, in particular, on the rights of indigenous peoples to their land and the extent to which they possess the right to self-determination.

Human Rights

Distinctions among various categories of human rights—civil, political, economic, social, cultural, individual, collective, positive, negative, first- or second- or third-generation, and so on—are often misleading and rarely result in greater protection for individuals or groups. Indeed, the most common purpose for identifying such categories is to deny the status of "right" to one or more of them, rather than to expand international or domestic protections.

International human rights law has only infrequently been applied to protect the interests of groups per se. Rather, its provisions have extended to individual *members* of groups, even in those few instances—such as article 27 of the Covenant on Civil and Political Rights—where the protection of groups is clearly the primary concern. At the same time, however, certain human rights are of particular importance in the protection of group or community rights.

While freedom of religion is commonly considered a classic "civil" or "individual" right, religious rights are fundamental to the protection of the rights of minority, indigenous, and other groups. As the cornerstone of many cultures, religious practices have often been the object of discrimination by the majority; state intolerance of religious diversity has perhaps surpassed racial discrimination as the primary motivator of human rights violations in the world today.

Linguistic and educational rights also are of particular significance to groups, since they constitute the vehicles through which culture is transmitted. The recognition (or nonrecognition) of a language as "official" or "national" has contributed to violent conflicts in countries as diverse as Sri Lanka, Belgium, Canada, Bulgaria, and Turkey. Even where the free use of minority languages is permitted, the obligation (if any) of the state to support the propagation or maintenance of such languages through the provision of educational or other facilities is unclear.

With few exceptions, a territorial base also is essential to the preservation of a group's culture. Seizure of land, for population expansion or the exploitation of natural resources, is perhaps the most common complaint of indigenous peoples; those European "minorities" that were not able to maintain a separate territory are in the process of disappearing. No specific right to land is mentioned in any major human rights instrument, however, perhaps reflecting the desires of states to retain absolute control over their territories.

The right to popular participation in government, as expressed in article 21 of the Universal Declaration of Human Rights and article 25 of the Covenant on Civil and Political Rights, should be interpreted as implying more than simple majority rule through the electoral process. As this right has been developed in subsequent UN studies, it suggests the right of effective participation in the political and economic decision-making processes of government.[25] If a situation exists in which an identifiable segment of the society is consistently excluded from any real share in economic or political life, alternative means of ensuring participation may be required.

Other rights commonly designated as collective—such as the right to development, peace, or control over natural resources—are more properly seen as claims of the state rather than rights of nonstate groups. The legitimacy of such state claims may rest on whether the individuals and groups that make up the state participate equitably in the benefits of such rights.

Finally, it should be recognized that most groups are threatened primarily by gross violations of rights to personal security. Mass and individual killings, torture, arbitrary and indefinite arrests, induced starvation, and discrimination in employment, housing, and public services are the most common *causes* of the assertion of group rights by the powerless. In addition, they constitute the most common *responses* by central governments to perceived threats to national unity and territorial integrity. Such violations are often linked to imposition of states of siege or emergency, and the violation of human rights by the security forces (or minority group terrorists) almost universally renders the resolution of conflicting assertions of rights impossible through the normal legal or political process.

Conclusion

International law guarantees the protection of individual human rights, whether those rights are exercised alone or in association with others. While the precise limits of internationally protected human rights may be unclear (apart from obligations assumed under international treaties), the essential philosophical underpinnings of human rights include the right *to be* and *to live in community with other members of one's own group.*

The state is and will continue for the foreseeable future to be the most significant international legal actor, but its sovereignty has never been absolute. Increasing international restrictions on state action reflect the increasing interdependency of the international legal and economic order and should not be seen as impermissible infringements on sovereignty. The fundamental attributes of sovereignty—independence from external control and international equality with all other states—remain intact.

At the same time, however, it must be recognized that the ideal of the "nation-state," which was held from the mid-nineteenth to the mid-twentieth centuries, is not only impracticable but undesirable. Attempts to create "national" states free of minorities or diversity have failed and have led more often to repression than to freedom, as the history of Europe from 1878 to 1945 amply demonstrates. Genocide against native Americans, Armenians, and Jews are only the most extreme examples of fulfilling national destiny; the attempted eradication of Kurds in Turkey, Turks in Bulgaria, indigenous peoples in Latin America, and Tibetans in China simply constitutes historical continuity.

Yet minorities and indigenous peoples, too, may need to abandon the "nation-state" as an ideal, so long as their "nation" can otherwise be preserved. Political loyalty to an existing state does not necessarily imply disloyalty to one's nation or culture, any more than the recognition of diversity by a central or majority government need encourage disunity or fragmentation.

As international actors—states, liberation movements, international organizations, transnational corporations, nonsovereign entities, and so on—become more diverse, appropriate responses to demands for group identity and recognition should become more common. As domestic constitutional arrangements become more inventive and flexible—as demonstrated from Greenland to Hong Kong—the securing of meaningful autonomy should respond more effectively to demands for self-determination.

The balance to be found between territorial states as they are presently constituted and the legitimate expressions of national or cultural identity upon which smaller groups will continue to insist cannot be found by resorting to simplistic formulas of federalism or decentralization, although these concepts may contain the seeds of potential solutions in many situations. Neither should the search for that balance be perverted by incantations of the largely formless notions of "sovereignty" or "self-determination."

It may be that violence by aggrieved nondominant groups is necessary in order to convince the established central authorities to share power, but the chances of avoiding violence might be enhanced if conflicts could be addressed in what is essentially a conservative, but nevertheless responsive, manner. Central governments or those groups which exercise effective political and economic power must redress minority grievances or escalation of the conflict is almost certain.

First, violations of widely accepted individual rights must be ended, since it is precisely such violations that make ethnic or group politics seem to be the only means of protection for the victims. While equality before the law and nondiscrimination may not satisfy the needs of communities that feel themselves under attack, the guarantee of these rights is an essential prerequisite to the resolution of any minority-majority conflict. Gross violations of human rights against powerless groups—including land seizure and economic exploitation, as well as the more obvious violent attacks by government or private armies—must cease, and the state must fulfill its obligation to protect the human rights of all those within its jurisdiction, or the individuals and groups under attack may legitimately reject the authority of that state.

Second, effective means for minority or indigenous groups to participate in the larger society (insofar as such participation is desired) must be adopted, even if this means some deviation from the classic democratic principle of "one person, one vote." When minority groups are permanently excluded from influence due to the ethnic (or religious or linguistic) nature of politics and the resulting permanent domination by the majority, constitutional structures must be adapted so that the whole population of a state feels that its voice is heard. While this does not necessarily imply a veto for the minority over national programs and goals, it may well be appropriate to adopt important or sensitive decisions on the basis of consensus or weighted voting rather than purely numerical majority rule.

Third, minorities and indigenous peoples must be given the opportunity to maintain and develop those social and cultural attibutes that are essential to the preservation of any community: the right to use of their own language, including facilities for publication and reasonable access to radio and television; the ability to provide for the education of their children, which might include establishment of their own schools or the insertion of minority values and language into national public schools; maintenance of minority or traditional religions, in the context of a secular state, or retention of various areas of personal jurisdiction over their members in a religious state; and perservation of sufficient political, economic, and environmental control so that the minority is not wholly at the mercy of the dominant culture. The preservation of minority cultural values should be considered as important as the provision of governmental assistance to disadvantaged members of society, so that special incentives or contributions to minority or indigenous groups will be seen as part of society's overall commitment to equality and pluralism.

Fourth, in exchange for the majority's acceptance of the legitimacy of minority cultures and values and the minority's ability to participate effectively in national political and economic life, minority groups must accept the obvious fact that the majority culture and values (where there is a single dominant majority culture) will predominate at the state/national level. While every attempt should be made to promote pluralism where possible, formal "equality" of, for example, language, may not be possible in a state where there are many minorities, a single small minority, or a well-established majority culture to which immigrants may, in time, be expected to adapt. Minorities or indigenous peoples that enjoy a high degree of autonomy or self-government also should respect fundamental internationally recognized human rights norms—at least those which have developed into customary international law—within their own societies.

Fifth, state societies should recognize that statehood or sovereignty in and of itself has no meaning; it is relevant only insofar as it contributes to the development of societal consensus and responds to the needs of those who live within its jurisdiction. Autonomy and self-government are modern responses to the principle of self-determination, and a multitude of internal constitutional arrangements, analogous to the multitude of international relationships that has developed since 1945, should be viewed as not only possible but desirable. The goal of "unity within diversity" remains elusive, but it may contribute to a more stable society than the coerced unity sought by both state governments and ethnically or religiously exclusive minority movements.

Conflict and tension are inherent in society; so are differences in individuals and cultures. One goal of the state under the most fundamental of international human rights norms is to eliminate discrimination, not to destroy all differences. Recognition of the right to personal autonomy and group identity is essential to ensure that the principles of self-determination, participation, and tolerance are allowed to flourish.

NOTES

1. IAN BROWNLIE, PRINCIPLES OF PUBLIC INTERNATIONAL LAW 287 (Oxford: Clarendon Press, 3d ed. 1979).

2. Among many works dealing with limitations on sovereignty, *see, e.g.*, INGRID DELUPIS, INTERNATIONAL LAW AND THE INDEPENDENT STATE (New York: Crane Russak, 1974); ALAN JAMES, SOVEREIGN STATEHOOD (London: Allen & Unwin, 1986); ARTHUR LARSON, C. WILFRED JENKS, ET AL., SOVEREIGNTY WITHIN THE LAW (Dobbs Ferry, N.Y.: Oceana, 1965); THE NATION-STATE (Leonard Tivey ed.; New York: St. Martin's Press, 1981).

3. On diplomatic immunity, *see* United States Diplomatic and Consular Staff in Tehran, Judgment, *I.C.J. Reports* 1980, p. 3.

4. *See, e.g.*, Reservations to the Convention on the Prevention and Punishment of the Crime of Genocide, Advisory Opinion, I.C.J. Reports 1951, p. 15, 23; Barcelona Traction, Light and Power Company, Limited, Second Phase, Judgment, I.C.J. Reports 1970, p. 3, at 33.

5. *Cf., e.g.*, Legal Consequences for States of the Continued Presence of South Africa in Namibia (South West Africa) notwithstanding Security Council Resolution 276 (1970), Advisory Opinion, I.C.J. Reports 1971, p. 16, at 57: "[T]o enforce . . . distinctions, exclusions, restrictions and limitations exclusively based on grounds of race, colour, descent or national or ethnic origin which constitute a denial of fundamental human rights is a flagrant violation of the purposes and principles of the Charter."

6. *See generally* JOHN BREUILLY, NATIONALISM AND THE STATE (New York: St. Martin's Press, 1982); ALFRED COBBAN, THE NATION STATE AND NATIONAL SELF-DETERMINATION (New York: Thomas Y. Crowell, rev. ed. 1969); HANS KOHN, NATIONALISM, ITS MEANING AND HISTORY (Princeton, N.J.: Van Nostrand, rev. ed. 1965).

7. UN CHARTER arts. 1(2) and 55.

8. GA Res. 1514, 15 UN GAOR Supp. (No. 16) at 66, UN Doc. A/4684 (1960).

9. GA Res. 1541, 15 UN GAOR Supp. (No. 16) at 29, UN Doc. A/4684 (1960).

10. The only partial exceptions might be Biafra, which was recognized by five states before its defeat by Nigerian forces, and the Turkish Republic of Northern Cyprus, which has been recognized only by Turkey and remains occupied by that country's armed forces.

11. The two most widely cited definitions have been put forward by members of the UN Sub-Commission on Prevention of Discrimination and Protection of Minorities: United Nations, Study on the Rights of Persons Belonging to Ethnic, Religious and Linguistic Minorities (F. Capotorti, Special Rapporteur), UN Sales No. E.78.XIV.1 (1978) at para. 568; Proposal Concerning a Definition of the Term "Minority" Submitted by Mr. Jules Deschenes, UN Doc. E/CN.4/

Sub.2/1985/31 & Corr. 1 (1985) at 30. Capotorti defined a minority as a "group numerically inferior to the rest of the population of a State, in a non-dominant position, whose members—being nationals of the State—possess ethnic, religious or linguistic characteristics differing from those of the rest of the population and show, if only implicitly, a sense of solidarity, directed towards preserving their culture, traditions, religion or language." The similar Deschenes definition is "[a] group of citizens of a State, constituting a numerical minority and in non-dominant position in that State, endowed with ethnic, religious or linguistic characteristics which differ from those of the majority of the population, having a sense of solidarity with one another, motivated, if only implicitly, by a collective will to survive and whose aim is to achieve equality with the majority in fact and in law."

12. *See generally* INIS L. CLAUDE, JR., NATIONAL MINORITIES 17–20 (Cambridge, Mass.: Harvard Univ. Press, 1955; reprinted, New York: Greenwood Press, 1969); OSCAR I. JANOWSKY, NATIONALITIES AND NATIONAL MINORITIES 112–15 (New York: Macmillan, 1945); C.A. MACARTNEY, NATIONAL STATES AND NATIONAL MINORITIES 273–94, 502–6 (London: Oxford Univ. Press, 1934); United Nations Sub-Commission on Prevention of Discrimination and Protection of Minorities, Treaties and International Instruments Concerning the Protection of Minorities 1919–1951, UN Doc. E/CN.4/Sub.2/133 (1951) at paras. 2–12.

13. *See,* in particular, CLAUDE, *supra* note 12.

14. RAYMOND PEARSON, NATIONAL MINORITIES IN EASTERN EUROPE *1848–1945,* at 148–49 (London: Macmillan, 1983).

15. *Supra* note 11.

16. UN Doc. E/CN.4/L.1367/Rev.1 (1979).

17. The text approved by the working group and proposals submitted concerning the remainder of the declaration may be found in the working group's 1987 report to the Commission, UN Doc. E/CN.4/1987/32 (1987), Annexes I and II.

18. 36 UN GAOR Supp. (No. 51) at 171, UN Doc. A/36/51 (1982).

19. *See* Comm. on Human Rights Res. 1986/20, UN ESCOR Supp. (No. 2) at 66, UN Doc. E/1986/22 (1986); Sub-Commission Res. 1983/31, UN Doc. E/CN.4/1984/2 (1983) at 98.

20. United Nations, Study of the Problem of Discrimination Against Indigenous Populations (Jose R. Martinez Cobo, Special Rapporteur), UN Doc. E/CN.4/Sub.2/1986/7/Add.4 (1986) at 50–51. This is the final installment of a five-volume work completed in 1983 and issued in consolidated form in 1986; the other volumes are UN Docs. E/CN.4/Sub.2/1986/7 & Adds.1–3. Since the reissued set of documents is not widely available, the original documents also might be consulted; they are, in order of their original appearance, UN Docs. E/CN.4/Sub.2/476/Adds.1–6 (1981); E/CN.4/Sub.2/1982/2/Adds.1–7 (1982); and E/CN.4/Sub.2/1983/21/Adds.1–7 (1983).

21. Convention (No. 107) concerning the Protection and Integration of Indigenous and Other Tribal and Semi-Tribal Populations in Independent Countries, INTERNATIONAL LABOUR ORGANISATION, INTERNATIONAL LABOUR CONVENTIONS AND RECOMMENDATIONS, 1919–1981, at 858 (1982).

22. *Supra* note 20.

23. ESC Res. 1982/34 of 7 May 1982.

24. Communication No. 24/1977, Lovelace v. Canada, *reprinted in* Human

Rights Committee, Selected Decisions under the Optional Protocol, UN Doc. CCPR/C/OP/1 (1985), UN Sales No. E.84.XIV.2, at 83.

25. *Cf., e.g.,* United Nations, Study by the Secretary-General on Popular Participation in its Various Forms as an Important Factor in Development and in the Full Realization of Human Rights, UN Doc. E/CN.4/1985/10 (1984).

2

United Nations Machineries on Women's Rights: How Might They Better Help Women Whose Rights are Being Violated?

SANDRA COLIVER

United Nations actions to promote women's rights have expanded markedly during the past decade. The Convention on the Elimination of All Forms of Discrimination Against Women, adopted in 1979, entered into force in 1981 and has now been ratified by more than ninety states.[1] Conferences—in Mexico in 1975, Copenhagen in 1980, and Nairobi in 1985—focused world attention on obstacles to women's advancement and developed strategies for addressing those obstacles. The Commission on the Status of Women (Women's Commission), the chief intergovernmental body charged with monitoring and promoting women's rights recommenced annual meetings in 1988 after nearly two decades of only biennial sessions.

Yet surprisingly little of an analytic nature has been written about the effectiveness of either the Women's Commission or the Committee on the Elimination of Discrimination Against Women (CEDAW) established by the Convention.[2] This paper does not attempt a comprehensive evaluation of those two bodies but rather addresses the question: How effective are the Women's Commission and CEDAW in helping women whose human rights have been violated? The Vienna-based Women's Commission and CEDAW are compared with their Geneva-based human rights counterparts: the Commission on Human Rights and the expert committees established to monitor implementation of three major human rights treaties: namely, the Human Rights Committee established by the International Covenant on Civil and Political Rights, the Committee (CESC) established by the Economic and Social Council (ECOSOC) to implement the International Covenant on Economic, Social and Cultural Rights, and its predecessor working group, and the Committee (CERD) established by the International Convention on the Elimination of All Forms of Racial Discrimination. The aim of the comparison is to identify areas where the women's procedures appear more or less effective than comparable Geneva-based procedures and to suggest ways of strengthening the weak procedures.

Some observers, conceding the relevance of CERD, CESC, and the ECOSOC working group, may question the drawing of recommendations from the work of the Human Rights Commission and Committee. Perceived differences result from the nature of the rights examined: rights scrutinized by the Human Rights Commission and Committee are primarily civil and political in nature, while women's rights are widely viewed as essentially economic and social in nature, despite the fact that nondiscrimination between men and women, the core right promoted by the Women's Commission and CEDAW, is a fundamental civil right. The difference, in any event, is significant only to the extent that traditional concepts persist; namely, that civil and political rights imply immediately binding obligations on governments, whereas economic and social rights impose obligations merely to strive for progressive achievement of rights in keeping with the country's available resources. Governments that engage in gross violations of civil and political rights often are censured and urged, shamed, and even pressured to stop the violations and provide relief to victims. Because, in many instances, violations of economic and social rights are a result of long-prevalent social patterns rather than direct government action, because curtailment of the violations may require costly programs, and because under the traditional analysis governments do not have immediate and clearly defined obligations to remedy the violations, some commentators maintain that condemnation of governments for violating women's rights is both inappropriate and ineffective.

While that reasoning may have some validity regarding advancement of certain rights by poorer countries, has not the time arrived when governments at least should be called to task for failing to remedy gross discriminations they perpetuate or condone (e.g., unequal opportunities and pay for public sector employment, unequal opportunities in public education, discriminations by private bodies that receive public benefits)? Should not all countries, regardless of resources or religious and other beliefs, be required to address assaults on women's rights such as harassment of women in detention, failure to enforce laws prohibiting bride-burning and other forms of domestic violence, toleration of female circumcision and other mutilations, and maintenance of inequitable laws regarding marriage and succession rights? Meaningful progress in promoting women's rights requires emphatic and authoritative responses to those and other questions. In helping to develop responses, the Women's Commission and CEDAW undeniably could benefit from experiences of the Human Rights Commission and other human rights treaty committees.

Commission on the Status of Women

The Women's Commission was established by ECOSOC in 1946. It consists of representatives (mostly women) of thirty-two governments elected for four-year terms by ECOSOC to reflect the geographical distribution of UN membership.[3] Since 1980 it has met in Vienna, where it receives staff support from the Advancement of Women Branch of the UN Centre for Social Development and Humanitarian Affairs.

The Commission's original charge was "to prepare recommendations and reports to ECOSOC on promoting women's rights in political, economic, civil, social and educational fields."[4] Its early work, focusing on drafting international treaties and declarations, culminated in 1979 in the adoption by the General Assembly of the Convention on the Elimination of All Forms of Discrimination Against Women.

Currently, the Commission's chief function is to monitor programs to promote the roles of women in economic and social development adopted by world conferences. The Commission was the principal monitor of the World Plan of Action on the Implementation of the Objectives of the International Women's Year, adopted in 1975 by the Mexico City World Conference, and of the Programme of Action for the Second Half of the UN Decade for Women: Equality, Development and Peace (1976–85) adopted by the Copenhagen Conference in 1980. It continues to monitor implementation of the Forward-looking Strategies for the Advancement of Women adopted by the World Conference to Review and Appraise the Achievements of the UN Decade for Women held at Nairobi in July 1985. The Commission regularly adopts resolutions on topics such as elimination of discrimination against women and exercise of all their rights; violence in the family; violence against detained women; women and development; elderly women; Palestinian women; and women and children under apartheid.

A second function of the Commission is to make recommendations, via ECOSOC, to the Secretary-General and appropriate UN bodies regarding (a) increased participation of women within the UN system, particularly in the implementation of the Forward-looking Strategies and at policy-making levels, and (b) implementation and coordination of UN programs to advance the rights of women.[5]

In 1987 ECOSOC expanded the Commission's terms of reference to encompass a third function; namely, making policy recommendations to ECOSOC concerning "priority themes" of the Forward-looking Strategies.[6] The Commission's deliberations are informed by Secretary-General summaries of information received from governments and UN agencies.[7]

The Commission's monitoring work is the focus of the following comments because it appears to offer the greatest potential for helping to curb instances of serious and systematic discrimination.[8] The resources and procedures of the Women's Commission are compared with those of the Human Rights Commission in order to highlight ways in which the Women's Commission might be strengthened.

Comparison with the Human Rights Commission

The Human Rights Commission, like the Women's Commission, was established by ECOSOC in 1946. Its mandate was and continues to be to help elaborate and promote the full range of economic, social, cultural, civil, and political rights prescribed by the UN Charter. Like the Women's Commission, it reports to ECOSOC and is composed of government representatives. Its membership of forty-three states currently is 25 percent larger than that of the Women's Commission, but that discrepancy is likely to be addressed soon since the Women's Commission, at its 1988 session, requested that its membership be enlarged to forty-three, with seats to be allocated in the same manner as those of the Human Rights Commission.[9]

One difference between the two commissions involves the lengths of their sessions. Whereas the Human Rights Commission meets annually for six weeks, the Women's Commission, between 1972 and 1986, met only biennially, and only for between one and two weeks. In 1988, at its request, it recommenced annual meetings. It did not request longer sessions, however, despite General Assembly encouragement to do so.[10]

A second difference concerns the expert assistance each commission receives. The Human Rights Commission is assisted by a number of individual experts (called special rapporteurs or representatives) who work throughout the year, generally for a period of several years, investigating patterns of violations wherever they may be committed or allegations of violations in particular countries. Most experts are authorized to conduct on-site investigations (with the consent of the investigated governments), to identify violations, and to make recommendations regarding measures to be taken by governments, the Commission, the UN Secretariat, other UN and intergovernmental organizations, and NGOs. Some experts are authorized, in addition, to make urgent appeals to governments to prevent threatened violations in particular cases and to report to the Commission on the outcome of such appeals.[11] The Human Rights Commission also is assisted by its Sub-Commission on Prevention of Discrimination and Protection of Minorities, a body of twenty-six experts that meets annually for four weeks. Several Sub-Commission members serve as special rapporteurs, generally for at least three years, to prepare studies on a wide spectrum of topics, many of which involve elaboration of rights set forth in the Universal Declaration of Human Rights and human rights treaties. The experts all receive some measure of ongoing assistance from Human Rights Centre staff members, many of whom have developed considerable expertise in the substantive areas in which they have worked.

In contrast, the Women's Commission only recently began to rely on assistance supplied by meetings of experts, on violence in the family in 1986 and on national machineries for the advancement of women in 1987.[12] While these meetings are a welcome development, they cannot match the contribution made by experts to the Human Rights Commission because they are convened on an *ad hoc* basis, and no institutional mechanism exists for follow-through either by the experts or by the staff who produce the reports.

The Human Rights Commission also has made considerably more effective use of working groups than has the Women's Commission. The

Human Rights Commission has several working groups, some that meet before its plenary session and others that meet during it. Some, like the rapporteurs, investigate allegations of violations or patterns of violations; others are charged with elaborating rights, which may include drafting a declaration or treaty. One, that meets before the plenary, reviews confidential communications alleging violations. The Women's Commission, in contrast, has only one working group—on confidential communications—which meets during the plenary session, seriously limiting the time it can devote to the communications.

A third difference between the two commissions is that the Human Rights Commission meets in Geneva, whereas the Women's Commission until 1978 normally met in New York or Geneva and since then has met in Vienna (except for a special session held in New York in 1987). Although the official reason for moving the Women's Commission to Vienna was to permit enhancement of its staff's status (from a section of the Human Rights Division to a branch of the Centre for Social Development and Humanitarian Affairs), the effect has been detrimental.[13] The Geneva-based Human Rights Centre, which staffs the Human Rights Committee, CESC, CERD, and the new Committee Against Torture, in addition to the Human Rights Commission, its Sub-Commission, individual experts, and working groups, has developed an expertise in rights implementation not yet matched by the Branch for the Advancement of Women. Isolated in Vienna, the Women's Branch does not have the opportunities of the Geneva staff for informal contacts and exchanges of information that facilitate the Geneva staff's energetic, occasionally even forceful, implementation efforts. Similarly, government and NGO representatives who attend Women's Commission sessions cannot benefit from consultations with human rights colleagues who pass through Geneva in greater number and with greater frequency.

Another, and perhaps the most significant, difference between the two commissions concerns the sophistication and effectiveness of procedures to deal with communications concerning patterns of serious violations. In 1948 ECOSOC granted both commissions authority to receive confidential and nonconfidential lists of communications prepared by the Secretariat. The commissions were authorized only to "take note" of the complaints.

In 1967 and 1970, after repeated requests from the Human Rights Commission, ECOSOC granted it authority to investigate allegations of consistent patterns of gross and reliably attested violations of human rights committed by named governments. The procedure established by ECOSOC Resolution 1235 (XLII) (1967) permits public debate of such allegations. NGOs that have consultative status with ECOSOC may intervene orally and in writing concerning violations in countries named on the agenda. In addition, since the mid-1970s, NGOs have been permitted to address, in oral statements, situations in countries not under Commission scrutiny.[14]

The Human Rights Commission has addressed rights of women in public debate on several occasions. For example, it has called for particular protection of women and children from armed conflicts in Afghanistan and El Salvador and under apartheid, and its Sub-Commission produced a report on traditional practices, such as female circumcision and some birth practices, that affect women's health (UN Doc. E/CN.4/1986/42).

A second procedure, established by ECOSOC Resolution 1503 (XLIII) (1970), authorizes action by the Commission and its Sub-Commission on complaints of "situations which appear to reveal a consistent pattern of gross and reliably attested violations of human rights" from any individual or group that has direct information. The procedure remains confidential unless the Commission decides to make public its findings. Since it began announcing the names of countries under investigation in 1978, the Commission has named some thirty countries. The only country it has expressly criticized is Equatorial Guinea. In 1985 it released its files on Argentina and Uruguay but only after requested to do so by the newly elected governments of those countries.[15]

The 1235 and 1503 procedures derive their effectiveness from the Commission's ability to "mobilize shame."[16] They are most likely to have an impact when the investigated government is sensitive to international scrutiny and condemnation, when publicity or the threat of publicity is substantial, and when the Commission identifies concrete steps that must be taken if the government is to escape further scrutiny. A few countries appear impervious to UN condemnation but most are not. On several occasions governments have announced planned reforms during Commission or Sub-Commission meetings as concessions to escape further criticism.[17] Most governments respond to requests from rapporteurs concerning specific cases; even when they deny allegations, their treatment of victims often improves.

The experience of the Women's Commission in dealing with serious violations stands in disappointing contrast to the steadily expanding role of the Human Rights Commission. In 1974, after nearly thirty years of "taking note" of undisclosed violations, the Women's Commission came close to relinquishing even that limited prerogative. Pursuant to a Soviet proposal, the Commission voted to stop receiving communications on the ground that ECOSOC resolution 1503 created a single, preemptive system for receiving complaints. Following strenuous lobbying by a few governments and NGOs, ECOSOC invited the Commission to reconsider. In 1976 the Commission did so, voting to reaccept complaints but seeking no expansion of its authority. In 1980 the Commission requested authority to appoint a five-member working group to review communications in order to identify those that appeared to reveal "a consistent pattern of reliably attested injustice and discriminatory practice against women." ECOSOC approved the request in 1982 (Resolution 1983/27), and in 1984 the procedure was initiated.[18]

The Commission's handling of communications in 1984, 1986, and 1988 provides scant encouragement for predicting that the procedure will contribute significantly to protection of women's rights, at least not without concerted NGO and government effort. The 1984 working group reported that it considered 121 communications as well as replies from some governments, that many of the communications dealt with problems encountered by women wishing to marry or divorce, and that the group did not consider those complaints to lie within its mandate since they applied equally to men and women. The group did identify one trend, "the widespread physical violence against women while in official custody," including "cases of rape, sexual abuse and violent treatment of pregnant women in detention." The Commission adopted a resolution calling on UN member states to eradicate such violations and invited them to submit views to the Secretariat, which was requested to prepare a report to the Commission for its 1986 session.

That report (UN Doc. E/CN.6/1986/11) was less than three pages long and was based on replies from only seventeen governments. According to paragraph 3, "All the responding Governments stated either that their laws and regulations guaranteed all prisoners the right to humane treatment and to respect for their dignity or that the problem was not evident in their countries since measures had been taken to prevent it." Some Commission members expressed concern that so few governments had responded, but there was no proposal on how to encourage greater response or on how to analyze those responses that had been received. The Commission adopted a resolution that was substantially the same as its 1984 resolution.

In 1988 the Commission's summary of the working group's report was even briefer than in 1984 and 1986.[19] The Commission reported that the working group identified one new trend, sexual harassment of women at the workplace; noted that many communications alleged "very serious and extensive" violations including discrimination in education, employment, and political rights; and expressed concern at the low number of governments that responded to requests for comments on communications. Despite the allegations of "very serious and extensive" violations, the working group's only recommendation reported by the Commission was that the Commission should urge ECOSOC to invite countries to take "legislative and other appropriate measures to halt the current negative trends related to the status of women in their countries." The Commission failed to adopt any resolutions based on the working group's conclusions, even on the working group's weak recommendation or, as in 1984 and 1986, on violence against women in detention.

To supplement its communications procedure, the Women's Commission also examines patterns of discrimination identified during its monitoring of the Forward-looking Strategies. As part of its monitoring work, the Commission reviews reports prepared by the Secretariat based on responses from governments and UN bodies to questionnaires that seek statistical and descriptive information concerning women's representation and achievements in specified areas. While the process is sometimes referred to as a reporting procedure, there is no opportunity for Commission members to question a government's representative about the report or to request supplemental information. All reports are filtered through the Secretary-General. His summary for the Commission discusses patterns that emerge from the government reports but does not identify governments that appear to be in violation of their obligations.

Further, though governments receive several questionnaires over the course of a four-year reporting period, often the questions are insufficiently specific to elicit information that can be analyzed comparatively. At its 1987 special session the Commission requested the Secretary-General to take steps to consolidate the different questionnaires, to simplify them, and to include clearly stated requests for relevant statistics and other measurable indicators. While that was a commendable step it is unlikely to be sufficient.

Even when the Commission has identified patterns of discrimination, its resolutions have been decidedly weak. Most simply call on states to take steps to curtail identified violations or request the Secretary-General to take note of the Commission's conclusions. South Africa and Israel are the only governments that have been singled out for criticism. Yet the fact that those two have been consistently censured suggests that the Commission finds nothing inappropriate in principle in condemning governments when warranted. The Women's Commission appears to be at a point in its development that the Human Rights Commission moved beyond in 1975 when it appointed a five-member working group on the human rights situation in Chile. Until 1975 the Human Rights Commission, like the Women's Commission today, had identified as violators only South Africa and Israel. The Chile working group was the precedent that broke through resistence to naming and condemning government violators, opening the way for investigations of human rights practices of numerous governments of all ideologies. Is it not time for the Women's Commission to grapple with its own "Chile case" and begin to investigate allegations of "consistent pattern[s] of reliably attested injustice and discriminatory practice" wherever they are alleged to occur?

Committee on the Elimination of Discrimination Against Women

The Convention on the Elimination of All Forms of Discrimination Against Women entered into force in September 1981. As of March 1988, ninety-four states had ratified it.[20] "Discrimination" is defined as

> any distinction, exclusion or restriction made on the basis of sex which has the effect or purpose of impairing or nullifying the recognition, enjoyment or exercise by women, irrespective of their marital status, on a basis of equality of men and women, of human rights and fundamental freedoms in the political, economic, social, cultural, civil or any other field. (Article 1)

The Committee on the Elimination of Discrimination Against Women (CEDAW) was established for the purpose of promoting implementation of the Convention (article 17(1)). Since 1982, it has met annually, generally for two weeks, alternating between New York and Vienna. Future sessions all may be held in Vienna in order to reduce costs.

CEDAW consists of twenty-three experts elected by states that are parties to the Convention to serve in their individual capacities for staggered, four-year terms, consideration being given to "equitable geographical distribution and to the representation of the different forms of civilization as well as the principal legal systems" (article 17(1)). In 1987 all were women and from countries that roughly reflected the desired equitable distribution (an improvement over previous years when Eastern European countries were over-represented). Although members of treaty-supervisory committees are supposed to be independent of their governments, geographic distribution generally is significant since most members in fact have been employed by their governments and many voice government views.[21] Despite that tradition, some observers have noted a refreshing collegiality among CEDAW members that has tended to reduce the influence of geographic loyalties and ideological differences, thus enhancing both willingness to compromise and CEDAW's potential for significant action.

Reporting Procedures

States are to submit reports within a year after they become parties and at least every four years thereafter on "legislative, judicial, administrative or other measures which they have adopted to give effect to the provisions of the Convention and the progress made" (article 18). Reports should include obstacles encountered in implementing the Convention fully and measures adopted to overcome such obstacles, and should pay particular attention to the status of women in rural areas (pursuant to article 14), the level of wages and unemployment of women and men, and measures to combat any differences in employment and wage levels.[22]

Reports are introduced by government representatives who are asked for explanations and supplemental information. CEDAW may make suggestions (of an informal nature) regarding specific countries or general situations and general comments (of a formal nature) regarding general situations.[23] Members also may offer "general observations" that may lead to formulation of suggestions or general comments.[24] CEDAW reports annually to the General Assembly, via ECOSOC, on its consideration of country reports and procedural matters, and its report also is transmitted to the Women's Commission (article 21).

In 1987 CEDAW took three actions that are likely to contribute substantially to its effectiveness. First, it instructed its chair to request states that had submitted reports that did not comply with its guidelines to forward to the Secretariat any missing information not later than three months prior to the session during which the reports were to be considered.[25] The chair's requests should result in reports that are more complete, reduce the amount of information states' representatives are asked to produce orally or on short notice, and thus facilitate more careful review.

Second, CEDAW decided to make general comments on states' reports following Committee consideration when consensus could be reached. Absent consensus, the only comment would be that the report had been received and considered and that not all questions had been resolved.[26] CEDAW members hope that this initiative will clarify what steps states are encouraged to take and will assist them in drafting subsequent reports.

Third, CEDAW decided that it was authorized, pursuant to article 21 of the Convention, to make suggestions and general recommendations addressed to individual states.[27] Suggestions and general recommendations differ from general comments because states are formally entitled (pursuant to article 21) to respond to suggestions and recommendations, opening the way for an interpretation that suggestions and recommendations therefore may be more pointedly critical. Regardless of whether it calls its statements comments, suggestions, or general recommendations, CEDAW's decision that it is authorized to address them to individual governments constitutes a major advance over other human rights treaty committees that have not yet decided to issue formal comments on individual states.

Both decisions concerning comments on states' reports were made despite opposition from some members.[28] Their adoption signifies CEDAW's willingness to depart from its consensus approach in the face of a small dissent, a bold innovation considering the paralyzing procedure of other committees to require that all decisions be unanimous.

A major problem CEDAW faces is how to review the large number of reports it receives, given its limited resources. It has determined that it can adequately review only eight initial reports or seven initial and two second reports during a ten-day session (a rate of review that is at least as efficient as that of other treaty committees).[29] At that rate CEDAW would require more than twelve years to review just the initial round of reports. By the end of the 1987 session CEDAW had examined only thirty-four reports. An additional twenty (fourteen initial and six second reports) had been received (only two of which, to CEDAW's credit, had been submitted before 1986).[30] Thirty-seven of the eighty-five countries required to submit initial reports, and twenty-four of the thirty countries required to submit second reports, had not yet done so; ten countries were delinquent on both their initial and second reports.[31] During its 1987 session CEDAW established a six-member, standing working group to recommend measures to reduce the backlog.

Inability to review country reports in a timely fashion and delinquent and often inadequate reporting encouraged by that delay are problems that plague all of the human rights treaty committees.[32] To improve adequacy and promptness of reporting, the Committee should consider asking the Secretariat, directly or via the Women's Commission, to offer its advisory services to those countries that are most delinquent, perhaps beginning with the ten that owe both initial and second reports.

To reduce CEDAW's backlog will require more innovative, and more costly, measures. Of all the human rights treaty committees, CEDAW faces the largest backlog. That circumstance is due primarily to its considerably shorter sessions, which in turn are in large part attributable to the General Assembly's failure to expand CEDAW's resources in keeping with the rapid growth in Convention ratifications. In contrast to CEDAW's annual two-week session, CERD meets for six weeks, CESC for three weeks, and the Human Rights Committee for nine weeks. The Human Rights Covenants, the Racial Convention, and the Women's Convention all have a comparable number of substantive provisions, and the Covenants and Women's Convention have approximately the same number of ratifiers (some ninety each compared to the Racial Convention's more than one hundred and twenty). No differences among the committees justify the much shorter length of CEDAW's sessions.

Responding to CEDAW's plight, the General Assembly authorized four additional meeting days for its 1988 session, an extension that is particularly noteworthy given that the UN's financial crisis led to the cancellation of several weeks from the regular sessions of other expert bodies. The extension enabled CEDAW to review 50 percent more reports than at previous sessions (eleven first and two second reports). Nonetheless the backlog continues to grow. Regular three-week sessions appear to be the minimum necessary for CEDAW to be able to complete its work in a timely and responsible manner.

In the absence of longer sessions, CEDAW might consider a procedure similar to that employed by CESC and its predecessor working group; namely, to require more countries to report each year but only on compliance with perhaps one-third or one-half of the Convention's substantive articles. For instance, one year could be devoted to discrimination regarding civil and political rights and employment; the next year to discrimination in health care, education, development, marriage, and family matters. There are several advantages: (1) countries might be more conscientious in reporting since (a) their reports would be more promptly reviewed and (b) reporting on only a few articles would pose a less formidable task; (2) by considering implementation of certain articles by a significant number of countries at a single session, the Committee would have more information on which to base general recommendations on those articles; (3) participation of UN specialized agencies would be facilitated; and (4) government representatives, asked to address women's rights only in certain areas, would likely be better prepared to respond to questions.

A less drastic departure from its current procedure, and one that could accomplish some of those goals, was proposed on a trial basis by CEDAW during its 1987 session. Experts were urged to coordinate their questions on topics such as equality, education, health, employment, and general comments.[33] A next step would be to encourage governments that do not already do so to organize their presentations in similar fashion.

A further step would be to designate groups of members to assume principal responsibility for raising particular issues, thereby sharpening questions and facilitating members' development of expertise. The proposal, discussed though not yet adopted by CESC,[34] would make particular sense for CEDAW given its relatively large membership (twenty-three members compared to eighteen each on the Human Rights Committee, CESC, and CERD, and ten on the Committee Against Torture). A range of ideological and geographic backgrounds thus could be represented in each group without requiring members to participate in more than one or two groups.

Reporting Guidelines

Another problem in monitoring implementation of the Women's Convention, as well as with other human rights treaties, is that no consensus has been reached as to what minimum measures countries presently are bound to undertake in order to be in compliance. The Women's Convention requires governments "*without delay* . . . to pursue by all appropriate means [in particular, by taking actions specified in the Convention] . . . a policy of eliminating discrimination against women" (article 2, emphasis added). There can be little doubt that immediate action is required. The question, then, is what sort of action? What must be done without delay is "to pursue" (not achieve) gender equality, and to do so by all "appropriate" (rather than necessary) means. Nonetheless, some clauses are sufficiently precise that failure to take at least certain concrete steps may presently be found to constitute a treaty violation. For example, states are to "take all appropriate measures, including legislation, to suppress all forms of traffic in women and exploitation of prostitution of women" (article 6); to "grant women equal rights with men to acquire, change or retain their nationality" (article 9(1)); and "[t]o repeal all national penal provisions which constitute discrimination against women" (article 2(g)).[35] Other obligations could be made concrete by incorporation of compliance timetables.[36] Yet others will require elaboration of the obligation to take "all appropriate measures."[37] Questions to be addressed include whether "appropriate measures" to implement certain rights may require violation of religious precepts, and whether governments are under a greater obligation to eliminate public discrimination than to proscribe purely private conduct.

The Women's Convention will not have incisive teeth until questions like those are answered and authoritative interpretations approved. Establishment in 1987 of a six-member, standing working group to study and propose suggestions and general recommendations constitutes a promising step. The working group should be instructed to focus on identifying provisions that are sufficiently precise to be immediately binding, and also to begin the task of specifying obligations that require greater precision. Governments should be instructed to identify in their reports measures they consider to be the minimum necessary to realize each of the rights set forth in the Convention.[38]

Supplemental Sources of Information

For a monitoring system based on government reports to be effective it is crucial that monitors have recourse to sources of information in addition to the reporting governments. While that proposition may appear self-evident, whether information from nongovernmental and intergovernmental sources may be used to challenge government reports has been rigorously debated by supervisory committees. CEDAW is to be commended for having requested the Secretariat to compile statistics garnered from official UN sources relevant to members' reports (UN Doc. E/1987/28 (1987) at para. 320), and for having requested UN specialized agencies to submit information provided by states parties and relevant to CEDAW's agenda (Decision 2, UN Doc. A/42/38 (1987) at para. 580).

CEDAW left ambiguous whether its decision authorizes consideration of information concerning practices of individual states that appear to violate the Convention (*id.*, para. 61); such a construction undoubtedly would enhance CEDAW's review of reports and should be pressed.[39]

NGOs constitute a rich source of information and procedural suggestions. Because of their expertise concerning certain rights and countries, their devotion of time and energy to issues, and their publicizing of UN actions, they have contributed enormously to the activism and effectiveness of bodies, such as the Human Rights Commission, in whose sessions they are authorized to participate formally. A major benefit of formal participation is that written statements not only are translated into UN official languages but also are assigned UN document numbers and distributed through UN channels. Though NGOs are allowed to attend CEDAW sessions, and their information is accepted by some CEDAW members on an informal basis to assist in questioning government representatives, their information would be more useable if subject to official distribution.

In addition to supplementing information available to CEDAW members, NGOs have a crucial role to play—that does not require formal accreditation—in publicizing and critiquing government reports and CEDAW comments on them.[40] In the absence of publicity governments can make representations about national conditions and planned reforms, and even can be challenged by CEDAW members, without being held accountable by national constituencies. NGOs are needed to inform and mobilize audiences that are best able to pressure governments to report accurately and to implement recommended reforms in good faith. NGO critiques are of use to CEDAW members committed to promoting women's rights and provide a watchdog mechanism to spur careful CEDAW review.

Reservations to the Convention

Reservations to treaties made by countries upon ratification impede implementation of most treaties, but the problem is of special concern regarding the Women's Convention due to the number and breadth of the reservations made to it. Islamic countries account for many, but by no means all, of the most limiting reservations. For instance, Bangladesh and Iraq, as well as New Zealand regarding its administration of the Cook Islands, entered reservations to article 2(f), by which states pledge "to take all appropriate measures, including legislation, to modify or abolish existing laws, regulations, customs and practices which constitute discrimination against women."[41] Seven countries (Cyprus, Egypt, Iraq, Jamaica, South Korea, Thailand, and Tunisia) reserved the right to deny women equal rights with respect to the nationality of their children (required by article 9(2)). Twelve countries (Bangladesh, Brazil, Egypt, France, India, Iraq, Malawi, Mauritius, South Korea, Thailand, Tunisia, and Turkey) made reservations to all or part of article 16 regarding marriage and family relations reserving, in particular, the prerogative to deny women equal rights to divorce, to choose a profession or occupation, and to acquire, dispose of, and manage property. At least three countries (West Germany, Mexico, and Sweden) declared their objections to the above and other reservations pursuant to article 28 which provides that "[a] reservation incompatible with the object and purpose of the present Convention shall not be permitted."

CEDAW is aggressively pursuing various measures to encourage withdrawal of reservations. In reviewing government reports, it has conveyed its dismay concerning reservations and questioned their necessity.[42] It has asked countries to undertake studies to identify the exact obstacles to withdrawal of the reservations, including, where appropriate, the impact of Islamic law. It has called on UN specialized agencies and the Women's Commission to study the relation between rights set forth in the Convention and Islamic laws and customs, compliance with which is a frequently cited reason for reservations. A particularly promising initiative was the decision of states that have ratified the Convention to address the problem of reservations, beginning in 1988, at their biennial meetings. In contrast, states parties to the other major human rights treaties have tended to confine their meetings to electing experts to the treaty committee and procedural matters such as choosing dates and places for committee sessions.

Interactions Between Women's Commission and CEDAW

At its 1988 session, the Women's Commission adopted a resolution formally recognizing the relevance of government reports submitted to CEDAW to its own monitoring responsibilities.[43] To enhance that relevance, the Commission recommended: (1) that CEDAW schedule its sessions sufficiently in advance of Commission sessions to enable the Commission to consider CEDAW reports of the same year; (2) that the chairpersons of the Commission and CEDAW attend sessions of the other body; and (3) that the Branch for the Advancement of Women be enlarged so as to be able to better meet CEDAW's needs as well as the increased demands of the Commission resulting from annualization of its sessions.[44]

Efforts to increase coordination between the Commission and CEDAW are to be commended and, it is hoped, may prompt similar interactions between the Human Rights Commission and CERD, CESC, and the Human Rights Committee. The Commission, however, should not regard government reports to CEDAW as substitutes for its own investigations of alleged violations. Though CEDAW members review government reports, they do not investigate facts nor do they supply the sort of sustained oversight that, for instance, rapporteurs appointed by the Human Rights Commission are able to provide.

Moreover, members of CEDAW, and indeed of other treaty supervisory bodies, are inclined to engage government representatives in constructive dialogue at least so long as it appears likely that the process will stimulate national debate and reform. Much can be said for the view that a critical approach should be undertaken only after constructive dialogue is seen to be ineffective. Given CEDAW's backlog, and the many years before it will have reviewed a significant number of second reports, it is unlikely in the near future forcefully to question governments concerning their reports. The Commission, on the other hand, because it has reviewed allegations of serious violations for several years, and because an aggressive approach may be more appropriate for an intergovernmental body, should already now be undertaking rigorous fact-finding studies, to be followed by identification of violations and recommendations of concrete measures to be taken if governments are to escape further scrutiny.

The Commission also should find useful CEDAW's elaborations of rights set forth in the Women's Convention. CEDAW has begun the process of elaboration by issuing suggestions and general recommendations based on its examination of government reports. While the Commission has not expressly recognized the relevance of that work to its own mandate, it has commended CEDAW for it.[45]

Conversely, CEDAW has addressed the Commission's work and, in particular, has asked for its assistance in conducting studies. At its 1987 session, CEDAW adopted a decision asking the Commission "to promote or undertake studies on the status of women under Islamic laws and customs and in particular on the status and equality of women in the family . . . and . . . in public life. . . ."[46] That request followed CEDAW's review of Bangladesh's report and undoubtedly was motivated by the low status of women, apparently due to application of Islamic laws and customs, in Bangladesh and other countries.

Clearly, the relation between women's rights and Islamic law is highly controversial. Equally clearly, clarification of that relation is crucial to the advancement of the rights of millions of women. That the Women's Commission has not addressed that relationship, and at its 1988 session did not even discuss CEDAW's request to do so, is truly remarkable. Several reasons could be posited for the Commission's failure. What is significant, however, is that, despite the concerns of some critics that reporting procedures often are little more than exercises in self-justification, CEDAW's reporting procedure has proved to be effective in formally raising a highly sensitive issue.

The above discussion suggests that, if its resources could be expanded, CEDAW might well be able to meet some of the Commission's needs for expert assistance. Expansion of CEDAW's role and resources seems advisable for several reasons: (1) much of the work that is integral to its mandate, including its elaboration of the Convention's obligations, is relevant to the Commission's work; (2) there is likely to be less resistance from Commission members and relevant UN bodies to expansion of CEDAW's resources—for instance, to enable it to meet for at least an additional week annually, and to have more staff assistance—than to creation of a new expert body or even appointment of individual experts; and (3) CEDAW already has demonstrated a willingness to be more innovative and forceful in promoting compliance with the Convention than has the Commission itself.

Summary of Recommendations

Both the Women's Commission and CEDAW would benefit from:

1. longer sessions;
2. expansion of the Branch for the Advancement of Women;
3. institutional arrangements to facilitate closer working relations between staff members of the Advancement of Women Branch in Vienna and the Human Rights Centre in Geneva;
4. enhanced access to and use of the Secretary-General's advisory services to assist countries that are unable to comply with recommendations because of lack of expertise or resources; and

5. increased coordination of their work.

The Women's Commission, in addition, should consider

1. investigating allegations of "consistent pattern[s] of . . . discriminatory practices" occurring in individual countries, and identifying governments, in addition to South Africa and Israel, that fail to take measures urged by the Commission to address any discriminatory practices found to exist;
2. requesting ECOSOC to appoint experts to assist in analyzing violations and monitoring gross abuses on a year-round basis;
3. making greater use of CEDAW's expertise;
4. being more responsive to CEDAW's requests for investigative studies;
5. undertaking a study on the compatibility of the Women's Convention with Islamic laws and customs; and
6. expanding its scrutiny of patterns of discrimination to include human rights violations that primarily affect women, even when they do not involve discrimination in a narrow sense (such as enforcement of restrictive marriage, divorce, and property laws).

CEDAW, in addition, should consider

1. directing states to report on only some, perhaps half, of the Convention articles at a given session, thereby enabling more states to report at each session and facilitating prompt review of reports;
2. directing states to identify in their reports essential minimum requirements in their country for the realization of each right recognized in the Convention;
3. placing a high priority on elaborating obligations that are immediately binding; and
4. clarifying its authority to consider information on individual countries from UN specialized agencies and NGOs.

Conclusion

The Commission on the Status of Women has begun to grapple with allegations of consistent patterns of discriminatory practices. It has declined, however, to investigate allegations of those practices being committed in individual countries, or to identify governments, other than South Africa and Israel, that have failed to take adequate steps to address violations found to exist. It has yet to undertake a study on the relation between Convention rights and Islamic law, despite the issue's obvious importance to its monitoring work. When the Commission has identified a pattern of discrimination, such as violence against detained women, and requested governments to provide information on how they are confronting the problem, few governments have responded, demonstrating the need for tougher procedures if the Commission is to have a significant impact on government practices. One initiative the Commission should consider is appointment of experts or working groups to investigate allegations of serious violations.

In its first seven sessions, CEDAW has evidenced promise of being an assertive promoter of women's rights. Nearly 60 percent of the 159 countries that are members of the UN (including such population giants as China, the USSR, and Indonesia) have become parties to the Women's Convention, and the number of parties continues to grow (seven countries became parties between CEDAW's 1986 and 1987 sessions and another two between its 1987 and 1988 sessions). Though more than a third of the Convention's 94 parties currently are delinquent in meeting their reporting obligations, several have displayed a responsiveness to CEDAW's scrutiny.[47]

In addition, CEDAW has taken several innovative steps that are likely to improve its effectiveness: it has appointed two working groups, one to study ways to reduce its backlog and the other to study and propose suggestions and general recommendations; it has adopted decisions despite small dissents, departing from the sometimes-paralyzing consensus approach strictly followed by other treaty supervisory committees; it has interpreted its authority to include issuance of suggestions and general recommendations concerning named governments as well as non-country-specific situations; it has encouraged its members to cooperate in grouping together and where possible consolidating questions on related topics; and it has requested the Secretariat and UN specialized agencies to compile and submit statistical and other information pertinent to its review of government reports.

CEDAW's chief weakness results from circumstances beyond its control; namely, the failure of powerful countries and countries where some of the worst violations are being committed—including the United States, India, and many Muslim countries—to ratify the Convention, or to do so only with substantial reservations. Ratification by more countries, especially by the United States and India, would considerably strengthen CEDAW's influence as well as the influence and credibility of those governments in advocating compliance with human rights standards. Encouraging ratification should be a high priority of NGOs.

A major problem CEDAW confronts is the large backlog of government reports for it to review. In the short term, the measure most needed to enhance CEDAW's effectiveness is extension of its regular sessions by at least one week.

CEDAW appears willing to commence the long-term and immensely important task of clarifying the obligations imposed by the Women's Convention. Assisted by CEDAW's energetic efforts, perhaps the Women's Commission might show greater activism in identifying, investigating and, where warranted, condemning, discriminatory practices, wherever committed. Such activism is crucial if the Commission and CEDAW are truly to help women whose rights are being violated.

NOTES

1. GA Res. 34/180 of 18 December 1979, 34 UN GAOR Supp. (No. 46) at 193–198, UN Doc. A/34/46 (1980).

2. *See, e.g.*, N. Burrows, *Monitoring Compliance of International Standards Relating to Human Rights: The Experience of the United Nations Commission on the Status of Women.* 31 NETHS. INT'L L. REV. 332 (1984); M. Galey, *International Enforcement of Women's Rights,* 6 HUMAN RIGHTS Q. 463 (Nov. 1984) (re Commission and Committee); Galey, *Promoting Non-discrimination Against Women: The UN Commission on the Status of Women,* 23 INTERNATIONAL STUDIES Q. 273 (June 1979); N. Hevener, *An Analysis of Gender Based Treaty Law: Contemporary Developments in Historical Perspective,* 8 HUMAN RIGHTS Q. 70 (February 1986) (re the Convention but not the Committee); T. Meron, HUMAN RIGHTS LAW-MAKING IN THE UNITED NATIONS: A CRITIQUE OF INSTRUMENTS AND PROCESS (Oxford: Clarendon Press, 1986); M. McDougal, H. Lasswell, & L. Chen, HUMAN RIGHTS AND WORLD PUBLIC ORDER 612–52 (New Haven: Yale University Press, 1980) (review of women's rights instruments); L. Reanda, *Human Rights and Women's Rights: The UN Approach,* 3 HUMAN RIGHTS Q. 11 (1981).

3. For basic information about the Commission, *see* UNITED NATIONS ACTION IN THE FIELD OF HUMAN RIGHTS, UN Sales No. E.83.XIV.2, ST/HR/2/Rev.2 (1983) at 290–91.

4. ESC Res. 11 (11) of 21 June 1946, 2 UN ESCOR Annex (No. 4) at 405.

5. ESC Res. 1987/19 of 26 May 1987, UN ESCOR Supp. (No. 1) at 16, UN Doc. E/1987/87 (1987).

6. ESC Res. 1987/24 of 26 May 1987, *id.* at 18.

7. ESC Decision 1987/121 of 26 May 1987, *id.* at 53–54.

8. Encouraging various UN bodies and regional commissions to better coordinate their work on women's rights and to promote women within their own ranks undoubtedly is important but can result in general improvement in the status of women only to the extent that the UN bodies themselves prove effective. The conferences planned by the Commission are perhaps its most visible undertakings and have been successful in drawing world attention to issues of greatest concern to the Commission and NGOs; but the conferences aim to "review" and "appraise" and thus cannot be expected, in and of themselves, to promote curtail-

ment of particular violations. Making policy recommendations on priority themes currently is a new and only roughly defined procedure that risks addressing too many issues at the cost of sacrificing follow-through. Treaty-drafting has been a significant Commission activity in the past; the focus now should be on implementation and enforcement.

9. Report of the Commission on the Status of Women, Draft Res. XIII, UN ESCOR Supp. (No. 5) at 25, UN Doc. E/1988/15/Rev.1 (1988).

10. Report of the Secretary-General, Alternative Measures to Strengthen the Commission on the Status of Women, UN Doc. E/CN.6/1986/13 at para. 18.

11. D. Weissbrodt, *The Three "Theme" Special Rapporteurs of the UN Commission on Human Rights,* 80 AMER. J. INT'L L. 685 (1986).

12. Res. 32/1, Report of the Women's Commission (1988), *supra* at note 9, at 37.

13. Some observers believe the move was a concession to then Secretary-General Kurt Waldheim, who sought to enlarge the Vienna Office. Others recall that the then-Director of the Human Rights Division protested his being outranked in Geneva by the Advancement of Women Branch and its female director.

14. Kamminga & Rodley, *Direct Intervention at the UN: NGO Participation in the Commission on Human Rights and its Sub-Commission,* in GUIDE TO INTERNATIONAL HUMAN RIGHTS PRACTICE 186–99 (H. Hannum ed.; Philadelphia: Univ. of Pennsylvania Press, 1984).

15. Marc Bossuyt, *The Development of Special Procedures of the United Nations Commission on Human Rights,* 6 HUMAN RIGHTS L. J. 179, 182 (1985).

16. Frank Newman (quoting and elaborating the phrase suggested by Ernest Landy, former Chief of the Application of Standards Branch of the ILO), *The Mobilization of Shame,* in HUMAN RIGHTS DOCKET OF THE MEIKLEJOHN CIVIL LIBERTIES INSTITUTE (A .F. Ginger ed.; Berkeley: Meiklejohn Civil Liberties Institute, 1979).

17. For instance, at the 1986 Commission session the Foreign Minister of Guatemala announced that his country would permit the International Committee of the Red Cross to visit its prisons and detention centers. Japan conscientiously has undertaken several measures to improve its treatment of minorities and mentally disabled people in order to stave off Commission censure. Sri Lanka successfully managed, until 1987, to counter efforts to pass a Commission resolution condemning its campaign to quell the demands of Tamil rebels for self-rule by promising to take steps to respect human rights and humanitarian law; the unmistakable message was that stronger criticism was likely in 1988 if Sri Lanka did not take effective steps to control gross violations.

18. Galey, *supra* note 2, 6 HUMAN RIGHTS Q. at 469–71 (1984).

19. Report of the Women's Commission (1988), *supra* note 9, at 65.

20. STATUS OF INTERNATIONAL INSTRUMENTS, UN Sales No. E.87.XI.2, ST/HR/5 (1987).

The U.S., Israel, and the Netherlands are among the few western democracies that have not ratified the Convention. Of the more than two dozen predominantly Islamic states, only Bangladesh, Egypt, Indonesia, Iraq, Tunisia, Turkey, and Democratic Yemen are parties. All ten Eastern European countries are parties, as are most Latin American and many African countries. India's failure to ratify is particularly disappointing given the size of its population, the gross violations of women's rights (such as bride-burnings) occurring there, and its leadership of the nonaligned group.

21. *See*, Galey, *supra* note 2, 6 HUMAN RIGHTS Q. at 477; Alston & Simma, *First Session of the UN Committee on Economic, Social and Cultural Rights*, 81 AMER. J. INT'L LAW 747, 749 (1987) (noting efforts of Eastern European experts, in keeping with expressed positions of their governments, to block CESC's development of more effective procedures).

22. CEDAW Report (Fifth Sess., 1986), 41 UN GAOR Supp. (No. 45) at paras. 362, 365, UN Doc. A/41/45.

23. *Id.* at para. 359 (discussing art. 21).

24. *Id.* at para. 365.

25. CEDAW Report (Sixth Sess., 1987), 42 UN GAOR Supp. (No. 38) at para. 49, UN Doc. A/42/38.

26. *Id.* at para. 44.

27. *Id.* at para. 59.

28. *Id.* at paras. 45, 59–60.

29. *Id.* at para. 47.

30. *Id.* at paras. 6, 578, and 580.

31. *Id.* at para. 10 and Annex II.B.

32. Johan Nordenfelt [former CEDAW member], *Conventions in Crisis*, 1 NORDIC JOURNAL ON HUMAN RIGHTS (1987), updated in HUMAN RIGHTS INTERNET REPORTER 60 (Winter/Spring 1987).

33. CEDAW Report (1987), *supra* note 25, at paras. 33, 40, 42, 51.

34. Alston & Simma, *supra* note 21, at 751.

35. Article 2(g) clearly requires the repeal of laws that prescribe a lesser penalty for wrongful acts committed by men (*e.g.*, adultery) or against women (*e.g.*, bride burning). Clarification is needed regarding whether laws that fail to accord special protection to women, such as those that provide no or minimal punishment for spousal rape, are also to be repealed.

36. *E.g.*, "States Parties shall take all appropriate measures to ensure to women, on equal terms with men and without any discrimination, the opportunity to represent their Governments at the international level and to participate in the work of international organizations." (Art. 8.)

37. *E.g.*, parties are to take "all appropriate measures" to ensure nondiscrimination in "access to the same curricula, teaching staff, . . . and equipment of the same quality" (art. 10(b)); "the same employment opportunities" (art. 11(b)); social security (art. 11(e)); health care services (art. 12(1)); and all rights and obligations relating to marriage and family relations (art. 16).

38. *Cf.* Alston & Simma, *supra* note 21, at 750 (one of the most important procedural suggestions advanced during CESC's initial session was that reporting guidelines should direct states parties to "identify benchmarks or standards which they consider to be the essential minimum requirement in their country for the realization of each of the rights recognized in the Covenant").

39. *Cf.* Alston & Simma, *supra* note 21, at 751 (International Labor Organization's provision of country-specific information to the ECOSOC working group deemed to be of considerable assistance).

40. D. Fischer, *International Reporting Procedures*, in GUIDE TO INTERNATIONAL HUMAN RIGHTS PRACTICE, *supra* note 14, at 178–83.

41. STATUS OF INTERNATIONAL INSTRUMENTS, *supra* note 20, at 142–71.

42. *See, e.g.*, CEDAW Report, *supra* note 25, at paras. 512 and 569.

43. Report of the Women's Commission (1988), *supra* note 9, Draft Res. XII, at para. 9.

44. *Id.* at paras. 7, 8, 12, and 13.

45. *Id.* at para. 6.

46. CEDAW report, *supra* note 25, Decision 4 (1987).

47. For instance, the representative who presented Canada's report announced that his government had amended its laws on sexual harassment to comply with the provisions of the Convention, and was seeking repeal of a law that deprived Indian women, but not men, of Indian status upon marrying non-Indians (CEDAW Report [1986], *supra* note 22, at paras. 35 and 36).

3

Prospects for the Development of Intergovernmental Human Rights Bodies in Asia and the Pacific

JON M. VAN DYKE

Since World War II, the international community has made great strides in codifying human rights norms and building institutions to protect those rights from governments that oppress their citizens in order to ensure their own power. The Universal Declaration of Human Rights, adopted by the UN General Assembly in 1948; the International Covenants on Civil and Political Rights and on Economic, Social and Cultural Rights adopted in 1966 and now ratified by over eighty nations; and the three regional human rights agreements—in Western Europe, in the Americas, and most recently in Africa—are all designed to define the protections that must be afforded to all citizens and to provide mechanisms that will in fact protect individuals whose rights are abused by their governments.

In a relatively short period of time, commissions and tribunals have been created and have begun issuing opinions, resolving disputes, and providing guidance for future conduct. The European Human Rights Commission and Court have a rich jurisprudence already, and the Inter-American Commission and Court and the Human Rights Committee of the Civil and Political Rights Covenant are also beginning to issue significant opinions and reports that are helping citizens and minority groups. The African Charter has only recently achieved a sufficient number of ratifications to take effect so it cannot yet be fully evaluated, but the determination of African nations to draft this document and to achieve the necessary ratifications is strong evidence of the region's commitment to human rights.

The only part of the world (aside from Eastern Europe) that remains without a regional human rights charter and organization is the Asia-Pacific region. Many possible reasons may explain why this area has lagged behind, but certainly a central problem is that it cannot be considered a "region" in any realistic sense. It constitutes half the planet and contains more than half of the world's population. It encompasses large and small nations, rich and poor, members of all political and military alliances and alignments, and adherents to all the current economic arrangements. The cultural and political differences among the peoples of Asia and the Pacific are vast and, although common human rights issues can be identified that affect many of the nations of this area, it would be overly optimistic to expect that these nations will all work together to solve these issues during the present generation.

The United Nations (through the Economic and Social Commission for Asia and the Pacific [ESCAP]) sponsored a meeting in Colombo, Sri Lanka, in 1982 to discuss the possibility of establishing a regional human rights organization. It assembled an impressive group of human rights advocates and government officials. Their most important recommendation was that subregions be identified, because the Asia-Pacific area as a whole is too large to support a single effective intergovernmental human rights organization.

Dividing Asia and the Pacific into smaller zones is not, however, an easy task. South Asia is an obvious subregion; it has recently developed the South Asia Association for Regional Cooperation (SAARC), consisting of India, Pakistan, Bangladesh, Sri Lanka, Nepal, Bhutan, and the Maldives. But this subregion is currently torn by ethnic strife and significant interstate conflict, and several countries now have military governments. These nations are thus unlikely to construct a human rights program in which the actions of a government toward its citizens can be scrutinized in detail by experts from other nations.

Southeast Asia is another area that has some elements of cohesion, and some nations of this subregion—the Philippines, Indonesia, Malaysia, Singapore, Thailand, and now Brunei—have worked successfully together on economic problems through the Association of South-East Asian Nations (ASEAN). Other nations in the subregion—Vietnam, Kampuchea, and Laos—have not been involved in these efforts and are unlikely to work together with the ASEAN countries either on economic problems or on human rights questions in the near future. Another problem country is Burma; it has steadfastly avoided joining either ASEAN or SAARC and has demonstrated no interest in dealing with human rights questions regionally or subregionally.

The Middle East (or West Asia) is a region in geographic terms, and some regional organizations—like the Arab League—have functioned effectively on some issues. The area has been torn asunder by strife in this generation, however, and a number of ongoing conflicts resist easy solutions: the civil war in Lebanon, the armed confrontation between Israel and its neighbors, and the war between Iraq and Iran. The development of a human rights charter does not appear to be a very high priority for the nations of the Middle East.

Perhaps the subregion that is least likely to come together to form a human rights entity in the foreseeable future is Northeast Asia. In this area, the two Koreas, Japan, and China are nations that have been adversaries for millennia. Although they are now, in fact, working together on limited economic projects, it is improbable that they will want to form any formal regional organizations together in the near future.

That leaves the Pacific island area, where close political and economic ties have developed among the nations and where significant regional organizations are well-established. The South Pacific Commission (consisting of all the island entities) and the South Pacific Forum (consisting of the independent and free associated states) have been functioning effectively as regional organizations for a number of years, and they have spun off a number of other special topic organizations such as the Forum Fisheries Agency (FFA) and the South Pacific Regional Environmental Programme (SPREP). All these organizations include Australia and New Zealand and extend eastward to Tonga and the Cook Islands and northward to the Micronesian political entities. The French-affiliated islands and the U.S.-affiliated islands participate in the South Pacific Commission and SPREP but are excluded from the South Pacific Forum and FFA. The Pacific island area thus shows the greatest promise of forming a cohesive subregion for the purpose of developing a human rights organization.

In April 1985, the Law Association for Asia and the Pacific (LAWASIA), a nongovernmental organization based in Sydney, Australia, coordinated a conference in Fiji where attorneys, community activists, and government officials from the South Pacific presented papers on the types of human rights problems found in the region. Among the issues identified were:

- the self-determination of peoples;
- the rights of indigenous peoples;
- the rights of cultural minorities, often immigrants from elsewhere in the region;
- the status of women;
- the rights of children and youths, particularly with regard to education and jobs; and
- the right to participate in decisions affecting one's vital interests.

The papers submitted at the 1985 meeting have since been published, and the participants have now begun to develop a human rights charter for the region.[1] LAWASIA sponsored drafting-committee and working-party meetings in Sydney and Apia, Western Samoa, in 1986. The Model Charter that was drafted will be examined at meetings to be held throughout the Pacific in the hope of developing a constituency to persuade the governments of the region to support this effort.[2]

The drafters began by looking at the African Charter of Human and Peoples' Rights and then modified it as appropriate for the Pacific island region. The African Charter contains statements of civil and political rights; economic, social, and cultural rights; rights of peoples; and duties of governments and individuals. It is the most recent statement of rights and comes from a part of the world in which peoples have only recently obtained their independence or are still pressing for it. Not only does it grapple with the critical issue of the right to development but it also raises two other issues of considerable importance for Pacific nations: the duties of individuals to the group, community, and society; and the rights of indigenous peoples. Human rights declarations and treaties from other regions of the world do not address these two topics.

Many Pacific island communities have a strong sense of the structure of the village or group, which is frequently a large extended family. One finds in island communities, from Samoa and Tonga to Yap and Palau, and including many variations, a set of traditional relationships within the group that may in some instances be thought to override the rights of an individual member of the group. The challenge in drafting a human rights charter for the Pacific is thus to find language that recognizes and protects the values found in such traditional group relationships but also protects each individual against possible abuses.

The rights of indigenous peoples are also central in many Pacific island communities. In New Caledonia, the indigenous Kanaks, who are outnumbered by Europeans and other Pacific islanders, have been struggling to regain control over their islands, or at least some degree of autonomy within their regions. In Fiji, the election of a coalition government in early 1987 that included many persons of Indian ancestry and Fijian leaders drawn from outside the traditional Fijian chiefs led to a military coup by the army (which is dominated by native Fijians), and then to the reestablishment of a government that effectively excludes Fiji Indians from participation. This action was taken even though the 1970 Fiji Constitution appears to have strong protections to ensure that the land rights of the native Fijians cannot be altered, and it thus illustrates how strongly felt the claims of the traditional leaders of the indigenous people are. Other Pacific communities with problems relating to the rights of the indigenous people in relation to other members include Australia, New Zealand, Guam, the Northern Marianas, and Hawaii.

The LAWASIA working party and drafting group, in developing a Draft Model Pacific Human Rights Charter, modified the African Charter by examining all the constitutions of the Pacific, determining which principles are accepted throughout the region, and choosing language that best expressed those principles. All the constitutions of the Pacific have bills of rights, except those of Australia and New Zealand. The New Zealand Parliament is currently considering the enactment of a bill of rights, but Australia recently abandoned its attempt to enact a bill of rights which would have implemented Australia's obligations under the International Covenant on Civil and Political Rights. Both countries have indigenous and immigrant communities that would benefit from specifically articulated and enforceable constitutional rights.

The drafters decided that the Pacific island nations are not ready for a regional court that could issue decisions binding on governments. Instead they recommended—again following the African model—a commission with powers to receive complaints, conduct investigations, and make recommendations for the resolution of grievances. The first steps toward forming a regional human rights organization in the Pacific are thus under way, at least at the nongovernmental level, and it is possible that the next few years will see the establishment of a Pacific Human Rights Charter and a Pacific Human Rights Commission.

The question remains whether all or part of the rest of Asia will move toward developing human rights treaties or organizations. Do Asian countries have a cultural aversion toward this topic, or do other fundamental obstacles stand in the way of movement toward international human rights protections? Although generalizations are dangerous on a broad question like this one, certain observations can be offered.

First, the nations of Asia have been especially reluctant to allow third-party adjudication of disputes and strongly favor bilateral negotiations as the proper way to resolve controversies. They have been reluctant to accede to the compulsory jurisdiction of the International Court of Justice,[3] and no Pacific or Asian state has ratified the Optional Protocol to the International Covenant on Civil and Political Rights, which allows individuals to bring complaints against their government to the attention of the Human Rights Committee. Even though international human rights mechanisms are generally less confrontational than the International Court, having a goal of facilitating settlements rather than arriving at formal decisions whenever possible, Pacific and Asian nations remain skeptical about such approaches. Given their lack of receptivity to existing mechanisms for the resolution of international disputes, Asian nations are likely to be reluctant to create new organizations with the power to address violations of human rights.

Second, many Asian peoples are still influenced by the teachings of Confucius, which emphasize hierarchy and respect for authority and the proper place for each person within the hierarchy, and discourage individualism. This world view tends to deemphasize the importance of protecting individual human rights in relation to other priorities. Perhaps if "collective" or "group" rights were also protected in a human rights charter, it might be more acceptable to the peoples of Asia and the Pacific.

Third, communist regimes in other parts of the world have not generally supported regional human rights organizations, and those in Asia are not likely to be more interested in such initiatives than their counterparts elsewhere.

Fourth, many nations in Asia do have serious human rights problems that go to the very essence of their national identity, so that outside scrutiny is perceived as threatening. An illustrative list of such problems would include the ethnic strife in Sri Lanka, the conflict between Chinese and Malays in Malaysia, religious and linguistic conflicts in India, the ongoing boundary disputes between India and Pakistan, the status of Chinese in Indonesia and Vietnam, the situations in the West Irian and East Timor areas which were incorporated into Indonesia, the Moro rebellion in the Philippines, the treatment of ethnic Koreans in Japan, and the status of indigenous peoples in many of these countries. Free expression in many Asian and Pacific countries is suppressed, and the right to participate fully and in some cases even partially in governmental decision-making is forbidden. The death penalty is used extensively in many Asian countries: in Malaysia it is used for persons convicted of smuggling drugs, for instance, and in the People's Republic of China it is used for a broad range of offenses, including, according to a September 1987 report, the showing of pornographic movies.

Political opposition is barely tolerated in some Asian countries, including those theoretically committed to democratic principles. For instance, in Singapore in the spring of 1987, sixteen community activists were arrested and detained without trial, pursuant to Singapore's Internal Security Act, accused of being Marxists involved in a communist conspiracy to overthrow the government. When asked about the proof that these individuals were in fact subversives, Prime Minister Lee Kuan Yew replied that he did not intend to submit his proof to a court of law and that he would not "allow subversives to get away by insisting that I got to prove everything against them in a court of law with evidence that will stand up to the strict rules of evidence of a court of law."[4] The Singapore constitution specifically authorizes detention without charges or trial in such internal security cases and limits the freedoms of speech and association when the security or public order of the nation is affected. The Malaysian government similarly arrested over ninety persons under its Internal Security Act in October and November 1987, including the leader of the main opposition party, and shut down three newspapers.

The Pacific island nations have generally managed to avoid such flagrant human rights violations after gaining independence during the past two decades, but the Fiji coups in 1987 and their aftermath illustrate that a Pacific island government also is capable of detaining citizens without trial, interfering with press freedom, and nullifying the results of a free election. Another serious human rights conflict exists in New Caledonia, where the differences between the indigenous Kanaks and immigrant settlers also raise questions of the special legal status of indigenous people and how that status should be protected in a multiethnic community.

Conclusion

The road toward the development of international human rights protections is a long and bumpy one, and it is not surprising that some regions of the world have moved faster than others. Many reasons can be cited to explain why the Asia-Pacific area has been the slowest to make progress in developing regional human rights mechanisms, and some of those reasons are so central to some nations that it may be unrealistic to expect any significant steps toward the development of a regional human rights program in this century.

Democracies do, nonetheless, thrive in parts of Asia and the Pacific, and many activists continue to pursue the goal of creating a structure that can help individuals in nations where human rights are not fully protected. A group of academics at the Jawaharlal Nehru University in New Delhi is now compiling information on human rights conditions throughout Asia and is publishing regular reports, and LAWASIA is also continuing to promote interest in human rights throughout Asia and the Pacific. These nongovernmental organizations can do a great deal to increase awareness of human rights among the citizenry and to generate political pressure against governments that abuse these rights. On some occasions, one government may try to bring pressure against another government, particularly when the second government is abusing the right of citizens with ethnic or religious ties to the first. Examples include India's attempts to assist the Tamils in Sri Lanka and the ethnic Indians in Fiji, Pakistan's concern for the rights of Muslims in India, and China's attention to the treatment of Chinese communities in Southeast Asia.

Although such ad hoc efforts are useful, they are not a satisfactory substitute for a permanent regional body that can monitor human rights on a more systematic basis. The Pacific island region may be the first subregion in which the efforts to establish such an organization may bear fruit.

Most Pacific island nations have excellent constitutions and functioning democracies with independent judiciaries sensitive to the need to protect individual rights. Pacific islanders have worked together effectively on other issues, and a number of individuals throughout the region have shown strong interest in developing a human rights convention and commission. The issues of colonialism and the rights of indigenous peoples and other ethnic groups may provide an impetus to developing mechanisms that will permit regional input into festering local problems. Although this effort remains at the nongovernmental level as of this writing, attempts to promote a Pacific Human Rights Charter and Commission will undoubtedly continue and can be expected ultimately to be successful.

NOTES

1. Conference on Prospects for the Establishment of An Inter-Governmental Human Rights Commission in the South Pacific (April 12–14, 1985) (Patricia Hyndman & Sarah Waddell eds.; LAWASIA, 1985).

2. Report of the Working Party on a Proposed Pacific Charter of Human Rights (Nick O'Neill ed.; Sydney, Australia: LAWASIA, 1986).

3. Among Asian nations, only India, Japan, Pakistan, and the Philippines have accepted compulsory jurisdiction of the International Court of Justice.

4. (Singapore) Straits Times, 3 June 1987.

PART II

HUMAN RIGHTS AND ARMED CONFLICT

4

Ways International Organizations Can Improve Their Implementation of Human Rights and Humanitarian Law in Situations of Armed Conflict

DAVID WEISSBRODT

Governments are principally responsible for the implementation of international human rights and humanitarian law during periods of armed conflict. During noninternational armed conflicts, governments and armed opposition groups may each bear responsibility for their obedience to these norms.[1]

International organizations can only encourage the participants in armed conflicts to respect human rights and humanitarian law. The International Committee of the Red Cross (ICRC) has long pursued a leading role in working for the application of humanitarian law during periods of armed conflict; recently it has also begun to refer to human rights law in situations of internal strife or tensions not covered by international humanitarian law.[2] The United Nations General Assembly,

The author wishes to thank Kathy Ellis, of the University of Minnesota Law School Class of 1987, for her assistance in the preparation of this article. An expanded version of this article appeared as *The Role of International Organizations in the Implementation of Human Rights and Humanitarian Law in Situations of Armed Conflict*, 21 VAND. J. TRANSNATIONAL L. 2, 313 (1988).

the UN Commission on Human Rights, the International Court of Justice, the Inter-American Commission on Human Rights, and several other intergovernmental organizations have occasionally attempted to use their influence to seek the protection of human rights during armed conflicts and have irregularly referred to humanitarian law in such endeavors.[3] All these organizations have sought partially to fill the vacuum left by the failure of the UN Security Council and other international mechanisms to deal successfully with situations of armed conflict.

International nongovernmental organizations (NGOs) have recognized that human rights violations within their respective areas of concern may occur during periods of armed conflict. Indeed, serious human rights violations, including arbitrary killings, detention, and ill-treatment, are likely to increase at such times. For example, in its Annual Report of 1986 Amnesty International identified twenty-one countries where armed conflicts were occurring or had occurred[4] and in which human rights issues were noted; the report also notes Amnesty International's concern about prisoners held by the Polisario Front and thus tangentially mentions the conflict in Morocco and the Western Sahara. The report fails to mention the war between Iran and Iraq, however.

In dealing with human rights violations, the United Nations and NGOs have relied principally upon the Universal Declaration of Human Rights and the International Covenant on Civil and Political Rights, but these organizations have begun to refer more frequently to principles of humanitarian law applicable to armed conflict situations, for example, those norms found in the four Geneva Conventions of 12 August 1949 and the two Additional Protocols adopted in 1977.

This article first briefly reviews the practice of nongovernmental organizations and one principal intergovernmental organization—the United Nations General Assembly—in seeking the application of human rights and humanitarian law during situations of armed conflict. It then studies the reasons why the United Nations and international NGOs should cite or should be reluctant to refer to humanitarian law in support of their human rights work. Third, the article considers the preeminent position of the International Committee of the Red Cross and considers what role other—principally nongovernmental—organizations can play in situations of armed conflict. Fourth, the article examines factors affecting fact-finding in periods of armed conflict. Finally, it discusses the effectiveness of the work of nongovernmental organizations against human rights violations during armed conflicts.

Practice of International Nongovernmental Organizations and the UN General Assembly in Referring to International Humanitarian Norms

There is considerable diversity in the way nongovernmental and intergovernmental organizations use humanitarian law in their human rights work and how they approach situations of armed conflict. Indeed, even *within* particular nongovernmental organizations one can identify quite different policies and practices. The diverse approaches in reports by a single organization might be explained by different individual authors, by a failure to develop a consistent supervision over the content of reports, and by the slow learning process in recognizing the importance of humanitarian law.

For example, Amnesty International has sporadically made use of humanitarian law for many years in dealing with torture, the imprisonment of prisoners of conscience, executions, and unfair trials in political cases, arising during periods of armed conflict. The limited mandate of Amnesty International, for example, to work for the freedom of prisoners of conscience and for fair trials in "political" cases, does not fit easily within the legal structure of humanitarian law. Nevertheless, during the last few years there has been a significant improvement in the sophistication of Amnesty International's efforts during periods of armed conflict, although its practice is still not entirely consistent.

The International Commission of Jurists (ICJ) has used humanitarian law in a sophisticated and careful fashion on some occasions and has almost ignored it on others. The principal reason for this diversity of practice may be explained by the degree to which the authors of the various ICJ reports understood humanitarian law or carefully assessed the distinct challenge presented by armed conflict situations.

Other NGOs have issued fact-finding reports on situations involving armed conflicts with a considerable diversity in their apparent awareness of international humanitarian norms. For example, the Minority Rights Group issued a report on the Western Sahara which principally discussed the armed conflict in that area, but which cited only the Universal Declaration of Human Rights, other UN resolutions, and the Charter of the Organization of African Unity, without any reference to the Geneva Conventions or other sources of humanitarian law.[5]

A review of six recent reports by the Fédération Internationale des Droits de l'Homme on situations in which armed conflicts have occurred indicates that the Federation cited the Geneva Conventions only with respect to a mission to Jordan, Israel, Lebanon, and the Gaza Strip; it failed to mention any standards of human rights or humanitarian law in regard to missions to Afghanistan, El Salvador, Ethiopia, Guatemala, and Honduras.

A review of United Nations General Assembly resolutions and decisions from 1977 to 1986 indicates that the General Assembly has not been any more consistent than NGOs in its references to the Geneva Conventions of 1949 and the Additional Protocols. Once the UN began citing to the Conventions for a given armed conflict situation, however, it consistently cited to the Conventions in subsequent years. In addition, the frequency of UN citations to the Geneva Conventions increased over the period, with the most dramatic rise occurring in the 1986 resolutions.

Over the ten-year period from 1977 to 1986, the UN General Assembly adopted a number of resolutions regarding situations of armed conflict. With respect to the substantive resolutions and decisions adopted during this period, there were eleven conflict situations in which the UN could have cited to the Geneva Conventions. These conflicts occurred in Afghanistan, Chad, Cyprus, East Timor, El Salvador, Grenada, Guatemala, the Israeli Occupied Territories, Kampuchea, Namibia, and Nicaragua.

None of the General Assembly resolutions concerning conflicts in Chad (1981), Cyprus (1978–83), East Timor (1977–83), Grenada (1984), Kampuchea (1980–86), and Nicaragua (1979) cited humanitarian law norms.

Prior to 1986, resolutions concerning Afghanistan addressed refugees, the threat to international peace, and the withdrawal of Soviet troops from Afghanistan. In 1986, the UN showed increased concern about human rights violations by the combatants and "[c]all[ed] upon the parties to the conflict to apply fully the principles and rules of international humanitarian organizations, in particular the International Committee of the Red Cross, and to facilitate their operations for the alleviation of the suffering of the people of Afghanistan."[6]

With respect to El Salvador, the General Assembly began citing to the 1949 Geneva Conventions in 1982. In 1984, it began to include references to the Additional Protocols, admonishing the combatants to apply the standards in both the Geneva Conventions and the Additional Protocols "as a minimum standard of protection of human rights and humane treatment of the civilian population."[7] In 1986, the General Assembly issued an even stronger statement regarding the applicability of the Geneva Conventions and the Additional Protocols to the Salvadorian conflict. The resolution cited to the Geneva Conventions in the opening of the preamble. In addition, the resolution included the following:

> *Considering* that, while the armed conflict not of an international character continues, the Government and the insurgent forces are obliged to apply the minimum standards of protection of human rights and humane treatment set out in article 3 common to the Geneva Conventions of 12 August 1949, as well as Additional Protocol II, to which the republic of El Salvador is a party, . . . The General Assembly, . . . 3. *Expresses* . . . its deep concern at the fact that serious and numerous violations of human rights continue to take place in El Salvador owing above all to non-fulfillment of the humanitarian rules of war and therefore requests the Government of El Salvador and the insurgent forces to adopt measures conducive to the humanization of the conflict by observing scrupulously the Geneva Conventions of 1949 and the Additional Protocols of 1977.[8]

In its resolutions concerning Guatemala, the UN has never cited to the Geneva Conventions or Additional Protocols, although since 1984 it has referred to the Guatemalan conflict as "an armed conflict not of an international character."[9]

The UN General Assembly has continuously cited to the Fourth Geneva Convention in its resolutions on the "Report of the Special Committee to Investigate Israeli Practices Affecting the Human Rights of the Population of the Occupied Territories."[10] It began citing the Fourth Geneva Convention in its resolutions on "The Situation in the Middle East" in 1982 and in its resolutions on Palestinian refugees in 1986.

While the General Assembly has reviewed the situation in Namibia every year since 1977, it did not cite to the Geneva Conventions until 1984. The next year, the General Assembly declared

> that the liberation struggle in Namibia is a conflict of an international character in terms of article 1, paragraph 4 of Additional Protocol I to the Geneva Conventions of 12 August 1949 and, in this regard, demands the Conventions and Additional Protocol I be applied by South Africa, and in particular that all captured freedom fighters be accorded prisoner-of-war status as called for by the Geneva Convention relative to treatment of prisoners of war and the additional protocol thereto.[11]

The UN General Assembly repeated this declaration in the same or substantially similar form in 1985 and 1986.

The UN General Assembly thus has cited to the Geneva Conventions and Additional Protocols in resolutions relating to a number of armed conflict situations since 1977. It has not done so consistently, however, nor has it cited to the Conventions and Protocols in every instance where it would have been appropriate. Recent practice may represent the start of a trend in which the UN will increasingly use the Conventions and Protocols as a tool to raise the combatants' respect for the human rights of people directly or indirectly at risk in situations of armed conflict.

Should Nongovernmental Organizations and the United Nations Cite International Humanitarian Law in Support of Their Human Rights Concerns?

International human rights organizations and the UN General Assembly ordinarily refer in their actions, reports, and resolutions to the Universal Declaration of Human Rights, the International Covenant on Civil and Political Rights, and occasionally for the principle of nonrefoulement to the Convention and Protocol Relating to the Status of Refugees.

The United Nations and nongovernmental organizations, when confronted by human rights violations in the context of armed conflicts, may often find that international humanitarian law is applicable to such violations and provides an additional legal foundation for their concerns. In some cases international humanitarian law may even provide a stronger basis for human rights work than the Universal Declaration of Human Rights or the International Covenant on Civil and Political Rights.[12]

The principal multilateral treaties that legislate international humanitarian law are more broadly applicable than the main human rights treaties. As of 31 December 1986, the Geneva Conventions of 1949 had been ratified by 162 countries; the Additional Protocol I of 1977 had been ratified by 55 nations, while 48 nations had become party to Additional Protocol II of 1977. The International Covenant on Civil and Political Rights of 1966 had been ratified by 83 nations, while the International Covenant on Economic, Social and Cultural Rights had been accepted by 86 countries.

The Hague Conventions of 1899 and 1907 are broadly accepted as restating customary international humanitarian law applicable to all countries, and some of the principles of international humanitarian law are more specific or more exacting than the provisions of international human rights law. Humanitarian law also applies specifically to emergency situations; international human rights law permits significant derogations during these same periods.

Article 4 of the International Covenant on Civil and Political Rights provides that in situations threatening the life of the nation, a government may suspend most human rights protections so long as (1) such a suspension is strictly required by the exigencies of the situation, (2) the suspension does not conflict with the nation's other international obligations (such as the Geneva Conventions), and (3) the UN Secretary-General is immediately informed. No derogation is permitted from the right to be free from discrimination on the basis of race, color, sex, language, religion, or social origin. Also, no derogation is permitted from the rights to be free from arbitrary killing; torture or cruel, inhuman, or degrading treatment or punishment; slavery; imprisonment for debt; retroactive penalties; or the failure to recognize a person before the law.[13] Other rights, such as the right to be free from arbitrary arrest or detention and the right to a prompt and fair trial, would be subject to derogation in times of public emergency.[14]

Many governments are not parties to the International Covenant on Civil and Political Rights; therefore, they are not required to take even the formal steps to derogate from their obligations under that treaty and are arguably not bound by the nonderogable rights identified in the Covenant. They may still be bound to respect these nonderogable rights, including freedom from torture, arbitrary killing, and so on. In this respect human rights organizations rely on the rights defined in the Universal Declaration of Human Rights, which is applicable to all governments and contains no derogation clause similar to article 4 of the International Covenant on Civil and Political Rights. But article 29 of the Universal Declaration of Human Rights contains a general limitation clause for all the rights contained in that instrument, even including the prohibitions against torture, arbitrary killing, and so on. Article 29 states,

> In the exercise of his rights and freedoms, everyone shall be subject only to such limitations as are determined by law solely for the purpose of securing due recognition and respect for the rights and freedoms of others and of meeting the just requirements of morality, public order and the general welfare in a democratic society.

The terms "morality," "public order," and "general welfare in a democratic society" are quite vague. If they were broadly interpreted, they could undermine all the rights in the Universal Declaration. There are several reasons to believe that these limitations should not be so broadly interpreted. First, it is a standard tenet of treaty construction that limitation and exception clauses should be narrowly interpreted to preserve the substantive rights granted. The European Court and Commission on Human Rights have narrowly interpreted the similar exception clauses in the European Convention on Human Rights. Second, it might well be questioned whether morality, public order, or general welfare could ever justify torture, arbitrary killing, and so on. Third, many countries cannot claim to be democratic societies and cannot make use of article 29's broad limitations. Fourth, one might find in the International Covenant on Civil and Political Rights and the International Covenant on Economic, Social and Cultural Rights an authoritative interpretation of what is meant by the Universal Declaration of Human Rights—and particularly by article 29 of the Universal Declaration. Hence, article 4 of the International Covenant on Civil and Political Rights might be read into the rather vague limitations of article 29 of the Universal Declaration and might thus make at least certain rights (such as the right to be free from torture and arbitrary killing) nonderogable even in times of public emergency. But other rights—e.g., to be free from arbitrary arrest or detention, or to receive a prompt and fair trial—would still be subject to general limitation, or at least limitation in times of public emergency.

In any case, neither the International Covenant on Civil and Political Rights nor the Universal Declaration of Human Rights constitutes a completely satisfactory legal basis for the human rights concerns of NGOs and the UN—particularly when such concerns occur in periods of armed conflict or other public emergency. At the very least, humanitarian legal principles constitute an important body of international law which human rights organizations have used and can continue to use in appropriate situations.

There are, however, several impediments to the use of international humanitarian law. First, international humanitarian law includes a relatively unfamiliar and complex body of principles. Human rights organizations must communicate their concerns in a sufficiently simplistic fashion so as to attract media attention and to use the pressure of public opinion. Both staff and members of human rights organizations have only begun to understand humanitarian law norms sufficiently to use these norms in their reports and campaign work.

Most of the articles of the Geneva Conventions are not directly relevant to the principal concerns of human rights organizations, but there are a few provisions, such as common article 3 to the four Geneva Conventions, which are quite brief, easily explained, and directly applicable to the concerns of most human rights organizations. Common article 3 reads:

> In the case of armed conflict not of an international character occurring in the territory of one of the High Contracting Parties, each Party to the conflict shall be bound to apply, as a minimum, the following provisions:
>
> (1) Persons taking no active part in the hostilities, including members of armed forces who have laid down their arms and those placed *hors de combat* by sickness, wounds, detention, or any other cause, shall in all circumstances be treated humanely, without any adverse distinction founded on race, colour, religion or faith, sex, birth or wealth, or any other similar criteria.
>
> To this end, the following acts are and shall remain prohibited at any time and in any place whatsoever with respect to the above-mentioned persons:
>
> (a) violence to life and person, in particular murder of all kinds, mutilation, cruel treatment and torture;
>
> (b) taking of hostages;
>
> (c) outrages upon personal dignity, in particular humiliating and degrading treatment;
>
> (d) the passing of sentences and the carrying out of executions without previous judgment pronounced by a regularly constituted court, affording all the judicial guarantees which are recognized as indispensable by civilized peoples.
>
> (2) The wounded and sick shall be collected and cared for.
>
> An impartial humanitarian body, such as the International Committee of the Red Cross, may offer its services to the Parties to the conflict.
>
> The Parties to the conflict should further endeavour to bring into force, by means of special agreements, all or part of the other provisions of the present Convention.
>
> The application of the preceding provisions shall not affect the legal status of the Parties to the conflict.

The second obstacle to the use of international humanitarian law is the most problematic; in order to apply humanitarian law one must ordinarily determine which sort of armed conflict is occurring and therefore which set of humanitarian principles are relevant. The decision as to the sort of armed conflict is often a tricky question, involving issues which are politically sensitive and facts which are outside the normal research competence of human rights organizations, and involving potential conflict with ICRC judgments.

The Four Types of Armed Conflict

International humanitarian law was specifically designed to limit human rights violations, during periods of armed conflict, against protected persons such as soldiers who are wounded or otherwise *hors de combat* and against the civilian population. International humanitarian law distinguishes four types of armed conflicts, with different legal principles and instruments applicable to each: (1) international armed conflict to which the four Geneva Conventions of 1949, the Additional Protocol I of 1977, the Hague rules, and other legal principles apply; (2) wars of liberation or self-determination, which are principally defined by and made subject to Additional Protocol I of 1977; (3) noninternational armed conflicts which are subjected to the regulation of common article 3 in the four Geneva Conventions and some customary norms; and (4) noninternational armed conflicts which are narrowly defined and regulated by Additional Protocol II of 1977.

If there exists only sporadic violence, internal disturbances, or tensions, international human rights law would apply, rather than international humanitarian law.

It has been suggested that there exists yet a fifth category of armed conflicts, that is, internal armed conflicts that have become internationalized by virtue of the foreign assistance provided one side or the other. Among these conflicts might be the Civil War in Spain during the 1930s, Vietnam, Chad (at various times since 1968 including the present), Lebanon (1976–present), and Afghanistan (1979–present). The Geneva Conventions and other humanitarian law instruments do not contain specific provisions dealing with an internationalized civil war. Accordingly, such conflicts must be analyzed from a legal standpoint as falling within one of the other four categories. For example, between any two foreign states intervening on behalf of each side of a civil war, international humanitarian law in its entirety would apply. Similarly, between the established government of a country and another government that is aiding the insurgents in a civil war, the humanitarian law of international armed conflict applies, although there may be some practical difficulties in application. Between the two sides in the civil war, article 3 of the four Geneva Conventions and Protocol II might apply if their various conditions for armed conflict not of an international character are met. Finally, between the insurgents and a state assisting the established government, there would again be an analysis as to whether the conditions were fulfilled for a noninternational armed conflict because the insurgents lack the requisite status in international law. The assisting government may still wish to apply the full panoply of international humanitarian law because it is fighting on the territory of another country, although by invitation. Other possible relationships and circumstances may arise in the context of an internationalized civil war, but any such conflict must, in any case, be assessed under the four categories previously identified.

International Armed Conflict or Occupation Most of the provisions of the four Geneva Conventions of 1949 "apply to all cases of declared war or of any other armed conflict which may arise between two or more of the High Contracting Parties, even if the state of war is not recognized by one of them." In addition, the Geneva Conventions apply to partial or total occupation of the territory of a High Contracting Party. Furthermore, even if one or more of the parties to the armed conflict have not ratified the treaties, the ratifying parties are nevertheless bound to obey the Geneva Conventions.

The authoritative ICRC commentary on the Geneva Conventions defines international armed conflict as any "difference arising between two states and leading to the intervention of members of the armed forces . . . even if one of the Parties denies the existence of a state of war. It makes no difference how long the conflict lasts, or . . . the number of victims."[15]

Wars of National Liberation or Self-Determination Protocol I of 1977 adds that international armed conflicts include

> armed conflicts in which peoples are fighting against colonial domination and alien occupation and against racist regimes in the exercise of their right of self-determination, as enshrined in the Charter of the United Nations and the Declaration on Principles of International Law concerning Friendly Relations and Cooperation among States in accordance with the Charter of the United Nations.

Noninternational Armed Conflict Under Common Article 3 Common article 3 to the four Geneva Conventions applies a limited number of very basic protections to "armed conflict not of an international character." The article does not distinguish noninternational armed conflict from unorganized and short-lived insurrection or a mere act of banditry.

The authoritative ICRC commentary mentions a number of non-obligatory but convenient criteria for applying common article 3, which were proposed during the discussion preparatory to its adoption:

> (1) That the Party in revolt against the *de jure* Government possesses an organized military force, an authority responsible for its acts, acting within a determinate territory and having the means of respecting and ensuring respect for the Convention.
>
> (2) That the legal Government is obliged to have recourse to the regular military forces against insurgents organized as military and in possession of a part of the national territory.
>
> (3) (a) That the *de jure* Government has recognized the insurgents as belligerents; or
>
> (b) That it has claimed for itself the rights of a belligerent; or
>
> (c) That it has accorded the insurgents recognition as belligerents for the purposes only of the present Convention; or
>
> (d) That the dispute has been admitted to the agenda of the Security Council or the General Assembly of the United Nations as being a threat to international peace, a breach of the peace, or an act of aggression.
>
> (4) (a) That the insurgents have an organization purporting to have the characteristics of a State.
>
> (b) That the insurgent civil authority exercises *de facto* authority over persons within a determinate territory.
>
> (c) That the armed forces act under the direction of the organized civil authority and are prepared to observe the ordinary laws of war.
>
> (d) That the insurgent civil authority agrees to be bound by the provisions of the Convention.[16]

Even if some of these criteria are not met, it is the ICRC view that common article 3 should be applied as widely as possible, since it reflects the "few essential rules" which governments should be following in peacetime or in war, as well as in dealing with common criminals or rebels.

It has been argued that if a government is willing to derogate from its responsibilities under article 4 of the International Covenant on Civil and Political Rights for an "emergency which threatens the life of the nation," it should be willing to acknowledge in appropriate circumstances the existence of a noninternational armed conflict under common article 3 of the Geneva Conventions. Nevertheless, governments are often unwilling to accept the application of common article 3. There have been a number of conflicts in which the governments concerned have acknowledged the application of common article 3, for example, Guatemala (1954), the French-Algerian conflict of 1956, Lebanon (1958), Cuba (1958), the Congo (1960–64), Yemen (1962–67), the United States in Vietnam (1964), the Dominican Republic (1965), Nigeria (1967–70), Uruguay (1972), Chile (1973), and Cyprus (1974).

Noninternational Armed Conflict Under Protocol II Additional Protocol II of 1977 attempts to define more precisely than common article 3 the sorts of "armed conflicts not of an international character" to which Protocol II applies. Hence, in article 1(1) of Protocol II one finds specified several of the criteria which were only suggested by the ICRC for interpreting common article 3:

> This Protocol, which develops and supplements Article 3 common to the Geneva Conventions of 12 August 1949 without modifying its existing conditions of application, shall apply to all *armed conflicts* which are not covered by Article 1 of the Protocol Additional to the Geneva Conventions of 12 August 1949, and relating to the Protection of Victims of International Armed Conflicts (Protocol 1) and *which take place in the territory of a High Contracting Party between its armed forces and dissident armed forces or other organized armed groups which, under responsible command, exercise such control over a part of its territory as to enable them to carry out sustained and concerted military operations and to implement this Protocol.* (Emphasis added)

Protocol II establishes a higher threshold of applicability than the plain words of common article 3 by specifying several criteria which were only suggested by the ICRC for interpreting article 3 and some elements which are entirely new. Among the elements not stated in common article 3 are the requirements that armed forces of a High Contracting Party be involved in the conflict and that dissident armed groups exercise a degree of territorial control to enable them to "carry out sustained, concerted military operations." Hence, Protocol II appears to require for its application what would ordinarily be considered a civil war.

Nevertheless, since Protocol II does not replace common article 3 but rather "develops and supplements" it, conflicts which fall short of the

Protocol II requirements would still be covered by the broader terms of common article 3, so long as there is greater conflict than simply internal disturbance and tensions, to which only international human rights law is applicable.

Is There a Need to Distinguish Among the Four Types of Armed Conflict?

The factors that might indicate the application of humanitarian law—for example, the Geneva Conventions as to international armed conflict, common article 3 for noninternational armed conflicts, and the requisites for triggering Protocol II—are based upon objective factual determinations, but governments, insurgent groups, the ICRC, the UN, and human rights organizations may interpret those provisions and the relevant facts in quite different ways. Obviously, some of the provisions of humanitarian law will not be implemented if a government refuses to acknowledge its international responsibilities, but in such circumstances the government should be considered in violation of its treaty obligations.

The ICRC does not generally indicate publicly whether it classifies a particular situation as (1) an international armed conflict to which the Geneva Conventions and Protocol I apply, (2) a war of self-determination to which Protocol I applies, (3) a noninternational armed conflict to which common article 3 applies, (4) a noninternational armed conflict to which Protocol II applies, or (5) merely internal disturbances or tensions, which are not the subject of regulation in the Geneva Conventions and Protocols. Instead, the ICRC generally relies as a basis for its actions upon article VI of the Statute of the International Red Cross, which provides for a right of humanitarian initiative: "It takes any humanitarian initiative which comes within its role as a specifically neutral and independent institution and intermediary and considers any question regarding examination by such an institution."[17] While the Geneva Conventions and the Protocols may provide the ICRC with a stronger legal basis for its activities, the ICRC has found that it is easier to obtain access to prisoners without requiring the government concerned to acknowledge, even implicitly, that a certain sort of armed conflict might be occurring.

Although there are legal distinctions among these different sorts of armed conflicts, the ICRC, governments, and others often use the more detailed provisions of the Geneva Conventions (applicable to international conflicts) as a guide to the interpretation and use of the less exacting provisions applicable to other sorts of armed conflicts. For example, with regard to the internment in Switzerland of Soviet soldiers captured by an Afghan opposition group, the ICRC referred specifically to article 111 of the (Third) Geneva Convention, even though that Convention might not strictly apply to the armed conflict and the provision itself relates only to prisoners of war held by another State Party.

The ICRC's policy of not discussing its analysis of the application of the Geneva Conventions to specific situations does not prevent it from making statements which imply certain preliminary conclusions have been made. For example, in describing the work of the ICRC in southern Africa in its 1982 Annual Report, the ICRC mentions 104 Angolan "prisoners of war" held in Namibia, "two prisoners of war (a Russian and a Cuban) held in South Africa," "two Soviet citizens held by UNITA," and so on. The use of the term "prisoners of war" indicates that the ICRC has concluded that the Third Geneva Convention applies. The failure to use the same terminology for the two Soviet citizens held by the *União Nacional para a Independência Total de Angola* (UNITA) indicates correctly that the Third Convention could not apply because UNITA is a nongovernmental entity and not a party to the Geneva Conventions.

Another exception to the normal ICRC practice has been developed for particularly grave and longstanding problems. Hence, the ICRC was prompted by a resolution of the International Red Cross Conference in 1981 to acknowledge that the Geneva Conventions (or at least common article 3) apply to the Western Sahara, Ogaden, and Afghanistan. The International Conferences and the ICRC had previously stated that the Fourth Geneva Convention applies to the Occupied Territories of the Middle East.

If human rights organizations other than the ICRC are to apply humanitarian law principles, they must necessarily classify particular armed conflicts. But should these organizations announce their categorization of armed conflicts, when the ICRC is so reticent about such pronouncements?

International nongovernmental and intergovernmental organizations need not publicly announce every logical step leading to their decision to cite a particular provision of humanitarian law. Experts will understand that these organizations must have made the necessary preliminary analysis, but perhaps these international organizations should not divert their principal attention from human rights violations. For example, a human rights organization might simply observe that the Government of Country A, by torturing prisoners, has violated article 5 of the Universal Declaration of Human Rights, article 7 of the International Covenant on Civil and Political Rights, and common article 3 of the four Geneva Conventions. Such a statement might be amplified by stating that Country A had ratified the International Covenant on Civil and Political Rights in 1974 and the Geneva Conventions in 1964. It would not be necessary to state further that the human rights organization had concluded that common article 3 applied because an armed conflict not of an international character was occurring in Country A.

Israel provides another concrete example, since it has generally denied that the Fourth Geneva Convention applies to the Occupied Territories but nonetheless frequently proceeds to defend its conduct as complying with the substance of humanitarian law including the Fourth Convention. Although the UN, the ICRC, the US Department of State, and most other authorities reject Israel's position as to the application of the Fourth Geneva Convention to the Occupied Territories, a human rights organization need not take a position on this controversial issue. Indeed, it might be unnecessary to do so if the international organization's principal purpose is to persuade Israel to prevent human rights violations. But when the Israeli government cites the provisions of the Fourth Convention to defend its actions, an NGO might effectively respond on the basis of that treaty.

It should be clear that intergovernmental and nongovernmental organizations are not required to cite provisions of humanitarian law except where such citation would appear useful in protecting human rights. In addition, consideration should be given to the use of humanitarian law not as a primary source of applicable norms, but as a point of reference. For example, a human rights organization might not say: "These trial procedures violated common article 3 to the Geneva Conventions." Instead, the report might observe: "Such trial procedures are forbidden even in periods of civil war under common article 3 to the four Geneva Conventions." Such a use of humanitarian law would obviate the need for characterizing a situation as one in which a certain sort of armed conflict was occurring or even of stating that humanitarian law applied. Instead, this more subtle way of citing humanitarian law would make use of the public perception that the Geneva Conventions and Protocols establish the most basic, minimum standard of conduct for governments.

Red Cross Work in Periods of Armed Conflict

Since the Red Cross has long held the leading role in the protection of human rights in situations of armed conflict, it is useful for other organizations to study the work of the Red Cross in order to learn from their experience and to learn how this work can be supplemented by the efforts of other organizations.[18]

The Red Cross is a movement with three constituent parts. (1) The International Committee of the Red Cross (ICRC) is a private institution subject to Swiss law; its action is essentially on behalf of the victims of armed conflicts, but it may undertake "humanitarian interventions" on behalf of prisoners detained as a result of internal disturbances. (2) The 130 National Red Cross and Red Crescent Societies are voluntary organizations auxiliary to public authorities; they give assistance to the victims of natural disasters or armed conflicts, and engage in various humanitarian activities related to medical care, public health, and social welfare. (3) The League of Red Cross Societies is the federation of the National Societies; it coordinates their activities in peacetime.

Article 6, paragraph 4, of the Statute of the International Red Cross prescribes three roles for the ICRC in armed conflicts: "[1] To undertake the tasks incumbent on it under the Geneva Conventions, [2] to work for the faithful application of these Conventions and [3] to take cognizance of any complaints regarding alleged breaches of the humanitarian conventions."

Fulfilling the ICRC's Tasks Under Humanitarian Law

The tasks in the first role above are related to the specific provisions of the Geneva Conventions and Protocols that authorize ICRC action. (*a*) The ICRC visits prisoners of war and civilian internees, interviews them without witnesses, and repeats such visits under article 126 of the Third Convention and articles 76 and 143 of the Fourth Convention. The principal purposes of the visits are to assure that prisoners are not killed or ill-treated and in some cases to provide assistance to prisoners, including blankets, medicines, soap, warm clothing, food, educational material, medical care, and recreational material. (*b*) The ICRC provides relief to the population of occupied territories under articles 50, 59, and 61 of the Fourth Convention. (*c*) Pursuant to article 123 of the Third Convention and article 140 of the Fourth Convention, the ICRC has established a Central Tracing Agency (CTA), which collects information on prisoners of war and civilians in occupied territories (particularly those who are interned) so that contact can be established and maintained with their families. (*d*) The Central Tracing Agency also searches for persons missing in the event of armed conflict, pursuant to article 33(3) of Protocol I.

(*e*) If children are evacuated under article 78(1) of Protocol I, the ICRC monitors the relocation to assure the return of the children to their families. (*f*) The ICRC helps to establish and identify clearly hospitals and safety areas protected from international armed conflict under article 23 of the First Convention and article 14 of the Fourth Convention. (*g*) In the event of noninternational armed conflict the ICRC may under common article 3 of the four Geneva Conventions take humanitarian initiatives to offer its services to the parties for assisting victims and for activities similar to those performed in international conflict.

Encouraging Faithful Application of Humanitarian Law

The second role identified by article 6 of the Statute of the International Red Cross is that the ICRC should "work for the faithful application of" the four Geneva Conventions and presumably the more recent Additional Protocols. The ICRC thus monitors the actions of the parties to armed conflicts to assure that the parties comply with all the provisions of the four Geneva Conventions and two Protocols.

The three principal techniques of the ICRC for assessing the fulfillment of these humanitarian law norms are (1) visiting places of detention, (2) making official or unofficial approaches to the authorities, and (3) making use of its right to take humanitarian initiatives.

Visiting Places of Detention In connection with visits to places of detention, ICRC delegates are able to check if the detainees are being treated in accordance with the provisions of humanitarian law, to draw the attention of the authorities to any problems, and to ascertain through repeated visits whether appropriate remedial action has been taken.

Making Approaches to Authorities When the ICRC believes that a violation of humanitarian law has occurred or may be prevented, it may make approaches to the relevant authorities. In principle, such representations are made without any publicity. The ICRC communicates its concerns in confidence to the authorities because it does not wish to become engaged in public controversies which might jeopardize its assistance of and protection work for victims.

While the ICRC's efforts to put an end to violations of international humanitarian law or to prevent such violations are in principle confidential, the ICRC has reserved the right to make public statements concerning violations of international humanitarian law if the following conditions are fulfilled:

- the violations are major and repeated;
- the steps taken confidentially have not succeeded in putting an end to the violations;
- such publicity is in the interest of the persons or populations affected or threatened;
- the ICRC delegates have witnessed the violations with their own eyes, or the existence and extent of those breaches were established by reliable and verifiable sources.[19]

In fact, the ICRC's techniques are far more subtle. While the ICRC's approaches to governments are made in confidence, the mere fact that the ICRC has become aware of certain information presents the authorities with an implicit threat that the information will somehow become more broadly known, particularly if no remedial action is taken.

The ICRC publishes far more information than many people realize. In its monthly newsletter, Annual Report, Review, and occasional press releases, the ICRC often publishes information about the places of detention visited, when the visits occurred, and the number of detainees visited.

If the situation becomes particularly grave, the ICRC may occasionally publish full reports. It has previously issued such public appeals with respect to the killings in the refugee camps in Lebanon and the conflict in Southern Rhodesia. It has also occasionally called upon the parties to civil wars to refrain from attacking civilian populations, as it did, for example, in the Congo (1964), Nigeria (1967), and Vietnam (1967, 1968).

In May 1983, the ICRC issued a public appeal to both Iran and Iraq to honor their obligations under the Geneva Conventions.[20] The appeal describes Iran's failure to permit the registration of 15,000–20,000 prisoners of war, to transmit family correspondence for prisoners, to allow ICRC access to prisoners, and to repatriate wounded or sick prisoners, as well as Iran's intimidation, injury, or execution of prisoners of war. The appeal then describes in less detail the situation of 6,800 Iranian prisoners held by the Iraqi government, including satisfactory registration of prisoners; satisfactory family correspondence; ICRC visits to prisoners, which have been hampered by failure to permit access to certain prisoners; some ill-treatment; and a few instances of brutality against prisoners.

The appeal concludes with the statement that both Iran and Iraq have committed "grave breaches" by summarily executing captured or wounded soldiers, by abandoning the wounded on the field of battle, and by bombing civilian targets. The ICRC was compelled to repeat this public approach to Iran and Iraq in February 1984. These public reprovals apparently made both Iran and Iraq less willing to accept the humanitarian assistance of the ICRC, but the Iran/Iraq situation may have marked the limits of ICRC willingness to cooperate with governments that gravely breach their legal responsibilities.

Despite the fact that the ICRC rarely issues such public appeals, the Iran/Iraq case is useful in assessing the ICRC's methodology, which is essentially to use the balance of humanitarian law violations as a means of encouraging compliance. If each side of a conflict can be assured of the compliance of the other side, the Geneva Conventions will be better implemented. This sort of balance is somewhat less successful when both sides are criticized publicly because such criticism demonstrates to each side that the other is not fulfilling its treaty obligations and because inevitably one side will appear better than the other when the accounting is published.

Furthermore, if a confidential ICRC report to a government is partially revealed by that government, the ICRC reserves the right to release the complete reports. Accordingly, the ICRC was compelled to release reports on prison visits in Greece under the Colonels, and when the present government of Iran disclosed partial information about ICRC prison visits during the reign of the Shah, the ICRC released several pertinent reports.

Finally, periodic International Red Cross Conferences express concern about or even deplore grave and longstanding violations of humanitarian law. Such a resolution was adopted at the International Red Cross Conference of 1981 with regard to the conflicts in Western Sahara, Ogaden, and Afghanistan.

Taking Humanitarian Initiatives In order to work for the faithful application of the Geneva Conventions and the Additional Protocols, the ICRC also reserves the right to take humanitarian action (*a*) in all situations under article 4(2) of its own Statute; (*b*) in international armed conflicts under article 9 of the first three Geneva Conventions, article 10 of the Fourth Convention, and articles 5 and 81 of Protocol I; and (*c*) in noninternational armed conflicts under common article 3 to all four Geneva Conventions. The ICRC's right to take humanitarian initiative is intended to protect and assist persons protected by the Geneva Conventions and Additional Protocol I, as well as all others who may become the victims of armed conflict or internal strife, subject to the agreement of the authority concerned. Under its right of humanitarian initiative, the ICRC may provide relief for persons not protected by the Geneva Conventions, organize the exchange of prisoners, reunite families, ask for truces to bring care to the wounded, help refugees, and so on.

Receiving Complaints Concerning Alleged Breaches of International Humanitarian Law

The ICRC has distinguished between two categories of complaints about alleged breaches of international humanitarian law:

> "The first category includes complaints or communications concerning the non-application or inadequate application of one or several provisions of the Conventions by the responsible Power in respect of persons protected by those Conventions, in circumstances where the ICRC can take direct action in favour of such persons." The ICRC then approaches the authorities to prevail on them to correct any shortcomings notified on the spot and reported by its delegates.
>
> "The second category includes protests against grave breaches of international humanitarian law committed in circumstances where the ICRC is unable to take direct action to help the victims." The breaches may, for example, have taken place on the scene of hostilities to which the ICRC has no access. The procedure followed by the Committee is not to forward the protests, unless there is no other regular channel for doing so and a neutral intermediary is necessary and where such protests do not come from third parties.
>
> In the case of the first category of complaints, it is indisputable that the actions taken by the ICRC, for example, to put an end to ill-treatment inflicted on protected persons, represent a contribution to respect for human rights in the same way as the action taken by the Committee on its own initiative and mentioned in the previous section. And for the second category of complaints, the ICRC plays a very limited part, as noted by the International Conference of the Red Cross, after it has recognized that the procedure laid down between the two world wars had given no appreciable result. The function of the ICRC as forwarding agent seems rarely to lead to any improvement in the situation, since the complaints usually refer to events in the past which can no longer be put right.[21]

In addition, the four Geneva Conventions permit the parties to a conflict to establish ad hoc commissions of inquiry where there have been alleged violations of the Conventions, although no such ad hoc commission has yet been accepted by two parties to a conflict. Article 90 of the Additional Protocol I of 1977 envisions an International Fact Finding Commission to be established when twenty states parties have declared acceptance of the competence of the Commission to investigate allegations of grave breaches or other serious violations of the Conventions and Protocol I, but only six states out of twenty-seven parties to Protocol I have deposited declarations accepting the competence of the Commission.

The ICRC and Other Organizations

The above discussion of the ICRC's work in periods of armed conflict and internal strife raise several questions. First, what can other organizations learn from the ICRC's long experience in dealing with human rights violations in periods of armed conflict and internal strife? Second, how should other organizations relate to the ICRC in regard to fact-finding and action?

What Can Other Organizations Learn from the ICRC's Experience? The ICRC's skillful use of the implicit threat of publicity might be helpful to all other human rights organizations, which must at least consider whether to follow the ICRC's general policy of not relying upon international law in pursuing its humanitarian objectives.

If a human rights organization intends to comment on the human rights violations committed by the government on one side of an armed conflict, the organization may be expected to include some statements in its reporting about the abuses perpetrated by the other party in the conflict, whose misdeeds may be the cause or at least the excuse for the repression. In many cases failure to do so may leave the organization open to charges of prejudice in favor of one side, both at the time of the report and possibly in the future. Nevertheless, such efforts to balance human rights reporting may help one party to the conflict to find justification for their previous human rights violations or for their future reprisals. This paradox demonstrates the difficulty of any effort to balance reporting and, indeed, the extremely hazardous character of any increased activity in periods of armed conflict.

If a human rights organization were to publish information about only one side of a conflict with regard to torturing or killing prisoners of war, civilians, and so on, the organization would probably be criticized for taking sides in the war or for having purveyed enemy propaganda. For the ICRC such an accusation would be very damaging, because the ICRC attempts in many respects to serve as an intermediary between belligerent parties. Other human rights organizations do not attempt to serve in any such intermediary role. If human rights organizations wish impartially to pursue their concern for human rights in criticizing violations by governments even in times of armed conflict, these organizations must at least proceed with the awareness of the particularly quarrelsome and sensitive nature of governments at such times.

In considering these lessons, one must be aware of the important differences between the ICRC and other organizations in structure, principles, and techniques. Most human rights organizations apply human rights law during periods of peace, internal crisis, and armed conflict; in addition, these organizations may refer occasionally to humanitarian law principles where they are relevant to their work. The ICRC applies humanitarian law during armed conflicts and may take humanitarian action pursuant to its Statute at any time. The ICRC has occasionally made reference to human rights law, but it generally does not publicly use any legal principles in its work.

Such a formulation leaves a considerable area of overlap between the work of the ICRC and other organizations. There are, however, significant differences in the techniques they ordinarily employ. As discussed more fully above, the ICRC makes most of its approaches to governments in confidence. Most other human rights organizations use a range of approaches to governments, including direct contacts, membership appeals, and publicity campaigns. The ICRC has both a large central staff and regional offices which regularly visit places of detention, provide relief, work with National Red Cross and Red Crescent Societies, and so on. Amnesty International is based on a very diverse membership, which provides financial support for the organization and assists with appeals to governments; AI's research and fact-finding work is centralized in London. Americas Watch and most of the other human rights organizations identified in this article have central offices but no effective membership or grass-roots campaigning capacity. Americas Watch is unique in having experimented with the use of local stringers who remain on-site for extensive periods. The United Nations General Assembly, the Human Rights Commission, and other UN deliberative bodies have the ability to adopt resolutions but must rely principally upon the Secretary-General for the use of his good offices to pursue more diplomatic approaches. The United Nations is generally not very effective at mustering media attention or grass-roots campaigns.

How Should Other Human Rights Organizations and the ICRC Relate to Each Other in Working for the Protection of Human Rights During Periods of Armed Conflict? Bearing in mind the important differences between the ICRC and other human rights organizations, there remains the question of how these organizations might continue to work without undue interference with each other. One possible approach would be to recognize the ICRC's longstanding and very successful efforts in periods of armed conflict and internal strife. It might be argued that other organizations should generally leave this field to the ICRC.

Other human rights organizations have, however, increasingly found that human rights violations which they cannot ignore have occurred at the time of armed conflict. The fact-gathering capacity and diverse methods of action available to other human rights organizations may complement the ICRC's work. Indeed, the ICRC has indicated its acceptance of and appreciation for the role of other human rights organizations in bringing human rights violations to the attention of the ICRC and the public. Whereas the ICRC must maintain a discreet approach, generally avoiding publicity in order to preserve its access to prisoners, most other human rights organizations choose to publicize violations, even though such publicity may prevent them from having much access to prisoners. It is important, in other words, for all human rights organizations to protect their separate identities.

The Impact of Armed Conflict on the Fact-Finding Work of Human Rights Organizations

In order to work effectively and with credibility against violations of human rights, organizations must be able to gather and assess the relevant facts. Armed conflict may hinder the fact-finding work of human rights organizations and thus impair their ability to respond to human rights violations during periods of armed conflict.

Factors Affecting Fact-Finding in Periods of Armed Conflict

There are several factors that ordinarily affect a human rights organization's ability to gather information from any particular country on human rights violations.[22] Situations of armed conflict may have a significant impact upon several of these factors.

a. *Whether there exists a general climate of fear or whether an individual can report a violation without inordinate risk of reprisal.*

Armed conflict and internal strife will certainly increase the level of fear in a society and make more individuals afraid of reporting human rights violations. As violence increases, the fear of arbitrary detention or killing makes it less likely that information will be communicated. Indeed, information may be considered by the parties to the conflict as defense secrets or security matters, so that the release of information may conceivably be viewed as espionage.

b. *Whether there exists a popular awareness of human rights norms and whether there exists an expectation that basic rights should not be violated.* With armed conflict and internal strife often comes a breakdown of legal constraints on violence and a decrease in the expectation that anything can be done about human rights violations.

c. *Whether there exists an independent judiciary which can respond to reports of human rights violations from an independent bar.* Court proceedings and lawyers are ordinarily a significant source of information about human rights violations. An increase in the general level of lawlessness may adversely affect the independence of the legal profession.

d. *Whether there exist domestic organizations that concern themselves with human rights.* Domestic organizations, which ordinarily provide information, may become the subject of government opposition and/or repression such that they are unable to function or to gather information and/or communicate it. Or such organizations may become so involved in the conflict that their information becomes suspect.

e. *Whether the local media can report human rights matters freely.* Press censorship ordinarily increases during wartime. At the same time, the war may attract certain foreign journalists.

f. *Whether human rights information can be regarded as reliable.* Human rights data can become suspect and/or less available because of its use as propaganda during periods of armed conflict or internal strife. For example, Amnesty International's 1984 report on El Salvador observed, "The civil conflict also creates a context where allegations as to responsibility for violent deaths may also be expected to be manipulated by all sides for political ends. In some instances, such accusations have been based on alleged medical or forensic evidence which upon closer examination has proved to be of dubious authenticity and was evidently formulated with intentional bias."[23]

Furthermore, there is a considerable risk that much of the information gathered during periods of armed conflict may have been filtered through one party or another. Indeed, that party may have been publicizing the same information through other channels, such as the media. In such circumstances the credibility of the information may be doubted and may be seen as war propaganda. In the absence of a human rights organization's own authoritative and independent research, the organization's role might be reduced to that of a "rubber stamp" or supporter for one party's propaganda campaign.[24]

g. *Whether the common language is easily understood by foreigners so that information about human rights violations can be com-*

municated. This factor will not be significantly affected by armed conflict, but if the language of the country is so little understood by foreigners that the regular flow of information is feeble, armed conflict will diminish the information flow even further.

h. *Whether there exists a communication infrastructure (e.g., telephone, letters, business travel) linking the country to the outside world.* Normal means of communication may become difficult during periods of armed conflict, thus reducing sources of useful information. With fewer sources of information the researcher cannot easily cross-check material and assure reliability.

i. *Whether there exists a substantial refugee or expatriate community with access to human rights information and human rights organizations abroad.* Wars ordinarily increase the flow of refugees, but these refugees may not have access to international human rights organizations for some period after their departure.

j. *Whether there is a possibility of sending a fact-finding mission to the country or to places where refugees may be found.* During periods of armed conflict it may be difficult to obtain permission from the government to enter the country for research missions. Travel in some areas may be hazardous without government or opposition group assistance, which may in turn undermine the credibility of the fact-finding exercise.

All human rights organizations employ researchers, each of whom is assigned to monitor human rights developments in a region of the world. The International Commission of Jurists divides its work in such a way that each employee is responsible for a particular geographical area. Because of its small staff, the International League for Human Rights can only turn its attention from one country to another; it cannot maintain continual monitoring. Even Amnesty International, despite its very large staff in London, must assign almost all of its researchers to investigate violations in several countries at once. The United Nations largely serves as a passive receptacle for information produced by other organizations; it does almost no factual research itself.

Rarely can researchers for any of these organizations do more than collect and then sift information from such sources as press reports, texts of laws and decrees, reports of international organizations, and unpublished testimony that may become available at central offices from relatives of victims, former prisoners, lawyers, opposition groups, church people, journalists, and academics. For certain countries where research is particularly difficult, a more active research strategy is needed; refugee camps and border areas may be visited, and information sought from expatriate groups in countries that have received refugees and diplomats who have been stationed in the country. Such a concentrated effort is very difficult for a researcher who is assigned to several other countries where human rights violations are regularly occurring and where information may be easier to obtain. This problem is aggravated if no other international human rights organization has undertaken significant fact-gathering efforts.

Of course, the problem of research cannot be considered in isolation from the means available to perform fact-gathering and fact-finding. The Western Sahara presents a situation that illustrates some of the difficulties in undertaking an activist research strategy in the highly visible and politically sensitive context of an armed conflict. It is probable that a considerable store of information on human rights issues would be found among the inhabitants of the refugee camps organized by the Polisario Front around the Tindouf in Algeria. Unfortunately, human rights researchers cannot visit these camps independently; all that researchers would see or hear in such camps would have been orchestrated (even assuming that the information was accurate). Indeed, the visit of a human rights organization to these camps would be used in propaganda, which might be counterproductive for human rights objectives.

Despite all the difficulties, human rights research is possible during situations of armed conflict—particularly if a more activist fact-gathering approach is used. Indeed, in some cases armed conflicts may make research easier by drawing world attention to the situation. The conflict in El Salvador, for example, has attracted foreign journalists, members of the US Congress, international human rights organizations, and even tourists. While the gathering of specific information on events in areas of conflict has been impeded by the fighting, the disruptions of war, and the repression of domestic human rights monitoring organizations, the increased level of international attention has to some extent compensated for these impediments.

Problems of Research on the Existence of Various Sorts of Armed Conflict

The application of humanitarian law hinges on the characterization of the armed conflict. In trying to apply humanitarian law, human rights groups will not only have to make political and highly contestable conclusions about the existence of certain sorts of armed conflict, but they will need to base the decisions on factual information of a kind not customarily used for human rights research in the past.

The numerous human rights organizations normally collect information about torture and ill-treatment, judicial and extrajudicial executions, disappearances, fair trial and due process rights for detained prisoners, the detention of political prisoners, and so on. But human rights organizations do not normally collect the sort of facts necessary to determine the existence or nonexistence of an armed conflict. For example, some of the factors to be considered in applying common article 3 include whether insurgents possess an organized military force—an authority responsible for its conduct—acting within a determinate territory and having the means of respecting humanitarian law; whether insurgents have been recognized by the government; and whether the United Nations has recognized the conflict as a threat to peace. In the ordinary course of their work, human rights researchers may collect facts and make tentative conclusions about only some of these subjects. The additional requirement of collecting this information in order to apply international humanitarian law would distract researchers from their principal research tasks and would be beyond the information base and expertise of most researchers.

The Effectiveness and Impartiality of International Organizations in Combating Human Rights Violations in Armed Conflict Situations

Many international organizations focus primarily upon human rights violations and seek to persuade governments to fulfill their human rights and/or humanitarian law obligations. Persuasion can be accomplished by diplomatic contacts with the government concerned, appeals through the media, letter-writing campaigns, communications to intergovernmental organizations, and efforts to encourage other governments to intercede. Some organizations, such as Amnesty International, the UN, and the ICRC, also assist human rights victims.

Just as situations of armed conflict or internal strife have an impact on the research efforts of human rights organizations, such situations also have implications for the effectiveness of these organizations in halting human rights abuses. Indeed, there is a significant correlation between the ability to collect relevant human rights information and the ability to take effective action. Armed conflict may disrupt or distort normal government functions so that any approach by a human rights organization to the government may be impeded.

Impartiality

Maintaining impartiality is one of the most difficult problems human rights workers face in situations of armed conflict and internal strife. Armed conflicts polarize public opinion. A human rights organization acting in a polarized climate will almost certainly be called on to express itself on numerous issues outside the organization's mandate. This problem in turn may affect the organization's ability to act consistently. During periods of armed conflict, a human rights organization's image of impartiality may be severely damaged, since governments are particularly sensitive to criticism directed at only one side. Concern for the image of impartiality may, in such situations, place pressure on the organization to balance its criticisms—an approach that, as discussed above, has been difficult to maintain and that may result in reduced effectiveness in curbing human rights abuses.[25]

Approaches Used by Human Rights Organizations to Halt Human Rights Abuses

As seen above, human rights groups use several different approaches to stop abuses in a given situation. They may privately approach a particular government or entity with evidence of abuses and request the authorities to stop the violations. They may also publish reports and issue press releases about human rights violations. Publication serves the dual purpose of informing the international community of human rights abuses in the hope of enlisting widespread pressure on a country which is violating human rights and thereby possibly embarrassing the violating country into ending its violations. Finally, human rights organizations and their membership may place pressure on other governments to act to induce the violating country to stop abusing human rights.

These approaches may still be used in periods of armed conflict, although they may be less effective. The private approach to the responsible government entity may be ignored or given less weight when a country is more concerned with fighting a war, particularly where an internal conflict or war of liberation is involved. Governments will be particularly sensitive to questions of a balanced approach and impartiality at these times and will be less receptive to private appeals. Publication of information on human rights abuses also may backfire in times of armed conflict. Publicity will often help mobilize pressure on a government to stop abuses of human rights, but such publicity directed at only one side in a conflict may be used by the other side to justify its own abuses.

Finally, approaches by members of human rights groups to their own governments may also be less effective during times of armed conflict. States may be less willing to interfere with the decisions made by a government when its country is at war. Human rights groups should be aware, then, that their traditional approaches, when applied to situations of armed conflict, will encounter these problems. They may have to alter their traditional operations in order to prevent human rights abuses at these times.

Assisting Victims in Domestic and International Tribunals

Human rights organizations have invoked the assistance of international and judicial bodies in attempting to aid victims of human rights violations during periods of armed conflict.

For example, Disabled Peoples' International (DPI) filed a complaint with the Inter-American Commission on Human Rights of the Organization of American States (OAS) on behalf of residents of the Richmond Hill Insane Asylum who were killed or injured by United States bombardment during the 1983 conflict in Grenada.[26] The complaint alleged violations of articles 1 and 11 of the American Declaration of the Rights and Duties of Man[27] and the (Fourth) Geneva Convention Relative to the Protection of Civilian Persons in Time of War. DPI argued that the right to life was nonderogable in time of war and that, since there were no domestic remedies to exhaust, the Inter-American Commission had jurisdiction. The Commission accepted the petition as admissible and found at least a prima facie violation of the American Declaration's protection for the right to life.[28] Although it has not yet heard the case on its merits, the Commission eventually will need to consider whether the American Declaration prohibits killings during periods of armed conflict—particularly killings that might be either forbidden or permissible under humanitarian law.

Conclusion

Many international organizations in addition to the International Committee of the Red Cross play an important role in assessing whether governments and armed opposition groups are respecting their human rights and humanitarian law obligations. Americas Watch, Amnesty International, the International Commission of Jurists, the United Nations General Assembly, and other organizations have for some time been applying humanitarian law and human rights law to situations of armed conflict. They need to become more consistent and careful in using humanitarian law; they can also learn from the experience of the ICRC how to be more effective in safeguarding human rights during periods of armed conflict.

NOTES

1. *See, e.g.*, Geneva Conventions, common article 3.

2. Common article 9 of the First, Second, and Third Geneva Conventions; Fourth Geneva Convention, art. 10; Geneva Conventions, common article 3; INTERNATIONAL COMMITTEE OF THE RED CROSS, THE RED CROSS AND HUMAN RIGHTS 38–39 (Geneva: ICRC, 1983); Schindler, *The International Committee of the Red Cross and Human Rights*, 208 INTERNATIONAL REV. OF THE RED CROSS 3 (Jan.–Feb. 1979).

3. *See generally* Ramcharan, *The Role of International Bodies in the Implementation and Enforcement of Humanitarian Law and Human Rights Law in Non-International Armed Conflicts*, 33 AMERICAN U.L. REV. 99 (1983); Wolf, *L'OIT et la Croix-Rouge—Convergences de leur action*, in STUDIES AND ESSAYS ON INTERNATIONAL HUMANITARIAN LAW AND RED CROSS PRINCIPLES IN HONOR OF JEAN PICTET 1011 (C. Swinarski ed., Geneva: ICRC, 1984). For a review of historical efforts to implement the Hague Regulations through international adjudication, *see* Gross, *New Rules and Institutions for the Peaceful Settlement of International Disputes*, 76 PROC. AM. SOC. INT'L L. 131 (1982).

4. Afghanistan, Angola, Botswana (South African attacks), Burma, Chad, Colombia, El Salvador, Ethiopia, Guatemala, Honduras (Nicaraguan armed opposition groups), Israeli Occupied Territories, Kampuchea, Lebanon, Lesotho (South African attacks), Mozambique, Namibia, Philippines, Somalia, Sudan, Uganda, and Vietnam. AMNESTY INTERNATIONAL, ANNUAL REPORT 1986 (1986).

5. MINORITY RIGHTS GROUP, THE SAHRAWIS OF WESTERN SAHARA (Report No. 40, 1979).

6. GA Res. 40/137, 40 UN GAOR Supp. (No. 53) at 246, UN Doc. A/40/53 (1986).

7. GA Res. 38/101 (para. 3), 38 UN GAOR Supp. (No. 47) at 204, UN Doc. A/38/47 (1984).

8. GA Res. 40/139 (preamble, para. 3), 40 UN GAOR Supp. (No. 53) at 248, UN Doc. A/40/53 (1986).

9. *Id.*

10. *See, e.g.*, GA Res. 40/161, 40 UN GAOR Supp. (No. 53) at 112, UN Doc. A/40/53 (1986).

11. GA Res. 38/36A (para. 56), 38 UN GAOR Supp. (No. 47) at 29, UN Doc. A/38/47 (1984).

12. Scholars have begun to comment on the convergence of humanitarian and human rights law. *See, e.g.*, NEW HUMANITARIAN LAW OF ARMED CONFLICT (A. Cassese ed.; Naples: Editoriale Scientica, 1979); Dinstein, *Human Rights in Armed Conflict: International Humanitarian Law*, in HUMAN RIGHTS IN INTERNATIONAL LAW 345 (T. Meron ed.; Oxford: Clarendon, 1984); Draper, *Human Rights and the Law of War*, 12 VA. J.INT'L L. 326 (1972); Marks, *Principles and*

Norms of Human Rights Applicable in Emergency Situations: Underdevelopment, Catastrophes and Armed Conflicts, in 1 THE INTERNATIONAL DIMENSION OF HUMAN RIGHTS 175, 193–94 (K. Vasak ed.; Westport, Connecticut: Greenwood, 1982); Meron, *Human Rights in Time of Peace and in Time of Armed Conflict,* in CONTEMPORARY ISSUES IN INTERNATIONAL LAW (T. Buerganthal ed.; Kehl, Federal Republic of Germany: N. P. Engel, 1984); Paust & Blaustein, *War Crimes Jurisdiction and Due Process: The Bangladesh Experience,* 11 VAND. J. TRANSNATIONAL L. 1, 15–18 (1978); Robertson, *Humanitarian Law and Human Rights,* in STUDIES AND ESSAYS ON INTERNATIONAL HUMANITARIAN LAW AND RED CROSS PRINCIPLES IN HONOR OF JEAN PICTET 793 (C. Swinarski ed.; Geneva: ICRC, 1984); Schindler, *Human Rights and Humanitarian Law: The Interrelationship of the Laws,* 31 AM. U.L. REV. 935 (1982); L. Sohn, Fundamental Guarantees, Human Rights, Seminario Interamericano Sobre Seguridad del Estado, Derechos Humanos y Derecho Humanitario, San José, Costa Rica, 27 Sept.–2 Oct. 1982. At the same time, many scholars and significant actors in the field of human rights have ignored humanitarian law. *See, e.g.,* HUMAN DIGNITY, THE INTERNATIONALIZATION OF HUMAN RIGHTS (A. Henkin ed.; New York: Aspen Institute, 1978).

13. *See* Hartman, *Derogations from Human Rights Treaties in Public Emergencies,* 22 HARV. INT'L L.J. 1 (1981). Although war was the scenario which figured most prominently in the minds of the drafters of the derogation clauses, derogations have been invoked because of internal disturbances. *Id.* at 13.

14. The American Convention on Human Rights is more protective of human rights than is the International Covenant on Civil and Political Rights during periods of public emergency. Article 27 of the American Convention on Human Rights makes nonderogable rights to juridical personality, to life, to humane treatment, to nationality, to a name, and to participate in government; rights of the family and of the child; freedom of conscience and religion, as well as freedom from slavery and *ex post facto* laws. In addition, the American Convention protects the right to judicial guarantees essential to the protection of these rights, from which a government cannot derogate during periods of war, public danger, or other emergency. Common article 3 of the Geneva Conventions and article 6 of Additional Protocol II protect guarantees for fair procedure in periods of noninternational armed conflict. *See* INTERNATIONAL COMMISSION OF JURISTS, STATES OF EMERGENCY, THEIR IMPACT ON HUMAN RIGHTS 426–27 (1983). Article 75 of Additional Protocol I provides extensive procedural protections for the accused during periods of international armed conflict.

15. 4 J. PICTET, COMMENTARY ON THE GENEVA CONVENTIONS OF 12 AUGUST 1949, at 35–36 (Geneva: ICRC, 1958).

16. 1 J. PICTET, COMMENTARY ON THE GENEVA CONVENTIONS OF 12 August 1949, at 49–50 (Geneva: ICRC, 1952).

17. *See also* Statute of the International Committee of the Red Cross, art. 4(2).

18. Much of the material in this part of the study comes from ICRC, The Red Cross and Human Rights (1983) (ICRC Doc. CD/7/1, prepared for the Red Cross Council of Delegates, 13–14 Oct. 1983); *see also* Dominice, *The Implementation of Humanitarian Law,* in 2 THE INTERNATIONAL DIMENSIONS OF HUMAN RIGHTS 427, 439–43 (K. Vasak & P. Alston eds.; Westport, Connecticut: Greenwood, 1982); Forsythe, *Present Role of the Red Cross in Protection* in FINAL REPORT: AN AGENDA FOR THE RED CROSS (Geneva: ICRC, 1975); J. MOREILLON,

Le Comite International de la Croix-Rouge et la Protection des Detenus Politiques (Geneva: ICRC, 1973); J. Pictet, Red Cross Principles (1956).

19. ICRC, *Action by the ICRC in the Event of Breaches of International Humanitarian Law,* International Review of the Red Cross 40 (March–April 1981).

20. International Committee of the Red Cross, Appeal, 7 May 1983.

21. ICRC, The Red Cross and Human Rights 38–39 (1983).

22. Most of these factors were identified by Stephanie Grant in the testimony she prepared for Hearing on Africa: Human Rights Problems before two subcommittees of the U.S. House Committee on Foreign Affairs, 31 October 1979. Stephanie Grant prepared the testimony for Amnesty International USA, but her views obviously reflected her considerable experience as head of research at the International Secretariat.

23. AI, Extrajudicial Executions in El Salvador, AI Index: AMR 29/14/84, at 15 (1984). Americas Watch apparently encountered similar difficulties in assessing evidence in regard to human rights violations in Nicaragua. Americas Watch, Human Rights in Nicaragua 1985–1986 (New York: Americas Watch, 1986).

24. *See* the problems discussed in Americas Watch, Managing the Facts, How the Administration Deals with Reports of Human Rights Abuses in El Salvador (New York: Americas Watch, 1985).

25. For example, Americas Watch attempted to catalogue human rights abuses by both sides to the Nicaragua conflict from 1981 to 1985. The group noted that, while the Permanent Commission on Human Rights, an independent human rights organization in Nicaragua, could supply reliable, continuously monitored information about abuses by the Nicaraguan government, no similar organization was available to monitor the *contras.* Americas Watch, Violations of the Laws of War by Both Sides in Nicaragua 1981–1985, at 7 (1985). Because of this lack of symmetry in information, the image of impartiality of Americas Watch was questioned.

A similar experience occurred when Amnesty International issued its report on Israel and Syria in 1974. Amnesty International, Report of an Amnesty International Mission to Israel and the Syrian Arab Republic to Investigate Allegations of Ill-Treatment and Torture, 10–24 October 1974 (1975). The Israel-Syria report was subjected to severe criticism both inside and outside the Amnesty movement. Its effort to bracket Israel and Syria demonstrated the risks of seeking to establish balance by placing violations by two countries in one report. Those people who politically favored Israel were critical because they noted that the Israeli violations were much less serious than the Syrian violations and therefore they resented the placement of Israel in the same report. It is doubtful that the report served to ameliorate human rights conditions in the area. Indeed, the report may have had the unanticipated effect for some partisans of justifying the brutality of one side by reference to the brutality of the other. Although the report fully indicates the fact-finding problems encountered by the mission, the report was criticized for its methodology and, perhaps correctly, for its decision to make findings of fact on the basis of the flawed evidentiary base available.

26. Decision of the Commission As to the Admissibility: Application No. 9213 by Disabled Peoples' International, et al. v. United States. OEA/Ser.L./V/II.67 Doc. 6 (17 April 1986) [hereinafter cited as DPI v. U.S.].

27. "Every human being has the right to life, liberty and the security of his person" (art. 1); "Every person has the right to the preservation of his health through sanitary and social measures relating to food, clothing, housing and medical care, to the extent permitted by public and community resources" (art. 11).

28. DPI v. U.S., *supra* note 26, at 13.

5

Genocide and the International Community: The Case of Sabra and Shatila

ANTONIO CASSESE

The "Novelty" of the 1982 Massacre in Two Palestinian Camps

Massacres of the innocents in the Middle East produced by ethnic, religious, and political hatred are notorious. Yet what took place in Sabra and Shatila on 16–17 September 1982 was not just another of those irrational episodes whose very futility leaves us speechless before the spectacle of so many lives wantonly destroyed. That incident involved Israel, a state with strong democratic leanings and people who are not afraid to voice their indignation. Besides, the international press has always kept an eagle eye on Middle Eastern affairs. As a result of these two factors, the massacre became the subject of an inquiry by an Israeli judicial commission, a wide-ranging investigation conducted by eminent international scholars of diverse nationalities, and a solemn pronouncement by the UN General Assembly.

Thus, the significance of the massacre was not only that it produced profound anguish in the hearts of those who follow events in the Middle

This essay is a slightly revised version of a chapter in VIOLENCE AND LAW IN THE MODERN AGE (Princeton, N.J.: Princeton University Press, 1988).

East, but that it produced reverberations in official national and international organizations. Similar investigations and subsequent condemnations of the guilty parties have not been seen since the end of the Second World War—not in Burundi, Democratic Kampuchea, Uganda, Iran, or Iraq. Let us hope that the indifference with which these and other similar cases of slaughter have been received by the international community will no longer be tolerated (although the fact that subsequent massacres, perpetrated by other factions in the same camps of Sabra and Shatila, have not produced the echoes heard in September 1982 leaves little room for optimism).

What standards were followed by the groups that examined and evaluated the facts of Sabra and Shatila? The most obvious guide would have been to apply the legal rules of the international community: the massacre occurred during the military occupation by one state of the territory of another, during military operations that are by their very nature subject to international law. These precepts have developed from the views of many states regarding other episodes, in many respects similar to Sabra and Shatila, and have resulted in the formation of fairly precise and rigorous rules. Despite the existence of such clear-cut parameters, however, all three bodies which investigated Sabra and Shatila avoided any reference whatsoever to these rules, applied them in a surprisingly loose way, or did not draw the appropriate conclusions from their application.

The aim of this brief essay is to examine why this happened and to see what other standards of behavior were applied instead.

The Facts

During the military occupation of Lebanon by the Israeli armed forces, which began on 6 June 1982, the Lebanese President and Phalangist leader, Bechir Gemayel, was assassinated on 14 September, just a few days after his election. The Christian (Phalangist) forces blamed the Palestinians for the crime.

The Israeli army, fearing a series of vendettas, entered West Beirut "to prevent possible grave occurrences and to ensure quiet." However, the Israeli military command allowed the Phalangists to enter the Palestinian camps of Sabra and Shatila to ferret out and arrest any "Palestinian terrorists" they might find. The Israeli forces surrounded the two camps; according to their orders, "only one element and that is the I.D.F. [Israeli Defence Force] shall command the forces in the area." In other words, even though only the Phalangists actually entered the two camps, they were operating from the onset of the operation under the aegis and control of the Israelis.

The Christian militias entered the camps on Thursday, 16 September, at about 6:00 P.M. A few hours after their entry, an Israeli officer learned from a Phalangist liaison officer that the latter had told one of his soldiers, who had captured forty-five people in one camp and wanted to know what to do with them, "Do the will of God." An hour before this conversation, another Israeli officer had informed his superiors that he had distinctly heard a Phalangist officer telling soldiers who had captured fifty women and children in the camps and were awaiting further orders, "This is the last time you're going to ask me a question like that; you know what to do." This answer, transmitted via radio to all the forces operating in the camps, was greeted by loud laughter from the Phalangists standing near the officer.

Although various Israelis soon realized that the Phalangist operation was taking a sinister turn and informed their superior officers of this fact, the latter did nothing. Only on Friday evening (17 September), when news of the massacre had spread and even an Israeli journalist had begun to make inquiries, did the Israeli commanding officers start to examine the facts, discovering that the rumors they had heard earlier were quite true. Even then, however, the Phalangist forces were not ordered by the Israelis to leave the camps until 5:00 A.M. on Saturday, 18 September. Israeli Prime Minister Menachem Begin was not informed until he heard the news on Saturday afternoon on a BBC radio broadcast.

These facts, drawn from the Israeli Commission of Inquiry's report,[1] prove that (1) the massacre was perpetrated by the Phalangists; (2) the Phalangists entered the Palestinian camps with the knowledge and consent of the Israeli army; and (3) the latter discovered at once that the Phalangists were indiscriminately killing the camps' inhabitants and did nothing to stop the slaughter.

The Israeli Commission of Inquiry

On 28 September 1982, domestic and international pressures forced Begin to establish a Commission of Inquiry, based on a 1968 Israeli law.[2] The members of the Commission were nominated by President Yitzhaz Kahan of the Supreme Court of Israel and consisted of President Kahan himself, Supreme Court Judge Aharon Barak, and Major General (Reserve) Yona Efrat.

Given its wide powers of inquiry, the Commission was able to examine the facts with great care and call numerous witnesses. In its exhaustive report, it concluded that members of the Israeli Cabinet and army were, in varying degrees, "indirectly responsible" for the massacres. It recommended, *inter alia,* that Defense Minister Ariel Sharon be asked to resign; that the Director of Military Intelligence, Major General Yehoshua Saguy, be removed from his post; and that the Division Commander of the forces in Lebanon, Brigadier General Amos Yaron, be suspended for three years.

It is not easy to judge if the Commission's recommendations, later adopted by the Begin government, were an adequate "punishment" for Israeli responsibility. But given the scope of its mandate, it is difficult to understand why the Commision did not rule on the responsibility of the Phalangists or suggest what measures Israel should adopt to seek out and punish the actual perpetrators of the massacres. This is a serious shortcoming. Although the Israeli government was primarily responsible for this lacuna, the Commission might have interpreted its mandate more broadly and concluded that Israel was obligated to punish those directly responsible, since they were still subject to Israeli political and military control.

The standards utilized by the Commission in reaching its conclusions also leave much to be desired. Rather than utilizing either Israeli law (for instance, the 1963 Israeli military manual) or international law (the laws of war applicable to Israeli forces during the military occupation of a foreign country), the Commission instead referred exclusively to moral and religious imperatives.

The Commission first distinguished between "direct" and "indirect" responsibility, without identifying from what source this distinction was drawn. It then observed that only the Phalangists could be held directly responsible and that, with respect to the Israelis, all that remained to ascertain was "indirect responsibility." The Commission stated that the legal definition of "indirect responsibility" was not among its tasks, even if the question could be easily answered by reference to the status of Israeli forces as forces of occupation charged with responsibility for public safety. But, the Commission added, even if this status was not attributable to the Israeli forces, the question of "indirect responsibility" remained.

At this stage, the Commission quoted a Talmudic interpretation of a passage from Deuteronomy (the description of the reaction of the sages of a city on discovering the corpse of an unknown man) in support of the principle that men are responsible if they witness a crime being committed by others and do nothing either to prevent it or to help the victim. The Commission then invoked the tenets of morality, to which it referred again at the end of its long report.

It is difficult to understand why the Commission avoided the domain of international law, but two reasons might be suggested. First, by not adopting a rigorous position on the legal status of the Israeli forces in Lebanon, it avoided expressing opinions that could have embarrassed the Israeli government, which was pursuing a policy of occupying Arab territories despite widespread condemnation by other states. Second, the Commission may have wanted to underscore its view that moral and religious principles were above legal norms; whatever the dictates of mere human law, there is a superior law which all civilized nations and individuals must obey.

The International Commission of Inquiry

In August 1982, a group of private individuals had decided to create an international commission to examine whether Israel had violated international law by sending its troops into Lebanon in June. Chaired by Nobel and Lenin Peace Prize laureate Sean MacBride, the commission consisted of five eminent Western scholars. Although the task had not been foreseen when the commission was established, the commission included within its mandate an investigation of the Sabra and Shatila massacres.

The commission made a thorough inquiry into the facts, based on eyewitness and other accounts, and concluded that Israel was "guilty" on the grounds that (1) the suspicion of direct involvement by the Israeli army in the massacres had never been completely disproved; and (2) Israel was guilty of grave breaches of international law because its armed forces, despite their obligation to maintain order and exercise effective control over the Phalangists, had instead shielded the Phalangists and helped them plan and execute the massacres.[3]

The commission's conclusions were based on international conventions that Israel does not consider applicable: the Fourth Geneva Convention of 1949 on the Protection of Civilian Populations, and the 1977 First Additional Protocol to the 1949 Geneva Conventions. Article 4 of the 1949 Convention protects the rights of all those who are not citizens of the occupying state, which would include the Lebanese, Jordanian, or stateless Palestinians living in Sabra and Shatila.

Some authorities believe that the Convention grants insufficient protection to those who are refugees (whatever their nationality);[4] therefore, the majority of the inhabitants of the two camps might have been only partially covered. In any event, there is an insurmountable obstacle to the application of the Convention in the context of Sabra and Shatila: the Convention does not lay down rules with respect to acts committed by other armed forces not part of the occupying army. Indeed, when article 29 defines the occupier's responsibility for the treatment of "protected persons" in the occupied territory, it speaks only of crimes committed directly by the agents of the occupier. The issue of crimes perpetrated by other military forces is considered in the 1977 Protocol, which is cited frequently by the MacBride commission. However, the Protocol has been neither signed nor ratified by Israel, and Israel is not bound by it. The few casual remarks by the commission to the effect that Israel ought to have respected the Protocol in any event are not convincing.

It thus appears that, although the commission did invoke international law, it did so unskillfully and erroneously, for reasons that are difficult to understand. Like the Kahan Commission, it also did considerable harm (though for different reasons) to the legal rules that govern the international community, not to mention the requirements of humanity and justice which they reflect.

Action by the UN General Assembly

The UN General Assembly briefly addressed the question of Sabra and Shatila in December 1982, in the context of its wider debate on the Middle East situation. By a vote of 123 votes in favor, none against, and 22 abstentions, it approved a resolution in which it first mentioned the Genocide Convention and the Fourth Geneva Convention of 1949. The resolution "*[c]ondemns* in the strongest terms the large-scale massacre of Palestinian civilians in the Sabra and Shatila refugee camps" and "*[r]esolves* that the massacre was an act of genocide."[5]

At this point a judge might rest content. An authoritative political organ had spoken for the consciences of all mankind, condemning the massacre in unequivocal terms on the basis of a solemn legal act that the same Assembly had approved in 1948. Nevertheless, neither jurists nor those who believe in applying forward-looking norms that reflect those humanitarian values that are so frequently trodden underfoot should be satisfied with this result. Although the General Assembly was correct to address such a serious crime, its actions can be criticized in at least two important respects.

First, the resolution was preceded neither by a careful and impartial inquiry, nor by an exhaustive debate on the facts and the legal implications of labeling the massacre "genocide"; the Cuban delegate, who introduced the draft resolution, merely observed that it was "self-explanatory." The label of genocide was applied more for political or propaganda purposes than on legal or humanitarian grounds. It did not result from an unbiased evaluation of the facts or serious consideration as to how to punish the guilty.

Among those states expressing reservations about the resolution (such as Spain, Denmark [on behalf of the ten EEC countries], Israel, the United States, Finland, Sweden, Turkey, Canada, Singapore, and the Philippines), several criticized the tendency of the General Assembly to use vague and imprecise language even in referring to very serious events and rigorous legal concepts. They also noted that it was not within the competence of the General Assembly to describe the Sabra and Shatila massacres (or other similar events) as acts of genocide under the 1949 Convention.[6]

One can disagree with these criticisms (and the author does feel that to a certain extent they are untenable), but they did voice justifiable political and diplomatic concerns, couched in legal terms. There was understandable dismay at the hurried manner in which the Assembly delivered its verdict, a haste that was all the more worrisome since the Assembly's resolution could be exploited as a dangerous precedent on other occasions, when the facts might be less dramatic than those of Sabra and Shatila.

The second grave flaw in the resolution reveals an intention to use it as a political instrument and a tool for propaganda. The General Assembly took no further action after adopting the resolution, as if by designating the massacres as genocide it had obliterated all possible consequences of the crime. Instead, it should have taken the subsequent step of exhorting states to seek out and punish the perpetrators. It could also have requested Israel to mete out the necessary punishment.

While Israel proved its undoubted courage and moral uprightness in trying to punish those Israelis who were "indirectly responsible" for the massacres, it did not attempt to try the real perpetrators of the crimes. The General Assembly could have exhorted Israel, as well as Lebanon and other states, to pursue the guilty Phalangists, but this opportunity was not taken. Despite the fact that international law possessed the necessary tools to go beyond the mere verbal condemnation of genocide, the Assembly was either unwilling or unable to use them.

What Rules Should Have Been Applied?

The Sabra and Shatila massacres occurred during Israel's military occupation of the area. It is quite true that the Israeli armed forces entered Lebanon not to fight the legal government of that country, but, with the help of one of the warring factions (the Phalangists), to destroy the forces of another faction (the Palestinians). Nevertheless, it is impossible to deem Israel's presence anything else but military occupation by one state of the territory of another. Thus, the applicable rules were those that govern armed conflict, especially the rules of military occupation.

Under general rules of armed conflict, military commanders are responsible for crimes committed by the forces under their command or control, if they have done nothing to prevent such crimes or subsequently taken steps to punish them. Prior to the Second World War, commanders were responsible only if they had ordered their subordinates to commit war crimes (such as massacres of civilians or maltreatment of prisoners). However, the trial of Japanese General Tomoyuki Yamashita at the end of the war marked the adoption of a new norm. As commander of the Japanese forces that occupied the Philippines from 1944 to 1945, Yamashita was accused by the United States of not preventing his troops from committing war crimes against U.S. and other Allied citizens, including killing civilians and prisoners of war, looting, and destroying religious buildings. Yamashita was found guilty, first by a U.S. military commission and then by the U.S. Supreme Court, to which he had appealed.[7] He was subsequently executed by the Allied forces in Japan.

It became clear during the trial that Yamashita had not ordered the crimes committed by his troops and had purposely been kept unaware of them. In any event, he could have done little to stop them, because the U.S. forces were deliberately creating a state of chaos in order to destroy the organization and authority of the Japanese army. Yamashita thus was sentenced even though he had infringed no specific rule and there existed no specific precedent. Two Supreme Court Justices expressed their strong dissent, and the decision seems obviously unjust: Yamashita was executed for something that was not prohibited at the time it was committed.

Nevertheless, the Yamashita case led to formulation of a new international rule, *ex injuria jus oritur.* Proof that a new rule had emerged can be found, for example, in the military manuals of the United Kingdom,[8] the United States,[9] and Israel,[10] and in article 87 of the First Additional Protocol of 1977.

The situation of Sabra and Shatila should have been examined in the light of this general rule of military responsibility. The Israeli military commanders exercised effective power over the Phalangist troops. It was their duty to prevent the massacre, which was both a war crime and genocide. Once they knew that the slaughter had started, they were obliged to prevent its continuation. According to the Yamashita rule, the fact that the Phalangist soldiers were not part of the Israeli forces was immaterial, since the Israeli army had the effective power to direct and control the Phalangist actions.

After the massacres, it was Israel's duty to seek out and punish not only its own military commanders, who had done nothing to stop the killing, but also those directly responsible for the crimes. Israel's failure to punish those responsible could have been challenged by any state party to the Genocide Convention, which provides in article 9 that any dispute between the parties, "including those relating to the responsibility of a State for genocide," can be submitted for determination to the International Court of Justice.

In addition, article 8 of the Genocide Convention authorizes any party to call upon "the competent organs of the United Nations" to adopt such measures under the UN Charter as may be appropriate for the prevention and suppression of genocide. Unfortunately, this opportunity was not grasped during the Assembly's debate, and short-term political considerations were allowed to prevail over elementary requirements of justice.

Legal Imperatives and Political Expediency

Readers may feel that the discussion thus far only confirms that international law is impotent, because it does not possess the force necessary to impose respect for its imperatives. "Covenants, without the sword, are of no strength to secure a man at all."[11] I cannot agree.

In this particular case, the rules existed by which facts could be assessed, as did the international procedures for the application of these rules. If only a faint, deformed echo of the law reached us through the decisions and opinions of the three bodies that examined the massacre, this is because political or partisan considerations impeded or deflected strict observance of the law. Unlike instances of wholesale slaughter elsewhere, however, in the case of Sabra and Shatila the Israeli Commission of Inquiry at least ensured that ethical and religious concerns did not disappear and that limited responsibility was assigned to some of the guilty parties.

Unfortunately, the full potential of international law was not exploited. Above all, an important occasion was lost to prove how certain legal rules distill humanitarian values and, so long as sufficient political will exists, can affect relations between states as well as between states and individuals. At least the names of Sabra and Shatila will not be forgotten, although it is sad that they must be added to the long list of formerly unknown villages and towns that recall abhorrent misdeeds: Auschwitz, Dachau, Oradour-sur-Glane, Katyn, Hiroshima, Nagasaki, Soweto, My Lai, Phnom Penh, . . . One can only hope that the obvious failures to utilize international law with respect to Sabra and Shatila will not be repeated.

NOTES

1. *Reprinted in* 22 International Legal Materials 473 (1983).

2. The text of the law is reprinted in P. Elman, *The Commissions of Inquiry Law,* 6 Isr. L. Rev. 398, 410 (1971).

3. Israel in Lebanon, Report of the International Commission to Enquire into Reported Violations of International Law by Israel during the Invasion of the Lebanon (MacBride Report) (London: Ithaca Press, 1983).

4. *Cf.* International Committee of the Red Cross, Draft Additional Protocols to the Geneva Conventions of August 12, 1949. Commentary 80 (Geneva: ICRC, Oct. 1973).

5. UN GA Res. 37/123 D of 16 Dec. 1982, 37 UN GAOR Supp. (No. 51) at 38, UN Doc. A/37/51 (1982).

6. *See,* for a summary of the debates on this point, UN Doc. A/37/PV.108 (1982) at 33–101.

7. *In re* Yamashita, 327 U.S. 1 (1946).

8. The Law of War on Land 176–79 (London: War Office, 1958).

9. The Law of Land Warfare 178–80 (Washington, D.C.: Dept. of the Army Field Manual, 1956); at 178–80; International Law, The Conduct of Armed Conflict and Air Operations (Washington, D.C., 1976) at 15/2, paras. d–e.

10. Code of Military Laws 17–2, The Laws of War (1963) at chap. II, para. 9.

11. Thomas Hobbes, Leviathan 223 (Macpherson ed.; London: Penguin Books, 1983).

PART III

DOMESTIC APPLICATION OF INTERNATIONAL HUMAN RIGHTS NORMS

6

Lawyers Pro Bono Publico: *Using International Human Rights Law on Behalf of the Poor*

STEPHEN ROSENBAUM

Nongovernmental organizations (NGOs) in the field of human rights are generally viewed as single-issue groups with a membership base or strong secretariat acquainted with the workings of international organizations and human rights instruments.

One entity that does not fit this mold is the Legal Services office, a creature of urban neighborhoods and rural small towns across the United States. Staffed by attorneys and paraprofessionals, these relatively autonomous law firms represent America's poor on all legal matters, save those which involve the criminal justice system.

Unlike their colleagues in the private bar, legal aid lawyers do not ask their clients for a fee. They are paid salaries mainly from governmental coffers, but they do not work *for* the government. Their objective—like any attorney's—is to provide the best possible representation for their clients. There is much debate about how best to serve those clients, and no small number of limitations have been imposed by legislators, bureaucrats, and boards of directors on the kinds of assistance these lawyers can provide. Despite the disagreements and the obstacles, these offices have the potential for concerted creative lawyering. This chapter examines ways in which international human rights doctrine can be utilized by legal aid advocates to advance the interests of poor and disadvantaged Americans. The reader should not look here for a detailed explanation of the instruments and procedures or for an analysis of whether domestic application of international law is preferable to filing cases in international human rights forums. Those are subjects written about elsewhere. Rather, this is a sympathetic account of some encounters by Legal Services lawyers with this evolving area of law: what works, what does not, and what simply escapes analysis.

The first section describes briefly the history and structure of the American legal aid program. The next section gives some practical reasons why attorneys may want to choose the domestic route or the international route in order to achieve their clients' objectives and to meet the bureaucratic limitations imposed by the Legal Services Corporation. The third section is composed of synopses of actual cases, both closed and pending. Finally, there is a discussion of some high points and hazards that the practitioner faces. I do not offer a definitive conclusion on the utility of international law for serving the poor, but do offer some observations on strategy and style, forum and form, for those who seek to join the interests of poverty lawyer and international human rights advocate.

History of Legal Aid in the U.S.

Legal aid to the poor is a concept as old in the Anglo-American legal system as the Magna Carta. Yet it was not until the middle of this century that the concept became something more than a noble objective subscribed to by members of the bar.

The duty of each attorney to work *pro bono publico,* that is, to accept cases without fee "for the public good," took on an organized character in the United States in the early 1900s with the founding of legal aid societies affiliated with local bar associations. The American Bar Association championed the cause in the 1920s. Eventually, President Lyndon Johnson's War on Poverty spawned a government-funded battalion of storefront lawyers representing the poor on civil matters under the auspices of the federal Office of Economic Opportunity (OEO). By 1967, eight hundred neighborhood law offices were serving the indigent in over two hundred communities throughout the United States.

Lawyers were encouraged, according to the Legal Services program's first national director, to design new legal, social, and political tools and vehicles to move the poor from deprivation and despair to ambition and opportunity. This large attorney corps was meant to do battle against the enemies of tenants, debtors, elderly patients, unpaid workers, unhappy spouses, expelled students, and others. The war has mainly been waged in state courts and before federal judges, boards of education, labor commissioners, welfare department hearing officers, and immigration law judges. The "tools and vehicles" are primarily statutes, regulations, and court cases.

By the early 1970s, Legal Services attorneys had performed effectively enough to alienate local politicians and members of Congress. The program underwent major changes. First, restrictions were progressively placed on the most controversial kinds of clients—those seeking to obtain abortions, to desegregate schools, to organize laborers, or to resist military conscription. Second, in 1974 Congress removed the program from the executive branch and established the quasi-independent Legal Services Corporation (LSC). This was not enough for the Reagan administration and the conservative Congress that accompanied him into office in 1980. More restrictions were imposed: advocacy of gay rights and representation for undocumented aliens were prohibited, lobbying of legislatures and regulatory bodies was severely limited, and the filing of class action lawsuits was made more difficult.

Despite these restrictions, Legal Services lawyers have endeavored to develop new approaches to meet the legal needs of the poor in the 1980s. International human rights law and procedures offer one approach for *pro bono* lawyers.

Enhancing American Jurisprudence with International Theories and Seeking Resolutions to Problems in International Forums

The two principal methods of using international law and procedures are to apply them in domestic forums and to take complaints to international bodies concerned with human rights.

Domestic Application

There are several ways in which Legal Services' objectives can be enhanced through the use of international law in domestic legal arenas. First, there are a number of traditional poverty law causes that can be bolstered by language in the Universal Declaration of Human Rights and

International Human Rights Covenants, the American Declaration and Convention on Human Rights, International Labour Organization (ILO) Conventions, UN Resolutions, and the case law interpreting these documents. These include funding more subsidized housing, supporting the Equal Rights Amendment, improving child nutrition programs, revoking medical assistance cutbacks, improving the education of migrant children, enforcing indigenous peoples' treaty rights, and staffing long-term health care facilities.

Second, Legal Services staff can teach about international human rights to lay advocates and grassroots organizations dedicated to poverty issues. The trend toward community legal education has been growing in LSC circles and among lawyers' organizations generally. The most recent amendments to the Legal Services Corporation Act require local offices to engage in training eligible clients and providing support services for "significant segments" of the client population. Many legal aid offices and bar associations have designed workshops, forums, and other projects for the benefit of tenants, consumers, public welfare recipients, immigrants, and other members of the public. The objective is to teach people about their rights before a legal problem occurs, much as some doctors and public health officials teach preventive medicine. For instance, presentations might be made to parents' groups concerning the inter-American or international human rights principles that support their children's right to an education or to instruction in a certain language. Welfare rights organizations might be interested in the economic guarantees enunciated in the International Covenants or the American Convention. These presentations could be timed to coincide with domestic lawsuits that raise the same issues.

Finally, legal aid offices can use human rights law to reach out to the private bar. There is a growing interest in this substantive field among private practitioners, public interest attorneys, and academics. Law offices that operate on grants from the Legal Services Corporation are now required under federal regulations to devote at least 12.5 percent of their budgets to "private attorney involvement" in the delivery of legal services. This involvement may take the form of training, technical assistance, research, or community legal education.

Under LSC guidelines, the legal aid office must also make an effort to involve private attorneys in "new or unique areas of the law." Certainly the promotion of international human rights norms may be characterized as new and unique and an area ripe for training, technical assistance, and research. This kind of lawyer-to-lawyer exchange ensures promotion of international human rights norms and at the same time meets a bureaucratic goal.

International Procedures

There is no set format for filing complaints with most international and regional bodies. Each tribunal has adopted procedures that often mirror the language of the conventions that authorized their creation. There are no rules of court and no customary practices for stating a cause of action or briefing a legal point.

International bodies receiving human rights complaints do not apply *stare decisis* decision-making. Officially reported decisions with the analysis and holding fully set out are rare. At best, one finds a broadly worded resolution calling on a government to take certain steps, and possibly a reference to the article that has been breached by the offending state party.

This is not to say that legal advocacy is out of place or less rigorous than in U.S. forums. In presenting a petition alleging human rights violations to an international body, an attorney must fully set forth supporting factual and legal arguments, although this may be done with a freedom of form and style not usually acceptable to U.S. judges or administrative tribunals. In many instances, the persons reviewing a human rights complaint will not be jurists, or at least will not be trained in common law. Instead, the reviewing panel is likely to be composed of persons schooled in diplomacy, philosophy, political science, or a civil law system.

The petition process is clearly less expensive than almost any litigation filed in a U.S. court of law. There are no filing fees, and unless the petition leads to a hearing or on-site investigation, there are no fees to be paid to witnesses, court reporters, or interpreters, and no out-of-pocket travel expenses incurred by attorney or client.

To the extent that international commissions compel governments to change laws or policies, the petition process affects legislative or administrative decisions. Influencing legislation and rule-making is severely hampered under the present Legal Services Act and accompanying regulations. Legal aid offices are prohibited from lobbying Congress or state, county, and municipal legislative bodies, unless specifically invited to do so by the legislators, or where the advocacy relates to a particular client. The same prohibition applies to administrative and rule-making agencies.

One can still respect the letter of the law by indirectly influencing public policy through the international petition process, since the restrictions speak to advocacy before *domestic* entities and elected officials at the *national* and *local* level. It may be possible to achieve the same impact as testifying before a congressional committee, writing a letter to a state senator, or commenting on regulations proposed by the State Department by addressing a communication to one of the international human rights bodies.

Another advantage of the international petition system is that complaining parties have broad standing before most bodies. For example, under the American Convention on Human Rights, "[a]ny person or group of persons, or any [legally recognized] nongovernmental entity" may lodge petitions with the Inter-American Commission on Human Rights (IACHR) containing denunciations or complaints of violations of the Convention or its parent document, the American Declaration, on their behalf or on behalf of third parties. The procedure for receiving communications under Economic and Social Council (ECOSOC) Resolution 1503 (XLVIII) by the UN Sub-Commission on Prevention of Discrimination and Protection of Minorities (the Sub-Commission) allows complaints from a person or group "who have direct and reliable knowledge" of gross violations of the United Nations Charter, the Universal Declaration of Human Rights, and other international instruments or from NGOs who meet the above criteria and "act[ ] in good faith . . . not resorting to politically motivated stands." The UNESCO standing requirements under its Executive Board Decision 3.3 (1978) are similar to the Sub-Commission's.

Thus, parties may bring violations to the attention of the international human rights bodies with considerably more ease than to that of American courts. This broad standing conveniently permits the representation of underrepresented groups, such as undocumented aliens, whose access to legal assistance has been substantially reduced since the enactment of legislative restrictions after the Reagan administration came into office.

The petition procedure allows relief for a large number of persons without the hurdles contained in the LSC regulations or the federal and state rules for certifying a class. The UN Sub-Commission's Resolution 1503 procedure, by definition, concerns complaints of "gross violations," which usually entail a government's repeated or massive violations affecting a large number of persons. UNESCO distinguishes between "cases" (concerning individual and specific rights violations) and "questions" (concerning a state policy of violating human rights or an accumulation of individual cases forming a "consistent pattern") in its procedure for receiving communications involving violations in the fields of education, science, culture, and information. The Inter-American Commission process, with its provision for on-site investigations, would also seem suitable for petitions necessitating class-based relief. Some IACHR observers have also noted a developing doctrine of granting jurisdiction more readily over "general" cases, that is, in instances where a pattern or practice of violations has been alleged. The mechanisms are in place, therefore, to handle complaints affecting large numbers of persons who are similarly affected by a law or government practice.

None of these petitions or complaints should be subject to LSC regulations or local board of director policy requiring class action approval by a Legal Services executive director. Serving a broad class of people—the indigent—is very much in keeping with the original Legal Services mandate. Senate hearings held in 1970 revealed that the OEO's legal component was intended to change laws and institutions that adversely and unfairly affect poor people. Thus, the goal was to serve the poor as a group, not simply individual clients who happened to be poor. The international accords reflect keenly an interest in protecting the rights of groups, whether by fighting social oppression and racism or by organizing to promote cultural interests or better working conditions.

The international forums, then, offer complainants a flexibility not often available in U.S. judicial and administrative tribunals as well as a way around the bureaucratic obstacles put in place by the Legal Services Corporation and Congress.

Case Studies: The International Approach in Practice

The best way to illustrate the use of international human rights law by Legal Services practitioners is to describe actual cases. The following are accounts of closed and pending cases.

Closed Cases

Civil Rights/Immigrant Worker Drownings A study of raids on agricultural fields conducted by the federal immigration authorities, in search of aliens with no documentation of lawful status, revealed a disturbing practice: irrigation canals and natural waterways were being used as barriers during roundups in the state of California. For many farm workers, the water was the only perceived escape from apprehension, detention, and probable deportation. By 1982, the tenth such worker in an eight-year period had been drowned while being pursued by the Immigration and Naturalization Service (INS). The Equal Rights Council (ERC), a coalition of minority organizations in California, requested the help of Legal Services attorneys in notifying Amnesty International (AI) of the latest drowning. California Rural Legal Assistance (CRLA) and the Legal Aid Society of Alameda County (LASAC) took on the case, with help from Human Rights Advocates (HRA) and two law professors.

Amnesty International's Annual Report of the previous year had commented on the brutalities sometimes inflicted on undocumented workers by U.S. law enforcement officials. After an exchange of letters with Amnesty's Secretariat, CRLA was informed that the case did not fall within the scope of AI's mandate. The Secretariat did, however, express an interest in receiving more documentation on physical brutality used by INS agents on undocumented workers and ill-treatment of Mexican Americans and other ethnic minorities while in police custody. This was consistent with the concerns outlined in the Annual Report. The Secretariat's Americas specialist also indicated her willingness to discuss these issues personally during an upcoming visit to the United States.

Simultaneously, LASAC attempted to bring the case before the UN Sub-Commission on Prevention of Discrimination and Protection of Minorities, a UN forum it viewed as more favorable than the General Assembly working group drafting a convention on migrant workers' rights, because the former was better suited to review ongoing violations. Since "migrant workers" was not on the Sub-Commission's 1983 agenda, LASAC tried to relate the violations to the "detention" and "slavery-like practices" agenda items. The attorneys had to settle for *oral* interventions before the full Sub-Commission and working group, since the staff and chair had been increasingly unreceptive to permitting the more durable and detailed written submissions from participating NGOs. The medium of the interventions notwithstanding, the U.S. Observer responded at great length. He never really denied the allegations, but lavished praise on the president of the United Farm Workers union in an effort to deflect the grievances raised by LASAC about migrant worker mistreatment. To keep the issue alive, LASAC requested that a report on the exploitation of undocumented migrant laborers, which had been prepared a few years earlier, be published by ECOSOC and distributed for comments to governments, UN agencies, and NGOs. The Sub-Commission adopted a resolution requiring the Secretary-General to report on these comments and "other significant developments regarding the human rights of migrant workers" at the 1984 session of the Sub-Commission. LASAC had lobbied unsuccessfully for more explicit language on updating the report.

No substantive report was ever prepared by the Secretary-General. But in the meantime, the General Assembly working group issued several drafts of its proposed international convention on the rights of migrant workers and their families. The drafts include articles affirming the rights to life, liberty, and personal security of workers and their families; protection against violence, physical injury, threats, and intimidation; the right to due process if detained or arrested; and freedom from arbitrary arrest and detention.

On a third front, CRLA took the complaint to the OAS Inter-American Commission on Human Rights in 1983. A petition was drafted on behalf of the ERC, and numerous newspaper clippings and declarations were compiled. Since the United States has not ratified the American Convention on Human Rights, the ERC raised violations arising under the Declaration of the Rights and Duties of Man, most notably the rights to life, liberty, and personal security. Violations of humane treatment, due process, equal protection, civil rights, and the special protection of children were also raised in this petition. The relief sought were a hearing and an on-site observation by Commission members.

Anticipating objections to the admissibility of the petition, CRLA met the issue head-on by arguing that the exhaustion of domestic remedies doctrine did not apply. A protracted exchange of letters, telephone calls, and new documentation followed. The OAS Secretariat at first refused to refer the petition to the Commissioners, claiming that it was not admissible since all domestic remedies had not been invoked and exhausted. Shortly after the 1983 session ended, CRLA was informed that the case had been referred to a Commissioner who would act as a rapporteur on the admissibility issue and report back to the full IACHR at its next session. Not until 1985 did the Commission transmit the petition to the U.S. for a reply. That reply was serious and well-reasoned, and, not surprisingly, it opposed admissibility, largely because there were two pending lawsuits that would give the ERC the relief it sought and one appeal that was never pursued in domestic courts. The government also alleged that the petition was not meritorious and failed to state a cause of action under the Inter-American Convention. CRLA rebutted the exhaustion charge by emphasizing the "unwarranted delay" exception, relying on European Commission precedent since the inter-American system is based largely on the European model and lacks extensive case law of its own. The petitioner also used this opportunity to mitigate the stated and implied concerns of both the Secretariat and the U.S. government that the ERC allegations were too tenuous. This was accomplished by focusing on the most serious violations of the hemispheric human rights accord: the INS raids created a climate of fear by threatening the rights to life and security.

The IACHR passed a resolution in mid-1985 denying admissibility on the ground that petitioners failed to state facts constituting a violation under the Declaration. The resolution referred to the deaths as "regrettable" but said they did not flow from INS policy or practice. The ERC requested reconsideration, but the Commission's answer remained the same some two and a half years after the petition was filed: not admissible.

Social Rights/Maternity Leave Benefits The Legal Aid Society of Alameda County filed an *amicus curiae* brief with the U.S. Supreme Court on behalf of an indigent mother who sought to return to her job following her maternity leave. Attorneys for fellow *amicus* Human Rights Advocates joined the brief. In addition to lending its prestige, the private firm representing HRA shared the significant printing costs and could have helped LASAC satisfy part of its private attorney involvement obligation.

The case, *Calif. Fed'l Sav. and Loan Ass'n v. Guerra* (479 U.S. 272, 107 S.Ct. 683 (1987)), involved a challenge to a state statute making it unlawful for an employer to refuse to grant an employee a reasonable leave of absence due to pregnancy. The employer plaintiffs below had claimed that the state law was preempted by a federal law. *Amici* argued that the state statute should be upheld, since it was analogous to protection afforded under international law, as evidenced by such treaties as the International Covenants, the Convention on the Elimination of All Forms of Discrimination Against Women, ILO Convention No. 103, regional treaties of Africa, the Americas, and Europe, and bylaws adopted in 127 nations. *Amici* urged that, wherever possible, federal statutes are to be interpreted in a way consistent with international law. This interpretation, they said, was supported by the federal statute's legislative history, which made explicit reference to international norms concerning maternity leave.

The U.S. Supreme Court upheld the state statute guaranteeing pregnancy leave. The opinion does not directly refer to arguments raised by *amici* but does note that the legislative history of the statute includes "extensive evidence of discrimination" by employers, especially in their disability and health benefits for pregnant women and working mothers, and must not be read to preclude states from adopting laws like the one challenged in this case (*id.* at 692). One of the congressional witnesses, mentioned in a footnote by the Supreme Court, had testified that all countries in Europe and most in the Western Hemisphere had enacted laws to provide income protection to working women with children and that women in the U.S. stood almost alone in the lack of this kind of protection (*id.* at n. 18). Her testimony had in fact been cited by *amici*'s lawyers as evidence of internationally accepted norms.

Economic Rights/Welfare Relief Payments State courts have been receptive to human rights arguments during the past decade, and some scholars have suggested they are a much more hospitable forum than the federal courts.

One case brought by individuals represented by Legal Services attorneys is noteworthy both for its championing of *economic* rights in American jurisprudence and for the fact that the court—and not the litigants—raised the applicability of an international human rights instrument *sua sponte. Boehm v. Superior Court* (("Boehm II"), 178 Cal.App.3d 496 (1986)) was filed by attorneys with Fresno-Merced Counties Legal Services and the Western Center for Law and Poverty (a legal support center for Legal Services staff specializing in welfare law) on behalf of county welfare recipients. The recipients were challenging the county government's reduction of public assistance grants to a level of minimum subsistence.

Plaintiffs contended that subsidies for food and shelter alone did not adequately "relieve and support" that county's indigent population as required under state law. The court agreed that the grant reduction was aribitrary and capricious since no study had been conducted to determine whether the basic necessities were being provided.

The judge's opinion refers specifically to article 25 of the Universal Declaration of Human Rights in stating that "it defies common sense and all notions of human dignity" to exclude clothing, transportation, and medical care from the minimum subsistence allowance (*id.* at 502). These are among the items listed in article 25's definition of a standard of living adequate for the health and well-being of oneself and one's family.

None of the parties had cited the Universal Declaration in their memoranda or had pleaded any claims arising under the UN document. No mention of the Declaration was made in the first decision by the same judge on a similar issue, *Boehm v. Superior Court* (("*Boehm I*"), 163 Cal.App.3d 450 (1985)). The spark for the judge's analysis appears to have been a 1984 law journal article. The article is critical of the failure of U.S. courts to constitutionally protect subsistence rights by referring to international legal norms. The author cites the Declaration, the Covenant on Economic, Social and Cultural Rights, the OAS Charter, and the American Declaration as examples of customary international law which may inform an equal protection analysis. The court liked the sound of it and cited both the article and the Universal Declaration in what is now part of an expanding body of international human rights jurisprudence in state courts.

Pending Cases

Civil and Economic Rights/Immigrant Job Applicants and Employees Workers at Oregon food-processing plants were being fired and denied hiring opportunities in the mid-1980s. Immigration authorities had conducted an effective "Operation Cooperation" among area employers, convincing them not to hire anyone who could not furnish certain work authorization or immigration documents. This campaign was conducted before Congress passed legislation in 1986 requiring employers to verify the immigration status of their employees.

The local office of the Oregon Legal Services Corporation, the American Civil Liberties Union (ACLU), and a private attorney decided to sue the INS in federal court for violations of due process, privacy, and administrative procedure. One of the attorneys was interested in raising claims under international human rights law. Another Legal Services attorney working on immigrants' civil rights issues introduced the Oregon lawyers to some academic readings in this field.

The consulting attorney first proposed causes of action founded on the Universal Declaration and the American Declaration, alleging that the INS's effort to discourage the employment of aliens lacking work authorization violates the right to work under favorable conditions. A separate proposed claim would allege that the INS's operation violates the right to "a simple, brief procedure" (due process) protecting aliens from an infringement on their "fundamental, constitutional rights," that is, the right to work. Either way, the consulting attorney intended to assert that the Declarations are authoritative interpretations of the UN and OAS Charters and that the Charters, in turn, are treaties to which the United States is bound. The Oregon attorneys preferred the more cautious approach of using the Declarations and Charters to interpret, or inform, the U.S. Constitution and case law.

In the end, the class of plaintiff aliens filed a complaint pleading four claims based on due process, two grounded on constitutional violations, and two more generally stated. The parties have reached a settlement, the terms of which are not yet fully implemented. But if plaintiffs were to brief these claims on appeal, the legal aid lawyers would rely in part on the declaratory international law in interpreting domestic due process law.

The Right to Nonrefoulement/Political Asylum Applicants Salvadorans seeking asylum in the United States have for many years faced almost certain deportation; only a very small percentage have ever been granted asylum by this government. Short of asylum, many have argued for the internationally recognized right of *nonrefoulement*, that is, the right not to be returned to a country where one's life or personal freedom would be threatened on the bases of political opinion or membership in a particular social group, nationality, religion, or race.

With the aid of the National Center for Immigrants' Rights, Inc. (NCIR, Inc.), a Legal Services litigation support center, a Salvadoran refugee defense organization filed a petition in 1982 with the Inter-American Commission complaining of violations under the American Declaration and the UN Convention and Protocol Relating to the Status of Refugees. At stake are the right of *nonrefoulement;* the right to seek and receive asylum; the right to life, liberty, and security, and to humane treatment while in custody; special protection for mothers and children; and freedom from discrimination. A number of other religious and human rights organizations later signed the petition. Other counsel joined on as well, including the International Human Rights Law Group, the American Civil Liberties Union, and a private law firm.

The petitioners asked for a full, on-site investigation of INS detention facilities, an on-site review of the treatment of detainees, and interviews with INS officials and immigration judges. Unlike the petition filed in the drownings case, this one was quickly forwarded to the government. The U.S. response was prompt and predictable: the case was inadmissible because the plaintiffs and causes of action in the petition were identical to those in lawsuits pending before domestic courts. In particular, the government singled out the NCIR, Inc., attorney for having filed a federal suit the very day the OAS petition was lodged. Petitioners countered with a legal memo claiming, first, that the U.S. courts would not be able to address the discriminatory nature of the asylum decisions or the impermissible *refoulement* since the judges would defer to the political branches of government on these questions. Second, they claimed that any domestic remedy would be ineffective; only monitoring by the IACHR of the *substantive*—as opposed to *procedural*—due process afforded Salvadorans would be effective.

During the next fifteen months, the U.S. urged the Commission to rule on admissibility, arguing that the petitioners had not even begun to pursue provisional remedies available in the United States.

In October 1983, the IACHR President took the extraordinary step of cabling the U.S. Secretary of State. Although the Commission still had not made a decision on admissibility, he wished to "reiterate the principle of *non-refoulement*" and "for humanitarian reasons . . . exhorts the U.S. Government to suspend deportation of all Salvadorans" while the case was under consideration.

Almost one year later, the parties were still involved in a jurisdictional dispute. Petitioners asked the Commission to conduct an on-site investigation for the sole purpose of determining exhaustion, making the issue one of fact, not law. The IACHR agreed, but the State Department insisted many months later that the Commission could conduct an investigation only if the results were used to make a determination of justiciability—not a finding on the merits. Following an *audiencia* three years after the cable was sent to the Secretary of State, the Commission told the U.S. that this limitation was unacceptable.

After passage of the 1986 immigration reform bill authorizing "amnesty" for many undocumented immigrants and the issuance of a 1987 Supreme Court decision liberalizing the standard for political asylum, petitioners' counsel asked the IACHR to hold this case in abeyance and give those seeking asylum a chance to have their claims heard individually by judges of the INS administrative tribunals. Before making another move at the OAS, petitioners' attorneys will monitor the effect of the new statutory and case law developments.

Linguistic and Cultural Rights/English-Only Law "English-only" initiatives have appeared on state and local ballots during the past few years, affirming that English is the official language of a particular state or municipality. California's recently adopted constitutional amendment, "Proposition 63," was one of the more significant measures in the country, owing to the state's large immigrant population, diversity of linguistic groups, and array of publicly financed bilingual services.

Even before its adoption by popular referendum, groups had formed to oppose Proposition 63. Their counsel include Legal Services of Northern California, the Legal Aid Society of San Francisco, the Mexican-American Legal Defense and Education Fund (MALDEF), and two ACLU affiliates. For the moment these lawyers have a cause but no pending action. The amendment's ambiguity has made proponents and opponents alike uncertain of the next step. On its face, the amendment requires enabling legislation to breathe life into its mandate to the Legislature "to insure that the role of English as the common language of the State of California is preserved and enhanced," not "diminishe[d] or ignore[d]."

The traditional theories—that the amendment violates equal protection, freedom of expression, and fundamental rights guaranteed under the state and federal constitutions—are being considered along with the more unconventional theories that Proposition 63 contravenes provisions of the UN Charter: the Universal Declaration International Convention on the Elimination of All Forms of Racial Discrimination; UNESCO's Convention Against Discrimination in Education, Declaration of the Principles of International Cultural Co-operation, and resolutions on the rights of migrant workers and their families; and other pronouncements of customary international law.

The "Proposition 63 Legal Team" continues to debate the best theories of opposition and still has not decided whether the international violations should be raised directly, whether the law should be used to inform domestic statutes and constitutional law, or whether international law should figure in the lawsuit at all. If international law *is* invoked, it is too soon to tell whether it will be on behalf of plaintiffs, defendants, intervenors, or friends of the court.

A more daring route, not yet discussed by this group, would be to submit a communication to UNESCO's Committee on Conventions and Recommendations, under the Decision 3.3 procedures, alleging that Proposition 63 negatively affects schoolchildren in bilingual classrooms and voters needing bilingual election materials, violating rights guaranteed under some of the United Nations and UNESCO instruments mentioned above. These violations concern education, culture, and information—the so-called "fields of competence" associated with UNESCO. The fact that the United States left the Organization does not bar a claim against the U.S. government.

The Value of Applying International Norms and Procedures

There is perhaps no case discussed here where the use of international human rights law or procedure *ipso facto* made, or will make, the difference between a favorable or unfavorable decision for poor people. But then, cases rarely stand or fall on the basis of one legal principle. Sometimes the inclusion of human rights citations or the filing of a petition in an international forum may be the extra ounce needed to tip the scales in the claimant's favor. What follows are comments on how the application of international principles or procedures can help (or harm) Legal Services clients.

Publicity Value

One of the most successful uses of international human rights law has been to generate publicity. The novelty of the international perspective, particularly where a case has been raised in an international forum, is appealing to the media. The impact of the media on resolving cases must not be underestimated.

For example, the press conference announcing the filing of the IACHR petition on behalf of drowned immigrant workers and subsequent news coverage may have moved an influential bishop and the Mexican Consul to take a position against INS tactics and may have pressured the chief of the INS's local border patrol unit to meet with community activists and order his agents to carry lifesaving equipment.

Media coverage of the proceedings themselves can also be beneficial to claimants. A newspaper article on an OAS on-site investigation of asylee detention facilities or the remarks of an NGO intervenor at the Sub-Commission can bring an otherwise overlooked matter to the attention of opinion shapers and policy-makers. The ultimate effect is to persuade or shame governments into taking steps to resolve a particular case.

Promulgating Novel Theories and Fresh Approaches

The insularity of American legal scholars and practitioners blinds them to the existence of international legislation and jurisprudence that could enhance their own well-developed body of law. There are phrases and concepts in certain treaties and conventions that are more detailed or generous than the language contained in parallel clauses of the U.S. and state constitutions and statutes.

The Oregon attorneys wanted to promote the right to work. The domestic bills of rights and decisional law do not state as plainly the importance of this liberty as the Universal Declaration of Human Rights and the International Covenants and their OAS analogues. Even though the same lawyers later decided to frame their claims as due process violations, they reserved the option to cite UN or inter-American instruments in subsequent briefs. These latter documents speak more precisely of judicial access and procedural protection than the "due process" provisions of federal and state constitutions.

Similarly, the coalition fighting the English-only amendment to the California constitution might draw on more helpful language from the UN Charter or UNESCO resolutions on promoting linguistic, cultural, and educational rights than they would find in domestic sources of law.

Sometimes human rights advocates breathe new life into old concepts. When the Legal Aid Society of Alameda County took its migrant rights issue to the UN Sub-Commission, it compared the detention phenomenon to a "slavery-like" practice. This allowed the lawyers to address the question under an existing agenda item and to expand the meaning of slavery in a world where its traditional forms have decreasing relevance. Although the attorneys' oral interventions did not result in any concrete action by the Sub-Commission, indirect effects should not be overlooked. The NGO may have sent signals to the General Assembly drafters or to U.S. State Department officials. The former articulated their concerns about migrant workers in a proposed convention and the latter may have discreetly asked their counterparts in other departments of the executive branch to look into the INS's raids and treatment of apprehended migrants.

California Rural Legal Assistance also tried to attract the attention of the international human rights community to the plight of migrants by attributing a broader meaning to an extant term. By characterizing the round-up of immigrants as "detention," the complainant hoped to enlist Amnesty International in its dispute with U.S. immigration authorities. The AI Secretariat found the characterization to be too wide of the mark for direct action, but encouraged CRLA to continue sending evidence of brutality and mistreatment.

Poor people's advocates have also won some procedural victories.

Scoring procedural points may, of course, lead to substantive gains for one's clients in the short term and for future grievants in the long term. When the Equal Rights Council petitioned the Inter-American Commission about the continuing drownings, referral to a rapporteur may have seemed an insignificant step. Although the petitioner eventually lost on the merits of its complaint, the assignment of a rapporteur forced the Commission to keep the question alive for several sessions and to compel an answer from the U.S. government.

In a more dramatic move, the NGOs who sought the Commission's help in protecting Salvadoran asylum applicants were able to get some action from the IACHR before a ruling on exhaustion was made: the Commission President sent a cable to the Secretary of State asking for suspension of deportation of Salvadorans living in the U.S.

Expanding the limits of the law is an objective most attorneys can embrace. This is particularly important for poverty lawyers and international human rights proponents, whose clients or ideas are so far from the mainstream, because their interests are only advanced if notions of justice and fairness evolve further than those of society at large.

Spreading the Word on Human Rights

Poor people's advocates and NGOs are concerned not only with the expansion of ideas but the extension of their audience. Fellow lawyers, decision-makers, and the general public constitute the relevant interest groups. To reach these people it is important to pay as much attention to the medium as the message.

For instance, consider the effect of the *amicus curiae* brief which addresses human rights issues. Having a friend of the court as the messenger at least ensures the message will be delivered. *Amici* often have objectives that are distinct from those of the parties, and their lawyers may not see eye-to-eye on the questions that should be raised in the appellate court. The *amicus* brief also allows human rights law to be argued where litigants' counsel neglected to do so in the court below. Lastly, the brief is a vehicle for educating judges about unorthodox theories without detracting from or "discrediting" more conventional arguments made by the parties in their own briefs.

The brief filed by the defendants' friends of the court in the maternity leave case illustrates this usage. The weight given the legal aid society and HRA's brief may have been far more than the Supreme Court's single footnote reveals. If one justice or one law clerk read the brief closely, that person may have thought a little bit more about international norms or treaty obligations on protections for working mothers. This, in turn, may have amplified defendants' arguments on behalf of the contested statute. Education of the judiciary is an ongoing process and one that does not always manifest itself in written decisions.

Precedents, moreover, have been built as much from footnotes and parenthetical remarks as from textual commentary. References to the Universal Declaration of Human Rights by the judge deciding the adequacy of a local public assistance program in *"Boehm II"* were a small but important contribution to the new state court human rights jurisprudence. It is of little consequence that the court invoked the Declaration without assistance from the litigants. Judges, no less than litigators, have the opportunity to educate their peers on the bench about international standards.

Briefs and opinions are not the only vehicles of communication. Comments made outside the courtroom may also be influential. For example, the serious reception given to international human rights doctrine by the English-only legal team can be explained in part by the direct participation of attorneys who have pioneered in this area of law. In addition, California's chief legal officer, the State Attorney General, gave the idea a boost when he alluded to a possible preemption of the new constitutional amendment by a nineteenth-century treaty signed by the US and Mexico. The 1848 Treaty of Guadalupe-Hidalgo, which ended the war between Mexico and its northern neighbor, does speak of liberty, property, and religious protections—but not linguistic, ethnic, or national minority rights. The specific inaccuracy did not obscure, however, the greater notion that an international treaty may have an effect on California law.

Lay education and outreach was discussed above as an appropriate function and obligation of the legal aid office. When the Equal Rights Council approached CRLA about requesting the aid of Amnesty International in putting an end to the drownings of migrant workers, its leaders had some rudimentary understanding of international human rights machinery, and the mandate and investigatory and reporting procedures of Amnesty International. The appeal to AI was not entirely misplaced. The lawyer's task, after all, is to take the client's broad objective—publicizing a human rights violation in the international community—and frame it in the proper legal terms and convey it to an appropriate legal forum.

Once its petition was filed, the ERC—and the Salvadoran refugee groups who petitioned the Inter-American Commission for *nonrefoulement*—found themselves thrust in the spotlight by the media attention.

The organizations were able to gain more stature among their members and the grassroots communities in which they operate. This "celebrity" status in turn can stimulate greater constituent interest in the posture of cases at the Commission level and the doctrinal underpinnings of the petitions. Locals who read the news columns of small-town dailies and more distant readers of features and editorials in big-city papers can increase their understanding of international law and procedures.

Although the benefit to one's clients is indirect, there is some value in increasing the general public's understanding of international human rights standards. This popularization should complement efforts to speak and write to the professionals, that is, lawyers and judges, who are more closely tied to the forums where these cases are considered.

Convincing Colleagues

The problem is not always persuading the judge or opposing party. Sometimes there is disagreement about the international approach among one's own colleagues. Socialization in the poverty law milieu is not necessarily sufficient to offset the bias of attorneys schooled in the Anglo-American system. Well-meaning lawyers may indeed disagree on the best strategy or legal theory. For example, the Oregon Legal Services attorneys were interested in citing supportive international human rights law, but they preferred a more cautious approach than the one suggested by the consulting attorney. They decided to adopt the method offered by Justice Hans Linde of the Oregon Supreme Court in a previously published law journal symposium, that is, using provisions of international instruments to assist the court in interpreting the US Constitution.

Fellow attorneys may also misunderstand or not try to understand an unconventional way of practicing law. When the CRLA lawyer filed his petition with the OAS, he urged his colleagues to raise inter-American human rights claims in their related federal court complaint. The complaint was in fact later amended on other grounds, but there seemed to be little interest in adding causes of action arising under international human rights law or in using that law to brief previously pled causes of action. This resulted not so much from principled disagreement as from inertia and professional etiquette: the ERC's attorney did not aggressively "lobby" his colleagues who were working on a case on which he was not co-counsel, and the lawyers on the domestic case did not have much time or incentive to learn a new area of law in the midst of litigation.

None of plaintiffs' counsel in the *Boehm* cases raised international law in support of their claims for subsistence benefits. Ironically, the vocabulary of legal aid lawyers is built on the concept of "economic justice." Could they have been reluctant to ask a court to recognize a right that does not fit neatly in the matrices of freedoms and protections sanctioned by U.S. courts? Or were these litigators simply unfamiliar with the international instruments promoting economic rights?

Unfamiliarity may even breed a mild form of contempt. One of the lawyers working with the California coalition opposing the English-only referendum dismissed arguments based on United Nations law as destined only for the World Court. This is the view of a very experienced litigator in the area of language rights.

One may also have trouble convincing fellow advocates to try new forums. The international and regional bodies are perceived as distant, politicized, nonlegal, and foreign. Co-counsel may think it unwise to take a matter to the Sub-Commission at a time when the General Assembly is squeezing its budget, or to utilize the UNESCO communications procedures when the US is no longer a member and many Americans have condemned that organization's "undemocratic" policies and Third World leanings.

This is not to say that attorneys who advise against the use of international arguments or forums are ill-intentioned or lazy. Serious discussions, as well as sincere disagreement, can take place with fellow counsel. The resistance to change that has been noted here, however, does underline the need for more education and training within the firm and the greater Legal Services community.

A Few Cautionary Notes

Despite the potential advantages, care in using international human rights norms and procedures is essential. Both clients and the Legal Services Corporation are likely to look askance at international human rights law initiatives, and such initiatives may backfire if they are filed prematurely or are overly broad.

Not Reaching the Clients

Legal aid lawyers have already been barraged with charges that they use their clients to achieve their own political and social goals. The phenomenon of the "paper plaintiff," that is, the litigant who exists only on the pleadings but has no real contact with counsel, may be more prevalent than those in the profession care to admit. The risk of losing one's clients or losing sight of their objectives is also real.

As arcane as the law may be for a layperson, international law may be that much more mysterious. By its very nature, it involves foreign words, foreign places, and foreign concepts. It may be too remote and intellectual for the indigent and parochial client to fully appreciate. For example, despite the ups and downs of the complaint that finally was lodged at the Inter-American Commission, some Equal Rights Council members asked the CRLA attorney who worked on their behalf to file a new petition after another farm worker drowned nearly one year after the original case had been dismissed. Apparently they had not fully grasped the significance of the denial of admissibility the first time. This does not mean, however, that clients may not be enthusiastic about achieving results through international means. The ERC was instrumental, after all, in getting CRLA to seek the good offices of Amnesty International.

There will always be communication gaps between the initiated and uninitiated; that is not an insurmountable problem. The danger lies more in the attorney's failure to understand the client's needs. Arguably, the job of a poor people's lawyer is to help people organize themselves to escape poverty or to minimize it and "empower" themselves in the process. The lawyer's enthusiasm for using international law solutions may sometimes detract from that more down-to-earth goal.

Political Fallout

Doing this kind of work does not come without a price tag. Legal Services attorneys have learned over the years that they are responsible not only to their clients. Looking over their shoulders is the Legal Services Corporation. In recent years the Corporation's Office of Monitoring, Audit and Compliance has taken a hard-nosed look at some of the unorthodox work performed by its affiliated law offices. For instance, when California Rural Legal Assistance was visited by a monitoring team in 1985, the staff attorney who had filed the IACHR complaint was asked why the matter was taken to that body and why the client organization could not hire its own lawyer. He responded that the Inter-American Commission petition was one of a number of legal vehicles utilized and that the client met the eligibility guidelines for assistance. The attorney picked up the latest issue of a publication widely distributed to Legal Services staff and pointed to the listing of the International Human Rights Law Group under the heading of "Specialized Litigation and Support Centers" on the inside cover. This, he explained, was the Corporation's unofficial imprimatur of the use of international human rights law. In its written report, the monitoring team noted both the international petition and the immigration subject matter. No disciplinary action, however, has been taken against CRLA.

It is conceivable that a communication from the Proposition 63 coalition to UNESCO's specially designated committee would incense some members of Congress or LSC Board members for much the same reasons it would discomfit fellow attorneys in search of the best forum.

Undertaking claims grounded in international human rights law is not *per se* controversial. Nevertheless, legal aid staff whose work involves heavily regulated areas—e.g., group representation, alien assistance, suits against government, lobbying—should be prepared to defend their cases before Legal Services bureaucrats and public officials alike. As one poor people's advocate observed just before the formation of the LSC, the more successful poverty lawyers are, the more likely it is that the government will try to eliminate their jobs.

Premature or Overly Broad Claims

Legal Services insiders have long argued for the necessity of lobbying state and federal legislators—as have members of the private bar—if a change in legislation would bring the most favorable outcome to their indigent clients. So, too, the international avenues should be explored where they maximize the chances of vindicating a client's rights. One must resist novelty for the sake of novelty, however. The all-too-frequent response from the opposing government in international forums is that the moving party has failed to exhaust domestic remedies.

This strategy by the US was very effective in the cases before the IACHR. The US representative's written communiques were filled with citations to cases pending in domestic courts which were often identical with those actions lodged with the IACHR. Petitioners tried to distinguish these cases by asserting that the relief sought from the international forum was broader, as in the *nonrefoulement* case, or that the final judgments in the US litigation were unduly delayed, as in the drowning petition. Still, attorneys should pause before rushing to file claims in Switzerland or Costa Rica. One should at least consider the wisdom of filing pleadings the *same* day with the *same* parties and *identical* issues. Even though attorneys must not overlook the many ways to zealously represent a client's interest, simultaneous litigation in different forums can harm their credibility.

Once one has turned to the international rights tribunals, it is preferable to rely on a few solid violations rather than to use the "shotgun" technique of stating every possible cause of action, whatever its strength. The petitioners at the IACHR realized this when they submitted their final briefs on the drowning of migrant workers: they limited their petition to violations of the substantive rights to life and personal security and confined their rebuttal of the government's assertion that they had failed to exhaust domestic remedies to an argument relating to delays in domestic judicial remedies. Lawyers should also tone down legal jargon and write concisely. The lead counsel for the Salvadoran refugees, for example, decided to adopt a nonlegalistic, informal style rather than let the paper get in the way of his client's message.

Finally, recourse to international forums should not be undertaken lightly. The dramatic effect can easily become *melo*dramatic, as in a compulsive communication sent to UNESCO before the implications of the English-only amendment are clear.

Not overloading the complaint is equally apt advice for the litigator in domestic courts; human rights claims should be used sparingly in pleadings. It is bold enough even to cite regional or international accords or resolutions as applicable authority in the US. One should temper that boldness by seeing to it that the citations are not helter-skelter and that words are not stretched to a ludicrous limit. The food-processing workers' attorneys framed their causes of action in terms of due process violations, leaving references to the American Declaration for the briefing and, possibly, oral argument stages. Even then, the Declaration is not meant to be the plaintiffs' sole authority.

The public interest coalition meeting to ward off the English-only amendment has begun its consideration of human rights arguments at a modest level. One litigator who has been successful in domestic application has suggested that an *amicus* brief might be the best vehicle. The views of the "hands off The Hague" advocate notwithstanding, most of his colleagues seem willing to use international doctrines in defense of language, educational choice, or privacy in a complaint, answer, or memorandum of points and authorities.

Conclusion

The general advantages and disadvantages of using international law and procedures have been amply noted. There are other considerations for the practitioner that do not fit into broad categories. For example, lawyers should understand that there are rarely any formalized precedents or clearly enunciated principles that emerge from the international petition system. While trained to operate within boundaries, guided by established authorities, attorneys may welcome the opportunity to take risks and not bind one's successors with "bad law." The same may be said of confidential proceedings: the advocate has little influence over the examiners' review of the case but may bank on an expert's dispassionate analysis or a government appointee's political sensibilities to yield a favorable result for the client.

While operating in the more familiar territory of domestic courts, attorneys must be ever mindful of the intrinsically conservative nature of their profession. Traveling on a lightly treaded path, they have a duty not only to their immediate client but to their colleagues and future clients, who also seek to make new law. Perhaps this is no different from the unwritten operating code adopted by attorneys for other matters, but it bears special mention that one's credibility and integrity are on the line once the words "international" or "human rights" are uttered to fellow jurists.

Caveats to proceed cautiously notwithstanding, the poverty lawyer must not steer clear of the unconventional and uncertain. The temptation to experiment and forge new legal principles should be tempered by an awareness that the goal is to achieve the client's goals, with whatever tools are available. International human rights law is *one* tool in the lawyer's workshop; the legal aid artisan should not be afraid to use it, but must exercise due care.

7

The Relationship of International Human Rights Law and Humanitarian Law to the Political Offense Exception to Extradition

DINAH L. SHELTON

For any criminal justice system to function, it is essential that persons who commit illegal acts be held accountable for their crimes. In recent decades this requirement has been increasingly complicated by the existence of national frontiers that individuals can cross with relative ease and speed, but that limit the reach of a state's prescriptive and enforcement criminal jurisdiction. Sophisticated underground networks and modern means of transportation enable fugitives both to quickly flee their national jurisdictions after crimes have been committed and to enter foreign territories for criminal purposes.

However, the ability to cross national boundaries also provides an escape for persons whose crimes consist of acts of political dissent ranging from printing opposition newspapers to organizing trade unions to political assassination to civilian bombings. This ability to flee applies as well to those who are subject to persecution or discrimination because of race, language, religion, ethnic origin, or political opinion.

The need for states to cooperate in prosecuting criminals has led to a multitude of bilateral and multilateral treaties for the extradition of suspected offenders,[1] while the desire to protect political dissidents and persecuted minorities has resulted in widespread acceptance of an exception to extradition for persons being sought for political offenses.[2] The problem lies in distinguishing nonextraditable political offenders from extraditable common criminals. Depending on what distinguishing criteria are applied, those who use violence to achieve political goals may be labeled either terrorists or freedom fighters.

Recent United States extradition cases and treaties suggest that neither the judicial nor the executive branch has succeeded in elaborating and applying an objective, comprehensive test for the political offense exception to extradition. Nonetheless, this article suggests that the policies underlying the political offense exception have as much, or more, validity today as a century ago, when it became common to incorporate the principle into extradition treaties.[3] The article also suggests how changes in international law during this century offer useful guidelines for courts or legislatures to define the "political offense" exception to extradition.

Historical Introduction

There is little agreement on most aspects of the law of extradition, including its history. While some authors find examples of extradition practice in antiquity,[4] others argue that the development of extradition began only during the eighteenth century.[5] Similarly, though Hugo Grotius stated that nations are bound by international law to prosecute or return fugitive offenders,[6] other scholars find no such obligation, noting that "extradition has always been considered as an exception to the traditional hospitality of asylum."[7]

Until the French Revolution the major purpose of extradition was to obtain the return of those considered guilty of crimes against the government or the state, such as treason, desertion, or sedition.[8] Rulers only sought fugitives whose acts directly affected the state or the sovereign, in whose punishment all states had a mutual interest.

Attitudes toward political offenses changed with the American and French Revolutions. From being considered the most dangerous criminals and the *raison d'etre* for extradition treaties, political offenders, like religious minorities, came to be viewed as immune from prosecution. The French Constitution of 1793 declared that the country would "give asylum to foreigners banished from their countries for the cause of liberty" and refuse refuge to tyrants.[9]

In 1833, Belgium adopted Europe's first Extradition Act and codified an exception for political offenders.[10] The same year, France renegotiated its year-old extradition treaty with Switzerland to eliminate extradition of political offenders.[11] The first United States extradition treaty contained a similar exemption,[12] as have all subsequent U.S. extradition treaties.[13] Moreover, as early as 1853, United States courts protected political offenders from extradition, even in the absence of a treaty obligation or statutory provision.[14] Today international human rights law guarantees the right of asylum, which adds force to the protection afforded political offenders.[15]

Rationale for the Political Offense Exception

Three policies underlie the political offense exception: (1) protecting human rights, (2) not intervening in the domestic affairs of foreign states, and (3) upholding international public order.

The political offense exception predates international systems for the protection of human rights. Nonetheless, much like those systems, the exception is based upon a recognition that individuals may "be compelled to have recourse, as a last resort, to rebellion against tyranny and oppression."[16] In addition, trial by a regime of those who oppose that government may be unfair and retaliatory. The exception thus shields individuals from reprisals or persecution by the state.[17]

Second, determining the extraditability of political offenders may violate principles of neutrality and imply a judgment with respect to internal conflicts.[18] On the other hand, the refusal to extradite is not necessarily a neutral action; it may amount to *de facto* support for the political adversaries of the requesting government.[19] In addition, remaining "neutral" may be unwarranted when it serves to protect those who have committed serious international crimes.

Finally, non-extradition is deemed neutral in its effect on the policy of upholding international public order. This assumes that political offenses have a purely local character, being directed only against the public order of the requesting state. Consequently, political offenders do not threaten the larger social order of the state of refuge or the international community as a whole.

Defining "Political Offense"

Treaties do not define the term political offense. Nevertheless, agreements and legislation exclude certain conduct from its protection by creating exceptions to the exception.[20] The first and still most widely accepted of such exclusions is the *attentat* clause, originating in Belgium, which provides that attempts or acts against the person of a foreign head of state or a member of his family shall not be considered political offenses.[21] More recently, multilateral treaties exclude war crimes,[22] genocide,[23] and other international crimes[24] from the political offense exception.

Two categories of political offense have evolved through judicial interpretation: "pure" and "relative" offenses. Pure political offenses, rarely extraditable, are limited to crimes such as treason, sedition, and espionage, which are directed solely against the state and do not cause a private wrong.[25] "Relative" political offenses are common crimes linked to political acts.

In most cases "pure" political crimes would not be extraditable offenses even in the absence of an explicit political offense exception, because they are rarely included among the offenses listed in extradition treaties. As a result, early court decisions interpreted the term "political offense" to cover common crimes related to political offenses. One court stated that the exception was created

> because the [Belgian] legislature did not merely wish to exclude from extradition offenses against the state, but also certain connected offenses. It was considered that an offense against the state, especially when it took the form of an armed rising against the existing state authority, ought (in order to make the principle of non-extradition effective) to embrace other acts attending it and contributory crimes in themselves, in particular offenses against life and property, as well as offenses respecting the person and liberty of the individual.[26]

The political offense exception thus may exclude common crimes from extradition if they are committed with a political purpose or in connection with political activity, or have political consequences. The difficulty is to determine what facts and circumstances cause a particular type of conduct to fall within the exception.

In practice, various national courts have developed several different objective and subjective approaches to this problem which they apply with varying degrees of consistency and success. France sometimes relies on political motivation as a major factor.[27] In the *da Palma* case,[28] a Paris court held that participation in a robbery of the Portuguese National Bank was a political crime when committed by politically motivated members of a revolutionary movement. Similarly, France characterized an airline hijacking a political offense because of the motivations of the United States perpetrators.[29]

More recently, French courts have looked primarily to the nature of the act committed. In the extradition to Germany of an alleged supporter of the Baader-Meinhof gang, political motivation alone was held insufficient to consider an offense a political crime.[30] The court found the acts alleged were not political in nature because they could not be integrated in an organized struggle for or against anything in particular; moreover, the acts were characterized by contempt toward the lives of innocent victims.[31]

The latter point also was emphasized in the *Piperno* extradition,[32] sought by Italy for an accused participant in the Aldo Moro kidnapping and assassination. Based on the seriousness of the acts involved, including physical and mental torture, kidnapping and killing of an innocent hostage,[33] the French court refused to accept the political offense defense.

Switzerland and Germany[34] rely on other criteria. Swiss tribunals apply a test of predominance and proportionality: if the political element of the offense dominates over the common crime, it may be characterized as a political offense. If the crime is too remote from the ultimate political goal, the political element does not dominate. An additional test of proportionality weighs the seriousness of the crime with the alternatives available and ultimate goals of the individual and group. According to the Swiss courts, the interests at stake must be sufficiently important to excuse the infringement of private rights.

The common law applies a "political incidence" test, developed from John Stuart Mill's definition of a political offense as "one committed in the course of a civil war, insurrection or political commotion."[35] This test focuses on the context of the act, not the motivation of the actor, to determine the nature of the offense.

In the landmark British case *In re Castioni*,[36] the court refused to extradite to Switzerland the alleged killer of a public official, finding that the act was incidental to and in furtherance of a political struggle. The court narrowed Mill's definition by adding a requirement that the act be in furtherance of the political disturbance. This brings some subjectivity to the "incidence" test as it looks in part to the purpose or motive of the act.

Four years following the *Castioni* decision, Mill's definition was further limited in *In re Meunier*.[37] In this case, the court stated that for the political offense exception to be applicable "there must be two or more parties in the State, each seeking to impose the Government of their own choice on the other."[38] Acts committed by anarchists, being opposed to all governments and being mainly directed against private citizens, are therefore not within the exception.[39]

British courts recently have given broader application to the political offense exception. In *ex parte Kolczynski*,[40] where Poland sought extradition of seven crew members of a Polish fishing trawler for kidnapping and assault, the court looked beyond the political incidence test and recognized the close relationship between the political offense exception and political asylum. Extradition was denied even though there was no political uprising. Instead, the court focused on the treatment that would likely be afforded to the crew members should they be returned to Poland.

Generally, courts have had little trouble in applying the political offense exception to "pure" political crimes, but have struggled to define the circumstances which will allow application of the term to common crimes related to political action. Most of the cases involve political violence—the majority of reported cases concern acts of homicide—and drawing the line between nonextraditable political offenses and extraditable crimes remains difficult. As discussed above courts outside the United States have looked to various factors, including subjective judgments about the accused and the requesting state, motivation of the actor, the circumstances surrounding the act, and the nature of the act.

Motivation of the actor, though less determinative than it was in the past, remains a factor in virtually all cases. In part it is the political purpose with which a common crime is committed that allows its characterization as a political crime. While political motive alone probably will not be sufficient to succeed in invoking the political offense exception, absence of a political motive may preclude its application.

Regarding the circumstances surrounding the act, many courts focus on the internal situation in the requesting state: whether there was a political uprising, disturbance, or civil war, and the likelihood of persecution or unfairness in proceedings if the individual is returned. Tribunals may also evaluate the degree of repression in the requesting state to determine, in light of the availability or absence of alternatives to violence, the necessity of the acts done.

The nature of the act has recently become a major factor in many states in evaluating applicability of the political offense exception. While sometimes it is and should be determinative, in many cases it has not been applied with any theoretical foundation or justified by any coherent policy. This shift in the rationale underlying the political offense exception is best illustrated by recent decisions of United States courts.

Application of the Political Offense Exception by the United States

United States courts adopted the *Castioni* political incidence test in 1894 in *In re Ezeta.*[41] Ezeta, vice-president and commander-in-chief of the army of El Salvador, was accused of robbing a bank to pay his troops and of hanging a spy during a revolution against the government. The court denied extradition, holding that the offenses, occurring during a state of siege, were "associated with the actual conflict of armed forces" and thus were of a political character. The court defined a political offense as "*any* offense committed in the course of or furthering of civil war, insurrection or political commotion."[42] The result thus distinguishes violent political disturbances from mere political opposition, although it places no limits on the type of acts which may be committed. In fact, the judge noted:

> With the merits of this strife I have nothing to do. . . . During its progress, crimes may have been committed by the contending forces of the most atrocious and inhuman character, and still the perpetrators of such crimes escape punishment as fugitives beyond the reach of extradition. I have no authority, in this examination, to determine what acts are within the rules of civilized warfare, and what are not.[43]

In *Ornelas v. Ruiz,*[44] the only United States Supreme Court opinion to discuss the political offense exception, the court focused not only on the context of the alleged political offense but also on the type of acts committed. In *Ornelas,* the court reviewed a habeas corpus petition to determine whether three Mexican nationals should be extradited to Mexico on charges of murder, arson, robbery, and kidnapping. The accused were part of a group of between 130 and 140 persons who crossed into Mexico from Texas to attack Mexican soldiers stationed at the village of San Ygnacio. Some of the soldiers were killed, others wounded and captured. The barracks were burned, horses and equipment stolen. In addition, civilians were assaulted, their property was stolen and their houses were burned, and three civilians were kidnapped and taken into Texas.

On this evidence, the United States Secretary of State had argued in favor of extradition. He stated:

> The idea that these acts were perpetrated with bona fide political or revolutionary designs is negatived by the fact that immediately after this occurrence, though no superior armed force of the Mexican government was in the vicinity to hinder their advance into the country, the bandits withdrew with their booty across the river into Texas.[45]

The magistrate agreed with the Secretary, but the district court reversed the decision, finding that the raid was part of "a political movement, having for its purpose the overthrow of the existing government in Mexico,"[46] and that the offenses were an attempt to accomplish this purpose.

The Supreme Court reinstated the magistrate's judgment, finding that it was not "palpably erroneous." In the court's view, the test is one not of political intentions but of whether the acts are in aid of a political movement. This is to be determined by considering the nature of the acts: "the character of the foray, the mode of attack, the persons killed or captured, and the kind of property taken or destroyed."[47] It may be inferred from the opinions of both the magistrate and the court that the attacks on civilians and their property were a factor in rejecting the political nature of the offenses.[48]

Subsequent cases have looked primarily to evidence on the existence of a political disturbance. If a violent upheaval is lacking, the exception is rarely applied. On the other hand, if an insurrection or other conflict is found, virtually all acts committed are deemed political offenses, without regard to their character. Thus, the requirement of political upheaval determined Venezuela's extradition request for its overthrown president Marcos Perez Jiminez,[49] who was sought on charges of financial corruption. The court granted extradition, holding that there was no political offense because "there is no evidence that the financial crimes charged were committed in the course of or incidentally to a revolutionary uprising or other violent political disturbance."[50] The court reached a similar conclusion in the *Sindona* extradition on allegations of fraudulent bankruptcy brought by Italy.[51]

Once a violent political conflict is found to exist, courts often ignore the criteria set out by the Supreme Court in *Ornelas v. Ruiz.* In *Ramos v. Diza,*[52] a Florida district court denied extradition of two Cuban revolutionaries who had been convicted of the murder of a prisoner, one of a group they had been responsible for safeguarding immediately following the revolution. The court relied upon the existence of a conflict in Cuba to characterize the offense. The court did not discuss the fact that murder of a prisoner during both international and civil wars is a grave breach of the international law of war.[53]

The existence of a political conflict, however, does not necessarily resolve the question of extradition. The character of the alleged crime was a factor in denying application of the political offense exception to Ziyad Abu Eain,[54] a Palestinian ordered extradited to Israel to stand trial for a bombing in Tiberias in which two Israelis were killed and others injured. The magistrate held that for the exception to apply, the accused must show a link between the crimes he allegedly committed and his political objective. For such a link to exist, the acts must be directed against the political organization of the state, rather than at the underlying social structure.

The Seventh Circuit affirmed, defining political offenses as "acts committed in the course of and incidental to a violent political disturbance such as a war, revolution or rebellion."[55] The definition is not met if there is no logical connection between the act and the political goal sought to be achieved. The court relied in part upon *In re Meunier* which excluded "anarchist" crimes from the political offense exception—these being offenses directed primarily against the general body of citizens. Further, the court deemed it necessary that there be two organized, nondispersed military forces engaged in armed struggle.

The tension between the strict *Castioni* incidence test applied in *Ramos* and the logical nexus approach of *Ornelas/Eain* is reflected in the three-decade-long litigation over extradition of Andrija Artukovic.[56] Beginning in 1951, Yugoslavia sought extradition of Artukovic alleging that he had directed the murder of more than two hundred thousand civilians while he was Minister of the Interior in a Nazi puppet government during World War II. In a 1956 opinion, the district court took judicial notice that German armies had invaded the country during the period in question.[57] Based upon this it concluded that "the plain reading of the Indictment here makes it immediately apparent that the offenses for which the surrender of the petitioner is sought, were offenses of a political character."[58] The court of appeals agreed and specifically declined to hold that war crimes against civilians were beyond the political incidence test.[59]

After reversal by the Supreme Court on a procedural point, a 1959 magistrate's hearing found lack of probable cause on the allegations.[60] Conceding that it was unnecessary to discuss the political offense exception, the commissioner nonetheless adopted the prior opinions of the district court and Ninth Circuit on the question.

Yugoslavia continued to seek Artukovic's extradition and ultimately was successful. In 1985, after a magistrate found probable cause for extradition, the district court denied Artukovic's petition for habeas corpus.[61] Applying the *Ornelas* test, the district court held that there was no "rational nexus between the alleged crimes and the prevailing turmoil although uprisings and disturbances did exist during the period in question."[62] It found that to determine applicability of the political offense exception, the focus must be on the circumstances of the offense and on the status of those harmed, and not on whether the acts merely were committed during the disorder. The court found that Artukovic's crimes consisted of impermissible vengeance upon disarmed enemy soldiers and efforts to rid the country of some of its population which could not be considered crimes of a political character.[63]

In a similar war crimes case, John Demjanjuk argued that Israel sought his extradition for political offenses.[64] Rejecting his defense, the court noted that Demjanjuk's alleged crimes included the murder of Jews, gypsies and others at Treblinka and held that "mere simultaneity between the alleged murders at Treblinka and World War II is insufficient to render the offense 'political.'"[65] Focusing on whether a rational nexus existed between the alleged crimes and the political disturbance, the court characterized Demjanjuk's invocation of the political offense exception as "frivolous and offensive," finding the civilian status of the victims "significant because the United States does not regard the indiscriminate use of violence against civilians as a political offense."[66]

Recent cases involving the conflict in Northern Ireland demonstrate the rather uncomfortable relationship between the "political incidence" and the logical nexus test. In *In re McMullen,*[67] the British government sought extradition of a former member of the Irish Republican Army for bombing a military barracks in Yorkshire, England. The magistrate denied extradition. Applying the political incidence test, he found the conflict in Northern Ireland to be a political uprising extending throughout Great Britain and held that an attack on a military target was incidental to and part of that uprising. In the magistrate's view,

> the political offense crime must be incidental to or formed as part of a political disturbance and committed as furthering a political uprising. Even though the offense be deplorable and heinous the criminal actor will be excluded from deportation if the crime is committed under these pre-requisites.[68]

In re Doherty[69] concerned an effort by the accused and other members of PIRA to ambush a convoy of British soldiers in Belfast. In a resulting shoot-out between the IRA members and members of the British Army, one of the latter was killed, and Doherty was arrested but escaped pending trial. The trial continued and he was convicted *in absentia.* Britain sought his extradition from the United States.

In rejecting extradition, the court had little difficulty finding the existence of a current political struggle in Northern Ireland and an offense committed during the course of that struggle. Nevertheless, it noted, that is not the end of its analysis, because strict application of *In re Castioni* "is hardly consistent with either the realities of the modern world, or the need to interpret the political offense exception in the light of the lessons of recent history."[70] In fact, said the court, not every act committed for a political purpose or during a political disturbance may or should properly be regarded as a political offense.

> Surely the atrocities at Dachau, Auschwitz, and other death camps would be arguably political within the meaning of that definition. The same would be true of My Lai, the Bataan death march, Lidice, the Katyn Forest Massacre, and a whole host of violations of international law that the civilized world is, has been, and should be unwilling to accept. Indeed, the Nuremberg trials would have no legitimacy or meaning if any act done for a political purpose could be properly classified as a political offense. Moreover, it would not be consistent with the policy of this nation as reflected by its participation in those trials, for an American court to shield from extradition a person charged with such crimes.[71]

Therefore, the court concluded, no act may be regarded as political "where the nature of the act is such as to be violative of international law, and inconsistent with international standards of civilized conduct."[72]

Under this test, not all acts of violence are impermissible. The court will evaluate the nature of the act, the context in which it is committed, the status of the party committing the act, the nature of the organization on whose behalf it is committed, and the particular circumstances of the place where it occurred. Applying that test to Doherty, the court found that his act was not one of indiscriminate violence against civilians or civilian representatives of the government. Nor did the violent act take place outside the territory of the conflict. In fact, none of the principles embodied in the Geneva Convention were clearly violated. "Instead, the facts of this case present the assertion of the political offense exception in its most classic form."[73]

Finally, the most recent case, *In re Quinn*,[74] concerned applicability of the political offense exception to charges of murder and conspiracy to cause explosions. The conspiracy charge centered around six specific bomb incidents against civilians in Britain. The murder charge involved the shooting death of an unarmed London police constable during an attempt to escape capture.

The district court agreed with the magistrate, and with the courts in *Mackin, McMullen* and *Doherty* that a political uprising exists in Northern Ireland.[75] But it disagreed with the magistrate's finding that the conspiracy offense was not incidental to the political uprising. The magistrate had applied the "in furtherance" language of *Castioni* to assess the acts undertaken by Quinn. The district court held that "the choices of action by an uprising group are not proper considerations for the extradition court when considering the applicability of the political offense exception."[76]

On appeal, the Ninth Circuit reversed the district court decision. In so doing, it stated that the political offense exception had by the 1850s "become a general principle of international law," incorporated into numerous extradition treaties.[77] The court acknowledged that the U.S. approach to the exception, while based upon *Castioni,* is more restrictive than the modern British view since it refuses to consider either the motive of the accused or that of the accuser.[78]

The court found merit in continued adherence to the restrictive approach yet it agreed that certain acts were "outside the original purposes underlying the exception."[79] Declining to state whether all war crimes are outside the exception, the court did exclude crimes against humanity, including genocide, as those acts whose "nature and scope . . . exceeded human imagination" and which violate international law.[80] They are crimes treated differently, constituting that part of international law which defines abuse of sovereignty. Thus the court explicitly disapproved its earlier *Artukovic* opinion.

The court then questioned whether it should exclude other activities from the exception. In spite of having just excluded crimes against humanity, the court declined to consider the legality of other types of conduct. Somewhat inconsistently, it stated that the exception should apply in an "ideologically neutral" fashion, and noted that a premise underlying recent opinions may be that "modern revolutionary tactics which include violence directed at civilians are not politically 'legitimate'."[81] Rather then viewing this as an application of international law the court found this to skew any political offense analysis because "we seek to impose on other nations and cultures our own traditional notions of how internal political struggles should be conducted."[82] The court concluded that "we believe the tactics that are used in such internal political struggles are simply irrelevant to the question whether the political offense exception is applicable."[83]

The situation changes, in the court's view, when the acts are committed outside the country whose government the individual or group is trying to change. First, the requirement of an uprising limits the exception to those situations where a certain level of internal violence exists, where political opposition "attracts sufficient adherents to create the requisite amount of turmoil."[84] Moreover, it excludes acts occurring outside the country in which the uprising is taking place. The political offense exception was designed

> to protect those engaged in internal or domestic struggles over the form or composition of their own government, including of course, struggles to displace an occupying power. It was not designed to protect international political coercion or blackmail, or the exportation of violence and strife to other locations—even to the homeland of an oppressor nation.[85]

In regard to the "incidental to" component of the test, the court applied what they termed "a liberal nexus standard," which requires no proof of the potential or actual effectiveness of the actions in achieving the group's political ends, nor of the motivation of the accused. The court specifically rejected a test that would distinguish civilian and military targets inside or outside the country.[86] Inside the country of conflict, everyone may be a target; outside the country no one may be. Under this analysis, Quinn was deemed extraditable since the uprising in Northern Ireland was not found to extend to England, where the offense took place.

U.S. Executive and Legislative Actions Regarding Political Offenses

Response from the political branches of government to recent U.S. extradition cases has been swift and generally unfavorable. Appealing for legislative changes, President Ronald Reagan called the political offense exception a loophole for terrorists.[87]

In judicial proceedings, the executive branch has increasingly sought to portray the exception as a matter for exclusive executive determination.[88] In *Eain, Mackin, McMullen, Doherty* and *Quinn*, the government argued the courts' lack of jurisdiction to decide the political offense question.

The government's position is based upon the language of extradition treaties and upon policy grounds. On the first point, it argues that extradition treaties define a political offense as one "which is regarded by the Requested Party as one of a political character."[89] In its view, "Requested Party" refers to the Secretary of State, not to the judiciary.

On policy grounds, the government claims that separation of powers renders the political offense as "unsuitable" matter for judicial consideration: it involves questions of foreign policy exclusively committed to the President;[90] judicial decision-making would constitute an intrusion upon the "unique resources available to the Executive to aid its determination of the political situation in foreign lands, and it could create a potential embarrassment to the country's conduct of foreign policy."[91] Finally, the government argues that the court lacks clearly manageable judicial standards.[92]

No court has accepted the government's arguments. The "Requested Party" language, in use at least since the turn of the century, has consistently been interpreted to refer to the country and not to any particular branch of government. Its usage is deemed merely to confirm longstanding, uniform practice in the United States that the political offense exception is a matter for judicial determination.

Responding to the policy arguments, courts have noted that where individual liberty is concerned, the Supreme Court has long accepted that "extradition without an unbiased hearing before an independent judiciary . . . is highly dangerous to liberty, and ought never to be allowed in this country."[93] This concern is not outweighed by foreign policy considerations, since placing the decision in the hands of the Secretary of State could heighten the country's foreign policy difficulties "unless the political offense exception were to be eviscerated in practice in the case of extradition treaties with nations with which we are allied or whose favor we especially desire."[94] As for the absence of manageable judicial standards,

> there has always been debate about the precise contours of the political offense exception. But the absence of perfect predictive ability in discerning whether a given act falls within the exception is not synonymous with an absence of manageable standards. . . . The determination whether there was a violent political disturbance in the requesting country at the time of the alleged acts and whether the

acts were incidental to the disturbance are mixed questions of law and fact . . . that do not require a political judgment.[95]

Failing to convince the courts that application of the exception lies within sole executive discretion, the government has sought to achieve the same result through legislation and treaty revisions. This effort has two objectives: to remove from the courts jurisdiction to apply the exception, and to redefine political offense so as to restrict or remove its application in many situations.

In Congress, the administration and those supporting its position sought to curtail the political offense exception through enactment of the 1981 Extradition Reform Act.[96] The Senate bill would have left to the sole discretion of the Secretary of State any question of the political character of an offense. Both Senate and House versions would have excluded hijacking, attacks on diplomats, genocide, war crimes, and narcotics offenses from the political offense exception. These limitations were probably unnecessary, as extradition or prosecution is required for these offenses under the provisions of multilateral treaties in force for the U.S.[97] Nonpolitical crimes also included acts of homicide, assault with intent to commit serious bodily injury, rape, kidnapping, taking of hostages or serious unlawful detention, and any offense involving the use of a firearm such as to endanger another person, "except in extraordinary circumstances." Neither the House nor the Senate version of the bill was enacted.

Treaty renegotiations, on the other hand, have succeeded in restricting the political offense exception. The 1985 Supplementary Treaty of Extradition between the United States and the United Kingdom[98] enacts the most far-reaching alterations. It limits the role of the judiciary by virtually abolishing the relative political offense exception. Article I refers to multilateral treaties concerning hijacking, attacks on diplomats, and taking of hostages. The Treaty goes further, however, by excluding murder, manslaughter, malicious assault, kidnapping, abduction, false imprisonment, offenses involving explosives and firearms, and property damage when lives are endangered.[99]

No consideration is given to the circumstances surrounding these acts. Thus, any killing may be extraditable, even if committed by one soldier against another during civil war or other major insurrection. While attacks by rebels on military targets are a preeminent form of political offense, the treaty suggests that such persons are extraditable and subject to victor's justice, clearly reversing a century of legal doctrine. In addition, the treaty also explicitly provides for retroactive application, a provision which has already been invoked to reinstitute an extradition request against McMullen.[100] The Legal Advisor to the State Department supported the revision, claiming that the "political offense exception has no place in extradition treaties between stable democracies, in which the political system is available to redress legitimate grievances and the judicial process provides fair treatment."[101] What cannot be overlooked is the possibility that stable democracies may become destabilized or autocratic.

Another Look at the Political Offense Exception

The effectiveness of modern state repression and the current inability of international machinery to adequately protect human rights victims reveal the need for continued application of the political offense exception. Those who are struggling to restore or improve internationally-recognized human rights should be protected. At the same time, political violence is a matter of considerable concern. The question is whether those using violent means to achieve political ends should be included in the political offense exception.

There are those who argue that the political offense exception is outmoded and unjustified in modern democratic regimes, that a rise in political violence necessitates abolishing what is in fact a loophole for terrorists.[102] In fact, the vast majority of states are not democratic regimes, but are societies in which political opposition is rarely tolerated. In addition, in many cases gross and systematic violations of human rights persistently occur.[103] Even in democratic societies, there may be periods of exception, such as Greece under the colonels,[104] where political opponents struggling to restore human rights required protection through the political offense exception. Or there may be particular problems as in the case in Northern Ireland, where generally guaranteed rights and liberties are not always respected.[105]

It is the existence of these problematic situations and of regimes that continually violate human rights norms which demonstrates continued need for application of the political offense exception to extradition. Not only are there often no legal avenues of political opposition under these conditions, but the effectiveness of modern repression may force political dissenters into acts of violence or terrorism because open rebellion is difficult, if not impossible, to initiate. Further, while acts of terrorism violate human rights, serious and repeated violations of human rights are likely to drive political opponents to turn to terrorism. To attack terrorism requires greater enforcement of human rights norms and other principles of international law rather than abolition of a doctrine designed to shield those opposing state violence.

Furthermore, despite much discussion of transnational terrorism, all recent United States extradition cases have concerned internal political violence. There appear to be no cases in which an international terrorist has escaped extradition through invocation of the political offense exception. Instead, through application of a test more than a century old, courts have struggled to respond to recent acts of political violence. Despite criticism leveled at the recent extradition cases in the U.S. and in spite of the different approaches and the often strained reasoning of the courts, the results of these cases were probably correct under international law standards: Eain and Quinn should have been extradited for bombing civilians and expanding the theater of conflict; Mackin, McMullen and Doherty attacked military targets during an ongoing internal armed conflict and should be considered political offenders.

The difficulty with these cases lies in the legal analysis used to reach the decisions. In *Eain*, the court found the PLO to be too dispersed to be conducting an armed uprising and stated that a civilian bombing is not an act in furtherance of such an uprising when one does exist. Earlier, Gonzales was extradited because no uprising existed, not because the torture and murder of prisoners is never permissible. The district court's decision in *Quinn* would have denied extradition upon finding an uprising throughout Britain, disregarding the attacks on civilian targets.

Both the judiciary and the political branches of government have failed to recognize that the international legal system has changed even more dramatically than has the world of extradition and political violence. First, a series of multilateral treaties aimed at international cooperation in criminal matters now explicitly provides for prosecution or extradition of persons who commit certain offenses, in effect creating a body of international criminal law.[106] Second, the status of the individual in international law has fundamentally changed from that of an object under exclusive jurisdiction of the national state to that of a person with internationally recognized human rights, freedoms, and duties.[107]

Multilateral treaties concerning international criminal conduct, which explicitly require prosecution or extradition, generally do not mention the political offense exception but merely imply its unavailability for the designated offenses.[108] Should the exception be deemed applicable, however, the result would not be immunity but prosecution in the requested state. The offenses regulated by such treaties are hijacking, genocide, the taking of hostages, terrorism, and war crimes.

The most detailed of these treaties is the European Convention on the Suppression of Terrorism.[109] It specifically deems nonpolitical a list of offenses that includes hijacking, attacks upon internationally protected persons, kidnapping and hostage-taking, and offenses involving bombs or firearms when these endanger persons.[110] States also may, but are not obliged to, consider as nonpolitical other serious violent acts against the life, physical integrity, or liberty of a person; or an act against property "if the act created a collective danger for persons."[111] The requested state may refuse extradition if it has substantial grounds for believing that the request is made for purposes of persecution based upon race, religion, nationality, or political opinion, or if the individual's position would be prejudiced for any of these reasons. In cases where extradition is not granted, if the person is suspected to have committed one of the listed nonpolitical offenses, the requested state must submit the case for prosecution.[112]

Such international treaties offer some guidelines for courts in determining the scope of the political offense exception, but they do not offer a comprehensive test. What is needed is a framework that offers objectivity to the greatest extent possible, reflects current international law, and serves the underlying purposes of protecting both human rights and world order.

A Proposed Standard for the Political Offense Exception

As a starting point, courts should continue to determine the existence of an uprising in the state in question or, in modern terminology, a non-international armed conflict. International law since Grotius has distinguished between the laws of war and the laws of peace.[113] For mostly humanitarian reasons, the laws of war are now in large part applicable to internal as well as international conflicts.[114] During armed conflicts, acts are permitted which would be illegal if committed during peacetime. Other acts, such as torture, genocide, or slavery, remain illegal irrespective of the context, since they are prohibited by both the laws of war and the laws of peace.

In most cases, the conduct itself, and not the existence of an armed struggle, will determine the applicability of the political offense exception. To require the existence of an armed struggle or uprising in order to apply the political offense exception arguably promotes violence as a means of political change. Moreover, given the repressive character of many modern day regimes, such a requirement restricts the applicability of the exception to the extent that it almost eliminates its usefulness.

For analytical purposes, it may be possible to characterize offenses according to three categories of conduct:

1. That which is always illegal, whether during armed conflict or peace. Acts within this category could not be termed political offenses and would oblige the state of refuge to either prosecute or extradite (*aut dedere aut judicare*).
2. Acts which are permissible during armed conflicts or uprisings, to use the *Castioni* language, but which may be illegal during peacetime. Whether an individual could invoke the political offense exception in this case would depend initially on finding an armed conflict.
3. Acts which would qualify as political offenses during both armed conflicts and peacetime.

Because much of the law in this area is undeveloped, the lines between the three categories will not always be evident or easy to determine. Nevertheless, there are some clearly accepted principles that can serve as guidelines.

Illegal Acts

International norms prohibit certain conduct under all circumstances and without regard to motivation. As the Secretary General of the United Nations has stated, "Even when the use of force is legally and morally justified, there are some means, as in every form of human conflict, which must not be used."[115]

The laws of armed conflict define war crimes and establish the limits of permissible conduct. For internal conflicts, article 4 of Protocol II Additional to the Geneva Conventions of 12 August 1949[116] prohibits "at any time and in any place" certain acts against those not actively engaged in hostilities. The prohibited acts are murder and cruel treatment such as torture, mutilation or corporal punishment; collective punishments; taking of hostages; acts of terrorism; humiliating and degrading treatment, including rape, enforced prostitution or indecent assault; slavery; and pillage. As President Reagan said in his letter transmitting the Protocol to the Senate for advice and consent to ratification: "This Protocol makes clear that any deliberate killing of a noncombatant in the course of a non-international armed conflict is a violation of the laws of war and a crime against humanity, and is therefore also punishable as murder."[117]

Under the Fourth Geneva Convention, those committing "grave breaches" or war crimes must be extradited or prosecuted.[118] Each contracting party, 187 states as of January 1, 1987, must "search for persons alleged to have committed, or to have ordered to be committed,"[119] such acts, which include willful killings, torture or inhuman treatment, and taking of hostages. This conduct, made criminal during the exigencies of battle, *a fortiori* must not be permissible in peacetime.

Several of the acts listed in the Fourth Geneva Convention and in Protocol II are also subjects of multilateral treaties, applicable during peacetime, which emphasize their illegality under all circumstances. These treaties include the Convention on the Prevention and Punishment of the Crime of Genocide,[120] the International Convention Against the Taking of Hostages,[121] the various antihijacking treaties,[122] and the Convention Against Torture.[123]

Thus, the first category excludes from the political offense exception any conduct currently deemed a war crime, whether war exists or not, both because such conduct is even less justifiable in peacetime than during war, and because international human rights instruments clearly prohibit such acts.

Protected Acts

At the other extreme is that category of conduct protected as political in all circumstances. Certainly this includes all traditional "pure" political offenses. In addition, it should include the exercise of any internationally recognized human right. Thus, for example, efforts to organize a trade union would be protected under article 23 of the Universal Declaration of Human Rights as well as other human rights instruments. Application of the political offense exception to acts in this category would serve to uphold international human rights norms by refusing to return to a state individuals who were engaged in the exercise of recognized rights and freedoms.

Dependent Acts

Probably the most difficult determination is the classification of acts in the middle category: conduct permissible under some circumstances but not others. The laws of armed conflict permit the killing of combatants;

indeed, that is probably the primary strategy of conflict. The central question is whether killing is ever permissible in the absence of an armed conflict.

The question is central because the overwhelming majority of extradition cases in which the political offense exception is invoked involve the taking of human life. It is also central because the effectiveness of modern governments to repress the opposition makes uprisings more difficult to initiate and thus forces dissenters into less open means of rebellion. Arguably the vast powers of such regimes may only be countered by the use of assassination as a political weapon. Even though there are circumstances in which one may sympathize with the motivations of those seeking to eliminate the personification of tyrannical and corrupt power—the Stalins, the Hitlers—the political offense exception should not extend to assassination.

First, summary and arbitrary executions are prohibited by human rights law.[124] As part of the right to life this extends to protect all individuals from those who would take it upon themselves to summarily determine when life is forfeit. Second, to permit invocation of the political offense exception for peacetime assassinations would place courts in an impossible position. Either they would have to allow that all politically motivated killings are political offenses or they would have to make the determination *ex post facto* whether the assassination was justified under the circumstances. While differences between the governments of Olaf Palme and Idi Amin are readily apparent, United States courts cannot be asked to determine whether these differences justify or excuse assassinating either man. Like torture, summary executions should be prohibited under all circumstances, whether perpetrated by or against a government. The only exception is the lawful killings of combatants during armed conflict.[125]

Apart from homicide, are there acts falling between the clearly legal and the clearly illegal which may be termed political offenses? One view would exclude all relative political offenses except during armed uprisings. The difficulty with this approach is that it puts a premium on effective repression by eliminating the exception as long as the government can prevent the uprising. Unless the courts want to promote violence, an armed uprising should not be required to invoke the political offense exception.

There is probably no single test that can be applied to determine the applicability of the exception to cases that fall in this murky area, cases which would include such things as economic sabotage, attacks on government property, and injury to persons. The courts could look at several factors: whether there exists organized opposition to the government or whether this is an individual action; the seriousness of the act; and the situation in the country, including the existence of available alternatives to political violence.

It may be argued that the latter would involve the courts in an impermissible intervention into the domestic situation in other countries. But courts already look into internal situations to determine whether an uprising exists and to determine whether the individual involved will be subjected to persecution upon return.[126] In addition, there is evidence prepared annually by the executive branch, the use of which would minimize intrusions into foreign policy. This evidence, contained in the State Department Country Reports on Human Rights,[127] may be used as a primary guide to the situation in the requesting country. Finally, there are credible and authoritative reports of intergovernmental and nongovernmental organizations.[128] The availability of widespread reporting on human rights throughout the world eases the burden of the courts in this regard.

There remains the question of whether the treatment to be afforded the individual upon return should affect extradition. It has been suggested that the political offense exception should be replaced by a requirement that the fugitive receive a fair trial in the requesting state. While this should be considered in cases where extradition is requested, it is not an adequate substitute for the exception. Trials are inherently suspect when political opponents are involved, and the existence of a normally fair process is not a guarantee that justice will be done in a particular case. In addition, the proposed test of fair trial is too narrow. Beyond the question of trial procedures is the question of motivation in prosecution: whether the individual is likely to be a victim of prejudice or persecuted on any of various grounds including race, religion, nationality, political opinion, or language. Furthermore, the consequences of conviction cannot be ignored. Even where there are fair trials there may exist cruel, inhuman, or degrading treatment or punishment.

Some authors object that these considerations are "premised entirely upon western and democratic notions of due process and other procedural safeguards afforded to individuals accused of crime."[129] These objections are sometimes raised to efforts to implement human rights, but they ignore the widespread participation by countries throughout the world in drafting and ratifying international norms, including basic protections of due process and fair trial, as well as prohibitions on cruel, inhuman, or degrading punishment. It is not imposing alien values to demand that a state implement legal obligations freely undertaken or to refuse to return an individual to a state where those obligations are routinely ignored.

Conclusion

Despite the confused case history of the political offense exception and the rather strained reasoning of recent U.S. extradition cases, the courts have the necessary law to coherently and consistently apply the political offense exception when extradition is requested. The central focus must be on the type of conduct involved. Whether the act is one protected at all times or conversely illegal in all circumstances can be determined using principles of international human rights and humanitarian law. For those cases that do not fall under either extreme, the court must determine whether the act occurred in the context of armed conflict or peace. Certain activities that are legitimate during armed conflict will not qualify as political offenses during peace. Other offenses may or may not qualify depending on the circumstances and the seriousness of the conduct.

The courts should also concern themselves with the treatment to be afforded the individual upon return. If the person is likely to be subjected to persecution, torture, or cruel, inhuman, or degrading treatment or punishment, or denied minimum standards of justice established by international human rights law, extradition should be denied and the option of local prosecution invoked.

Application of these principles would serve the interests of individual liberty while upholding international law and public order. In the United States both the courts and the legislature should take a new look at the political offense exception, maintaining it as a necessary protection of individual rights while confining it to avoid shielding those committing common crimes or acts illegal under international law.

NOTES

1. The United States is currently party to nearly one hundred bilateral treaties of extradition, listed following 18 U.S.C.A. § 1381 (supp. 1986). Multilateral treaties involving extradition obligations include the Convention for the

Suppression of Unlawful Seizure of Aircraft, *signed* 16 Dec. 1970, *in force* 14 Oct. 1971, 22 U.S.T. 1641, T.I.A.S. No. 7192; the Montreal Convention for the Suppression of Unlawful Acts against the Safety of Civil Aviation, *signed* 23 Sept. 1971, *in force* 26 Jan. 1973, 24 U.S.T. 565, T.I.A.S. No. 7570; and the Convention on the Prevention and Punishment of Crimes Against Internationally Protected Persons, Including Diplomatic Agents, *signed* 14 Dec. 1973, *in force* 20 Feb. 1977, 28 U.S.T. 1975, T.I.A.S. No. 8532.

2. Every United States bilateral extradition treaty contains the political offense exception. It also has been included in the constitutions of Brazil (art. 153), Mexico (art. 15), Italy (art. 1, App. A) and Spain (art. 1, para. 3), and in the domestic legislation of most other countries.

3. The 1834 French-Belgian Extradition Treaty first incorporated the political offense exemption. Convention on the Extradition of Criminals, 22 Nov. 1834, Belgium-France, 84 Parry's T.S. 457, 22 BRITISH AND FOREIGN STATE PAPERS 223, art. 5.

4. *E.g.*, Grotius. H. GROTIUS, 2 DE JURE BELLI AC PACIS LIBRI TRES 526–29 (F. Kelsey trans.; Oxford: Clarendon Press, 1925). An agreement concluded in 1280 B.C.E. between Egyptian Pharaoh Ramses II and the Hittite Hattusili is often cited as the oldest known extradition treaty. Langdon & Gardiner, *The Treaty of Alliance Between Hattusili King of the Hittites and the Pharaoh Ramses II of Egypt*, 6 J. OF EGYPT. ARCH. 179 (1920). For a discussion of this and other ancient precedents, see Blakesley, *The Practice of Extradition from Antiquity to Modern France and the United States: A Brief History*, 4 BOSTON COLLEGE INT'L & COMP. L. REV. 39 (1981).

5. *See, e.g.*, A. BILLOT, TRAITE DE L'EXTRADITION 35 (Paris: E. Plon, 1874); and M. VILLEFORT, DES TRAITES DE L'EXTRADITION DE LA FRANCE AVEC LES PAYS ETRANGERS 5 (Paris: 1851).

6. GROTIUS, *supra* note 4, at 527. Vattel and Bodin agreed with this view. E. DE VATTEL, LE DROIT DES GENS 311–13 (Liv. 3, ch. 6, § 76, 77) (1758) (Washington: Carnegie Inst., 1916); J. BODIN, LES SIX LIVRES DE LA REPUBLIQUE (1576), THE SIX BOOKS OF A COMMONWEALE 100–101 (Harvard Pol. Classics, K. D. McRae ed.; Boston, 1961).

7. CH. VAN DEN WIJNGAERT, THE POLITICAL OFFENSE EXEMPTION TO EXTRADITION: THE DELICATE PROBLEM OF BALANCING THE RIGHTS OF THE INDIVIDUAL AND THE INTERNATIONAL PUBLIC ORDER 4 (Boston: Kluwer Publ., 1980). *See also* B. AFRICA, POLITICAL OFFENSES IN EXTRADITION (Manila: Benipayo Press, 1926), p. 11. Modern state practice, codified in the United States, supports the view that extradition is not required or even permitted in the absence of a treaty in force between the requesting and requested states. *See* 18 U.S.C. § 1381; United States v. Rauscher, 119 U.S. 407 (1886); Valentine v. United States ex rel. Neidecker, 299 U.S. 4, 10 (1936).

8. VAN DEN WIJNGAERT, *supra* note 7, at 5.

9. Quoted in VAN DEN WIJNGAERT, *supra* note 7 at 9.

10. Belgian Extradition Act of 1 Oct. 1833. 67 BULL. OFF. (No. 1195).

11. BILLOT, *supra* note 5, at 109–10.

12. Treaty of Extradition, United States–France, 9 Nov. 1843, 8 Stat. 581, T.S. 89, 7 BEVANS 830, 1 MALLOY 526.

13. 6 M. M. WHITEMAN, DIGEST OF INTERNATIONAL LAW 799–800 (U.S. Dep't. of State, 1973). Eastern European countries do not include the political offense exception in their extradition treaties among themselves and with the Soviet Union.

14. *Ex parte* Kaine, 14 F.Cas. 79, 81–82 (C.C.S.D.N.Y. 1853) (No. 7597).

15. "Everyone has the right to seek and to enjoy in other countries asylum from persecution. This right may not be invoked in the case of prosecutions genuinely arising from non-political crimes or from acts contrary to the purposes and principles of the United Nations." Art. 14, Universal Declaration of Human Rights (1948), GA Res. 217A (III), UN Doc. A/810, at 74 (1948) (3d Sess. 1st Part). *See also* art 27, American Declaration of the Rights and Duties of Man, OAS Res. 30, *adopted by* the Ninth International Conference of American States, Bogota, 1948, and art. 22, American Convention on Human Rights, *signed* 22 Nov. 1969, *entered into force* 18 July 1978, OAS T.S. No. 36, at 1, OAS Off. Rec. OEA/Ser.L/V/II.23 doc. rev. 2. The latter provides: "Every person has the right to seek and be granted asylum in a foreign territory . . . in the event he is being pursued for political offenses or related common crimes."

16. Preamble, Universal Declaration of Human Rights, *supra* note 15.

17. In addition, there is concern about rendition of those who may be subject to torture, or to cruel, inhuman, or degrading treatment. Art. 5, Universal Declaration of Human Rights. *Id.*

18. Van den Wijngaert, *supra* note 7, at 3.

19. *Id.* at 204 n. 1071.

20. For example, art. 1 of the European Convention for the Suppression of Terrorism, *signed* 27 Jan. 1977, E.T.S. No. 90, excludes from the definition of political offense, *inter alia,* hijackings, attacks on internationally protected persons, kidnapping or taking of hostages, and offenses involving the use of bombs. Similarly, art. 5(2), para. 2, of the French Extradition Law of 10 Mar. 1927 states that acts committed during a civil war or insurrection may not be grounds for extradition unless they constitute acts of odious barbarism or vandalism prohibited by the laws of war.

21. Ann. Parl. Ch., at 312 (1855–56).

22. Art. 1(b), Additional Protocol to the European Convention on Extradition, 15 Oct. 1975, E.T.S. No. 86.

23. Art. 7, Convention on the Prevention and Punishment of the Crime of Genocide (9 Dec. 1948; *entered into force* 12 Jan. 1951), 78 U.N.T.S. 277.

24. *E.g.,* hijacking and attacks on internationally protected persons. *See* the multilateral treaties listed, *supra* note 1.

25. The distinction is discussed in *In re* Castioni, [1891] 1 Q.B. 149, at 152–68, and *In re* Ezeta, 62 F. 972, at 997–1004 (N.D. Cal. 1894).

26. *In re* Fabijan, Supreme Court of Germany, [1933–34] Ann. Dig. 360–61 (No. 156).

27. *See* Van den Wijngaert, *supra* note 7, at 122–23. Contrast *In re* Gatti, Judgment of 13 Jan. 1947, Cour d'appel, 1947 Ann. Dig. 145 (No. 70, France) where the court holds that an offense does not derive its political character from the motive of the offender, but from the nature of the rights it injures. *Id.* at 145–46.

28. Da Palma Inacio, Decision of 14 Dec. 1967, Cour d'appel (Paris), La semaine juridique, No. 15387 (1968).

29. *In re* Holder, *reprinted in* 1975 Dig. U.S. Practice Int'l L. 168–75.

30. *In re* Croissant, Judgment of 16 Nov. 1977, Cour d'appel (Paris), 93 J. Trib. 52 (1978).

31. *Id.*

32. *In re* Piperno, Judgment No. 1343–79 of 17 Oct. 1979, Cour d'appel (Paris).

33. *Id.* p. 14.

34. *In re* Fabijan, *supra* note 26. In this case, the court stated that political motive was insufficient where there was no political act. *Id.* at 367.

35. 184 HANSARD'S DEBATES 2115 (1866).

36. *In re* Castioni, *supra* note 25, at 152–68.

37. [1894] 2 Q.B. 415, at 419.

38. *Id.*

39. *Id.*

40. [1955] 2 Q.B. 540, 1 All E.R. 31. *See also* Schtraks v. The Government of Israel, [1962] All E.R. 529 (House of Lords).

41. *In re* Ezeta, *supra* note 25.

42. Ezeta, *supra* note 25, at 978. (Emphasis added).

43. *Id.* at 997.

44. Ornelas v. Ruiz, 161 U.S. 502 (1896).

45. *Id.* at 511.

46. *Id.* at 510.

47. *Id.* at 511.

48. AFRICA, *supra* note 7, at 61.

49. Jiminez v. Aristeguieta, 311 F.2d 547 (5th Cir. 1962), *aff'd* (per curiam) *sub nom.* Jiminez v. Hixon, 314 F.2d 654 (5th Cir. 1963), *cert. denied*, 373 U.S. 914 (1963).

50. *Id.* at 560.

51. *In re* Sindona, 450 F. Supp. 672 (S.D.N.Y. 1978), *habeas corpus den.* 461 F. Supp. 199 (S.D.N.Y. 1978), aff'd Sindona v. Grant, 619 F.2d 167 (1980). *See also In re* Pazienza, 619 F. Supp. 611 (D.C.N.Y.). Contrast *In re* Mylonas, 187 F. Supp. 716 (1966) where the court refused extradition on strikingly similar financial charges finding that "the offence for which extradition was sought was incidental to, formed a part of, and was the aftermath of political disturbances. . . ." *Id.*

52. Ramos v. Diaz, 179 F. Supp. 459 (S.D. Fla. 1959).

53. Art. 3, 130, Geneva Convention Relative to the Treatment of Prisoners of War, 12 Aug. 1949, U.S.T. 316, T.I.A.S. No. 3364, 75 U.N.T.S. 135.

54. Eain v. Wilkes, 641 F.2d 504 (1981).

55. *Id.* at 518.

56. Artukovic v. Boyle, 101 F. Supp. 11 (S.D. Cal. 1952), *rev'd sub nom.* Ivancevic v. Artukovic, 211 F.2d 565 (9th Cir. 1953), *cert. den.* 348 U.S. 818, 75 S.Ct. 28, 90 L.Ed. 645 *reh. den.* 348 U.S. 889, 75 S.Ct. 202, 99 L.Ed. 645 (1954), *on remand* 140 F. Supp. 245 (S.D.Cal. 1956), *aff'd sub nom.* Karadzole v. Artukovic, 247 F.2d 198 (9th Cir. 1957), *vacated and remanded*, 355 U.S. 393, 78 S.Ct. 381, 2 L.Ed.2d 356 (1958) (mem.), *surrender denied on remand sub. nom.* United States v. Artukovic, 170 F. Supp. 383 (S.D.Cal. 1959). Deportation efforts were unsuccessfully attempted in 1982, *see* Artukovic v. INS, 693 F.2d 894 (9th Cir. 1982). In 1984, Yugoslavia filed a new extradition request. The magistrate found probable cause, Extradition of Artukovic, CV 84–8743–R(B) (C.D. Cal. 1 May 1985). Artukovic's petition for habeas corpus was denied, Artukovic v. United States, 628 F. Supp. 1370 (C.D.Cal. 1986), *aff'd sub. nom.* Artukovic v. Rison, 784 F.2d 1354 (9th Cir. 1986), and after nearly thirty-five years, Artukovic was extradited.

57. Artukovic v. Boyle, 140 F. Supp. 245 (S.D.Cal. 1956).

58. *Id.* at 247.

59. Karadzole v. Artukovic, 247 F.2d 198, 205 (9th Cir. 1957).

60. U.S. v. Artukovic, 170 F. Supp. 383, 393 (S.D.Cal. 1959).
61. 628 F. Supp. 1370 (C.D.Cal. 1986).
62. *Id.* at 1376 (C.D.Cal. 1986).
63. *Id.*
64. 612 F. Supp. 544 (D.C.Ohio 1985), 776 F.2d 571 (6th Cir. 1985).
65. 612 F. Supp. 540, 570.
66. *Id.*
67. *In re* McMullen, No. 3–78–1099 MG (N.D.Cal. 11 May 1979).
68. *Id.* at 3. *See also* U.S. v. Mackin, 80 Cr. Misc. 1 (S.D.N.Y. 13 Aug. 1981), appeal dismissed *In re* Mackin 668 F.2d 122 (2d Cir. 1981), where the Second Circuit affirmed a magistrate's findings of a political offense and refused to extradite a member of the IRA accused of attempting to murder a British soldier in Belfast.
69. 559 F. Supp. 270 (S.D.N.Y. 1984).
70. *Id.* at 274.
71. 559 F. Supp. 270, 274 (S.D.N.Y. 1984).
72. *Id.*
73. *Id.* at 276.
74. 783 F.2d 776 (9th Cir. 1986).
75. Quinn v. Robinson, No. C–82–6688 RPA (3 Oct. 1983) (unpublished opinion).
76. *Id.* at 29–30.
77. 783 F.2d 776, 793.
78. *Id.* at 796.
79. *Id.* at 798.
80. *Id.* at 799.
81. *Id.* at 804.
82. *Id.*
83. *Id.* at 805.
84. *Id.* at 807.
85. *Id.*
86. *Id.* at 810.
87. 131 Cong. Rev. LS 9696 (Daily Ed. 17 July 1985).
88. Present federal law requires the requesting state to obtain approval of both the judicial and the executive branches before extradition will be granted. 18 U.S.C. 1384. While the judiciary determines that the correct person is in custody, that the offense is one listed within the extradition treaty and not a political offense, and that there is probable cause to believe that the accused committed the crime caused, it is exclusively for the executive to determine whether the request is politically motivated or whether there are humanitarian grounds for withholding extradition. In addition, if a court finds the accused is not a political offender, the executive may reverse the court. *See* Sternberg and Skelding, *State Department Determinations of Political Offenses: Death Knell for the Political Offense Exception in Extradition Law,* 15 Case W. Res. J. Int'l L. 127 (1983).
89. *In re* Mackin, *supra* note 68 at 132.
90. *Id.* citing United States v. Curtis Wright Export Corp., 299 U.S. 304, 57 S.Ct. 216, 81 L.Ed. 255 (1936).
91. Eain v. Wilkes, *supra* note 54 at 514.
92. "There is simply no justifiable standard to the political offense." *Extradition Reform Act of 1981: Hearings on H.R. 5227 Before the Subcommittee on*

Crime of the House Committee on the Judiciary, 97th Cong. 2d Sess. 24–25 (testimony of Roger Olson, Deputy Assistant Attorney General, Criminal Division, U.S. Department of Justice).

93. *In re* Kaine, 55 U.S. (14 How.) 103, 112, 14 L.Ed. 345 (1852).

94. *In re* Mackin, *supra* note 68 at 133.

95. Quinn v. Robinson, *supra* note 75 at 790.

96. 1981 Extradition Act, S. 1639, 97th Cong. 2d Sess. (1982); Extradition Reform Act, H.R. 5227, 97th Cong. 2d Sess. (1982).

97. *See* the Conventions listed, *supra* note 1. The U.S.–U.K. Supplemental Treaty, *infra* note 98, also mentions the Convention against the Taking of Hostages, 17 Dec. 1979, GA Res. 34/146, 34 UN GAOR Supp. (No. 39), UN Doc. A/34/819 (1979) *reprinted in* 18 INT'L LEGAL MATERIALS 1457 (1979).

98. *In force* 23 Dec. 1986. U.S.T. , T.I.A.S. No. , *reprinted in* 24 INT'L LEGAL MATERIALS 1105 (1985). Other recent bilateral treaties have also shifted authority over the political offense exception to the executive. *See* the Extradition Treaty United States–Mexico, 4 May 1978, art. 5(1), 31 U.S.T. 5059, T.I.A.S. 9656; S. Doc. No. 33, 97th Cong., 1st Sess. (1981) (United States–Netherlands Extradition Treaty); S. Doc. No. 33, 97th Cong. 1st Sess. (1981) (United States–Colombia Extradition Treaty).

99. *Id.*, art. 1.

100. Conversation with Attorney William Ong Hing, 28 Mar. 1987.

101. A. D. Sofaer, Statement to Senate Committee On Foreign Relations, 1 Aug. 1985, at 22.

102. A study by Cherif Bassiouni, *International Control of Terrorism: Some Policy Proposals*, questions the perception that terrorist acts are substantially increasing in number or that further legislation is necessary. 37 INT'L REV. CRIM. POL. 44 (1981).

103. *See, e.g.*, Dept. of State, COUNTRY REPORTS ON HUMAN RIGHTS PRACTICES FOR 1987, Report submitted to the Committee on Foreign Affairs, House of Representatives, and Committee on Foreign Relations, United States Senate, 100th Cong., 2nd Sess. (Feb. 1988).

104. *See*, Denmark, Norway, Sweden, Netherlands v. Greece, 11 Y.B. Eur. Conv. H.R. 690, 730 (1968); Report of the Commission, 5 Nov. 1969, Council of Europe Doc. 15.707/1 (1969); Res. DH (70)1: The Greek Case, Committee of Ministers, 15 Apr. 1970, Council of Europe Doc. D.36.782 (1970), 9 INT'L LEGAL MATERIALS 781 (1970).

105. *See* Ireland v. United Kingdom, Eur. Ct. H.R., Judgment of 18 Jan. 1978, 21 Y.B. Eur. Conv. H.R. 602 (1978).

106. *See, e.g.*, the multilateral treaties listed *supra* note 1. *See also* E.B. Lillich, TRANSNATIONAL TERRORISM: CONVENTIONS AND COMMENTARY (Charlotteville: The Michie Co., 1982).

107. For the texts of global international human rights instruments, *see* United Nations, HUMAN RIGHTS: A COMPILATION OF INTERNATIONAL INSTRUMENTS, UN Doc. ST/HR/1/Rev.2 (1983).

108. *E.g.*, the 1970 Hague Convention and the 1971 Montreal Convention on hijacking, *supra* note 1. An exception to this is the Genocide Convention whose article 7 prohibits characterizing genocide as a political offense. *Supra* note 23.

109. *Supra* note 20.

110. *Id.*, art. 1.

111. *Id.*, art. 2.

112. *Id.*, art. 7.

113. *See* Grotius, *supra* note 4.

114. *See* T. MERON, HUMAN RIGHTS IN INTERNAL STRIFE: THEIR INTERNATIONAL PROTECTION (Cambridge: Grotius Publications, 1987).

115. G. Gilbert, *Terrorism and the Political Offense Exemption Reappraised*, 34 I.C.L.Q. 695, 699 (1985).

116. Protocol II Additional to the Geneva Conventions of 12 Aug. 1949, and relating to the Protection of Victims of Non-International Armed Conflicts, *opened for signature* 12 Dec. 1977, *reprinted in* 16 INT'L LEGAL MATERIALS 1442.

117. Protocol II Additional to the Geneva Convention Relative to the Protection of Victims of Non-International Conflicts. Message from the President of the United States, 100th Cong., Treaty Doc. 100–2 (1987) at III.

118. Geneva Convention Relative to the Protection of Civilian Persons in Time of War of 12 Aug. 1949, *opened for signature* 12 Aug. 1949, *entered into force* 21 Oct. 1950, 6 U.S.T. 3516, T.I.A.S. No. 3365, 75 U.N.T.S. 287.

119. *Id.*, art. 146.

120. Genocide Convention, *supra* note 23.

121. *Adopted* 17 Dec. 1979, GA Res. 34/146, 34 UN GAOR Supp. (No. 39), UN Doc. A/34/819 (1979).

122. *See supra* note 1.

123. Convention against Torture and other Cruel, Inhuman or Degrading Treatment or Punishment, *opened for signature* 10 Dec. 1984, 39 UN GAOR Supp. (No. 51) at 197, UN Doc. A/39/51 (1985).

124. *See, e.g.*, art. 6. International Covenant on Civil and Political Rights, *opened for signature* 16 Dec. 1966, GA Res. 2200, 21 UN GAOR Supp. (No. 16) at 52, UN Doc. A/6316 (1966). *See also* A. Wako, REPORT ON SUMMARY OR ARBITRARY EXECUTIONS, UN Doc. E./CN.4/1985/17 (1985). In addition, it may be noted that the charter of the Organization of African Unity provides in its article III that the member states adhere to certain principles, among them "(5) unreserved condemnation, in all its forms, of political assassination as well as of subversive activities on the part of neighboring states or any other states." *Done at* Addis Ababa, 25 May 1963, *entered into force* 13 Sept. 1963. 479 U.N.T.S. 39, *reprinted in* 2 INT'L LEGAL MATERIALS 766 (1963).

125. Common article 3 of the Geneva Conventions, *supra* note 53, protects all persons taking no active part in the hostilities in a non-international armed conflict.

126. *See* Demjanjuk v. Petrovsky, 776 F.2d 571, 583 (1985); Gallina v. Fraser, 278 F.2d 77, 79 (2d Cir.), *cert. denied* 364 U.S. 851, 81 S.Ct. 97, 5 L.Ed.2d 74 (1960); Salome Bara Arnbjornsdottir-Mendler v. U.S., 721 F.2d 679, 683 (9th Cir. 1983).

127. *Supra* note 103.

128. *E.g.*, reports of Amnesty International, Americas Watch, the country reports of the Inter-American Commission of Human Rights and the Special Rapporteurs of the United Nations.

129. Gilbert, *supra* note 115.

PART IV

REDRESSING PAST ABUSES OF HUMAN RIGHTS

8

The International Legal Consequences of Torture, Extra-Legal Execution, and Disappearance

NIGEL S. RODLEY

The practices that are the subject matter of this article are what a long-standing member and former Chairman of the United Nations Committee on Crime Prevention and Control has called "criminal violations of human rights."[1] For him "the euphemistic expression 'violation of human rights' cannot be used to avoid the term 'criminal' when these violations constitute deliberate assaults on the personality and corporal integrity of a person whether by the State or by an individual."[2]

He was writing in reaction to the adoption, by the General Assembly of the United Nations, of the Declaration on the Protection of All Persons from Being Subjected to Torture and Other Cruel, Inhuman or Degrading Treatment or Punishment (Declaration Against Torture).[3] Significantly, this landmark document was drafted, not by the human rights organs of the UN, but by the Fifth UN Congress on the Prevention of Crime and the Treatment of Offenders.[4]

This essay is a revised and expanded version of *Torture, Extra-Legal Execution and "Disappearance" as Crimes Under International Law,* which appeared in CRIME AND CRIMINAL POLICY (United Nations Social Defence Research Institute, Pub. No. 25, Rome: Franco Angeli, 1985), p. 587, and draws substantially on parts of my THE TREATMENT OF PRISONERS UNDER INTERNATIONAL LAW (Oxford: Clarendon Press, 1987). The opinions expressed herein are my own and may not necessarily be attributed to any organization.

Indeed, since 1973 a year has not passed without the General Assembly adopting at least one resolution indicating its concern at the continuing problem of torture. More recently, and in particular since the Sixth UN Congress on the Prevention of Crime and the Treatment of Offenders adopted its Resolution 5 on "Extra-Legal Executions,"[5] the General Assembly has also been expressing alarm "at the occurrence on a large scale of summary or arbitrary executions, including extra-legal executions."[6] The Assembly has also adopted several resolutions on "enforced or involuntary disappearances" since it first in 1978 expressed itself to be "deeply concerned" by reports of the practice.[7]

The present article has a limited purpose, namely, to explore the legal consequences for states and for the individual perpetrator flowing from the perpetration of torture, extra-legal execution, or disappearance. Accordingly, it will not attempt to describe the geographic scope of the practices: the fact that they have elicited such attention by the General Assembly and other UN bodies is considered sufficient justification for their treatment.[8] Nor will comprehensive definitions of their meaning be attempted. For the purposes of this article, the definition of *torture* contained in article 1 of the Convention Against Torture and Other Cruel, Inhuman or Degrading Treatment or Punishment (Convention Against Torture) will suffice as a working description.[9] The following working description of *extra-legal executions* is offered: killings committed by public officials other than by way of lawfully prescribed capital punishment or by way of necessary and proportionate measures incidental to legitimate law enforcement objectives or by way of the conduct of armed conflict in accordance with the rules of international humanitarian law. *Disappearances* may be understood to be detentions by public officials, where the authorities refuse to acknowledge the detention, in circumstances raising fears for the lives or safety of the abducted persons.

I shall begin by giving the outlines of the none-too-controversial argument that the practices in question are violations of general international law. This will be followed by more substantial sections aimed at suggesting that such violations impose a responsibility on governments to investigate them, bring their perpetrators to justice, and compensate victims or their dependants, and that they are in fact "*crimes* under international law," that is to say, crimes in respect of which the alleged perpetrators may be tried wherever they may be found (universality of jurisdiction). Finally, I shall suggest approaches aimed at the eventual codification of what is partially, at present, a diffuse area of the law.

The Practices as Violations of International Law

Clearly, the practices in question all violate article 3 of the Universal Declaration of Human Rights: "Everyone has the right to life, liberty and security of person." One or more of the practices also violate other articles of the Universal Declaration, including article 5 ("No one shall be subjected to torture or to cruel, inhuman or degrading treatment or punishment"), article 6 ("Everyone has the right to recognition everywhere as a person before the law"), and article 9 ("No one shall be subjected to arbitrary arrest, detention or exile"). While many would argue that the Universal Declaration, although a resolution of the General Assembly[10] and therefore not automatically of legally binding status, has subsequently acquired formal juridical force, it is not necessary to rely on such an argument to maintain that the practices in question are violations of international legal standards. It is only necessary to show that the actual principles violated are ones recognized by general international law. In an important passage, the International Court of Justice in a recent case stated:

> Wrongfully to deprive human beings of their freedom and to subject them to physical constraint in conditions of hardship is in itself manifestly incompatible with the principles of the Charter of the United Nations, as well as with the fundamental principles enunciated in the Universal Declaration of Human Rights.[11]

This quotation confirms the approach just suggested. It also refers to practices that precisely violate articles 3, 5, and 9 of the Universal Declaration, that is, three of the very articles at issue in dealing with torture, extra-legal executions, and disappearances.

This view is also supported by the relevant international treaty law. Torture and extra-legal executions specifically violate those articles of the International Covenant on Civil and Political Rights (ICCPR)[12] prohibiting torture (article 7) and providing for the right to life (article 3). Moreover, these are articles from which no derogation is possible even in time of public emergency. The same is true for the analogous articles of the European and American Conventions on Human Rights.[13] This is a strong indication that the rules in question are not just rules of treaty law binding on the parties to the treaties but rules of general international law binding on all states. Combine the above with the Declaration and Convention Against Torture and Resolution 5 of the Sixth Congress on extra-legal executions, together with the repeated General Assembly resolutions condemning the practices, and the case for their international illegality becomes irresistible.[14] Extra-legal executions may also amount to genocide, which the World Court has considered to be a violation of international law, regardless of adherence or otherwise to the Genocide Convention.[15]

The case is not quite so vivid in respect of disappearances. This is because the main right violated by this practice is the right to liberty and security of person, which includes the prohibition of arbitrary arrest and detention (ICCPR, article 9). This article, like its regional analogues,[16] is one that *may* be suspended in time of public emergency. The fact that this is so, however, does not prevent the rule from being one recognized by international law. Certainly the language of the International Court of Justice described above suggests the opposite ("wrongfully to deprive human beings of their freedom . . . is . . . manifestly incompatible with the principles of the Charter of the United Nations, as well as the fundamental principles enunciated in the Universal Declaration of Human Rights"). Also, the fact that a rule can be derogated from does not give *carte blanche:* the derogation must be limited to that strictly required by the exigencies of the situation. Surely disappearances are never so required. Moreover, as noted in the above-mentioned Resolution 5 of the Sixth UN Congress, disappearances often cannot be separated from violations of the right to life—they become *extra-legal executions.*[17] Finally, it may well be that they are also a form of *torture.* This was the view of the Human Rights Committee (established by the ICCPR) in respect of the mother of a disappeared person: she was held to have been the subject of a violation of article 7 of the ICCPR.[18] A similar view has been taken by the Inter-American Commission on Human Rights.[19] Also, according to the Twenty-fourth International Conference of the Red Cross (Manila, 1981), "disappearances imply violations of fundamental human rights such as . . . the right not to be submitted to torture."[20] Thus, it seems that disappearances violate the right to liberty and security of person; this right, although derogable, remains a rule of international law that will always be violated by disappearances. Also, where death may be presumed, they constitute extra-legal executions violating the right to life as recognized by international law. In any event, they may be considered as violating the international legal right not to be subjected to torture.

Finally, it should be noted that torture, extra-legal execution ("wilful killing") and causing the disappearance ("unlawful deportation or transfer or unlawful confinement" of protected civilians) of persons in the hands of a party to an armed conflict (international or noninternational) are all roundly prohibited by the Geneva Conventions of 12 August 1949. Indeed, as far as their occurrence in international armed conflict is concerned they constitute "grave breaches" of the Conventions to which at the time of writing some 165 states (virtually the whole world community) are party.[21] The significance of the categorization "grave breach" will appear below.

State Responsibility for Torture, Extra-Legal Executions, and Disappearances

When a violation of international law occurs, there are consequences for the government that has committed it and possibly also for individuals, usually agents of the government, who may be personally liable. The responsibility of the government attaches to the state itself and is often known as "state responsibility." This state responsibility for torture, extra-legal execution, and disappearance will be dealt with in this section.

The Concept of State Responsibility

It is clear that when a state breaches its obligations under international law, its responsibility is engaged; it is less clear just how that responsibility operates. There have been attempts to find municipal law analogies to describe the juridical nature of the responsibility under international law: some have likened it to the English law of tort (noncontractual civil obligation); others prefer the analogy of contract law, especially in the case of noncompliance with treaties. Another approach, recognizing the essentially public law character of international law, is that which considers a violation of international law to be a "delict," understood as a general offense under public law.[22]

Recently, the International Law Commission has been propounding a dual approach: Breaches of an international obligation are generally categorized as "internationally wrongful acts," called "international delicts," and certain particularly grave "internationally wrongful acts" are considered to be crimes. Thus, the Commission follows the delictual approach in general but adds a further category of international crime. The latter would include "a serious breach on a widespread scale of an international obligation of essential importance for safeguarding the human being, such as those prohibiting slavery, genocide, and *apartheid*."[23] This formulation could reasonably be understood to cover systematic torture of prisoners.[24] At the time of writing, the Commission has not yet drafted articles specifying the consequences of internationally wrongful acts in general, or of international crimes in particular.[25]

Traditionally, the international law of state responsibility envisages reparation for the wrongful act. The reparation will usually take the form of restitution and/or compensation for damage or loss. Other types of reparation are also known, sometimes under the general rubric of "satisfaction." They include, in appropriate cases, and where there is an adjudication, a declaration by the court or tribunal that the violation has occurred, a formal acknowledgement and/or expression of regret by the state committing the wrong, the punishment of the individuals concerned, and the taking of measures to prevent a recurrence of the harm. But this traditional international law approach is not automatically applicable to all human rights violations. This is because, historically, the wrong in question has generally been one committed by one state to the detriment of another. Even where the wrong involved injury to individuals (normally nationals of the claimant state), it was to the claimant state, rather than to individuals, that reparation was to be made. In the case of a violation of the newer branch of international law concerned with human rights, the obligation is multilateral, with no single state having an interest in material reparation, while, in the absence of special agreement (between *states*), the individual victim has no standing to bring an international claim.

State Responsibility for Human Rights Violations

International legal instruments tend to require an "effective remedy" from the national authorities where a human rights violation has occurred,[26] but there is no explicit reference specifying what the remedy should be. In any case, the mode of reparation deemed appropriate will vary according to the nature of the wrongful act and its specific circumstances. Financial compensation will not always be the appropriate remedy, and where it is, its measure may be uncertain. As Professor Rosalyn Higgins notes in a rare treatment of the subject, "it is therefore perhaps not surprising that these underlying questions seem to remain unclear and uncertain in the leading international instruments on the protection of human rights."[27] Those instruments that establish courts capable of giving binding decisions envisage the award of "just satisfaction" or "fair compensation";[28] those that do not provide for courts are silent on the issue. Certain articles of the ICCPR specifically envisage a right to compensation in particular circumstances,[29] but strangely these do not include the nonderogable articles, including the prohibition against torture and the provision on the right to life.

State Responsibility for Torture Despite the absence of a reference to compensation in the ICCPR, the Human Rights Committee, which monitors compliance with the Covenant, has expressed the view that compensation is due in respect of violations of provisions *other* than those expressly envisaging compensation. Thus, having found that Argentine concert pianist Miguel Angel Estrella had been subjected to torture in Uruguay, it expressed the view that the state party "is under an obligation to provide the victim with effective remedies, including compensation, for the violations he has suffered and to take steps to ensure that similar violations do not occur in the future."[30] In similar cases, the Inter-American Commission on Human Rights, presumably recognizing that compensation is an issue for the Inter-American Court of Human Rights (where it has jurisdiction), confines itself to a call for investigation of the facts and punishment of those responsible.[31] The European Commission of Human Rights restricts itself even further, leaving all questions on reparation to be dealt with by the European Court of Human Rights in appropriate cases.[32] Further, the Court's own policy is to leave it to the state in question to give effect to its awards, except insofar as the Court may itself be willing to award compensation as "just satisfaction."[33]

It is difficult to draw firm conclusions from the practices just outlined, since these appear to be simply reflections of what each body considers to be within its competence, rather than substantive assessments of what reparation flows, as a matter of law, from a violation of the provisions of the instrument in question. Nevertheless, there seems to be a common denominator to the extent that compensation is deemed due for certain human rights violations, even where not specifically signaled in the text of the instrument concerned, and that violations involving torture or other ill-treatment do fall within this category.

As far as the prohibition against torture is concerned, the practice of the Human Rights Committee is arguably the most authoritative guide, not only to the impact of that instrument, but also to general international law. The Committee has formalized its approach in its "general comment" on article 7. Reading article 7 together with article 2 (the right to an effective remedy), it concludes

> that States must ensure an effective protection through some machinery of control. Complaints about ill-treatment must be investi-

> gated effectively by competent authorities. Those found guilty must be held responsible, and the alleged victims must themselves have effective remedies at their disposal, including the right to obtain compensation.[34]

All these requirements are also to be found in both the Declaration Against Torture and the UN and OAS Conventions against Torture. It may be that one or other of the requirements is beyond the competence of one or other body to award. But it would be difficult not to conclude that the requirements are applicable both to parties to the instruments in question and, to the same extent that torture is held to be prohibited by general international law, to all other states.

State Responsibility for Extra-Legal Executions It may be argued that similar legal consequences attach to the commission of extra-legal executions as attach to torture. As noted earlier, Resolution 5 of the Sixth UN Congress on the Prevention of Crime and the Treatment of Offenders concluded that extra-legal executions "also violate" the Declaration Against Torture. In that case, it is probable that such executions constitute a form of torture, in which case the same consequences automatically flow.

Further, the practice of the Human Rights Committee is to treat violations of articles 6 (right to life) and 7 (prohibition of torture and other ill-treatment) in the same way. The Committee's approach is illustrated in its findings in respect of a notorious incident in Suriname where "15 prominent persons . . . including journalists, lawyers, professors and businessmen, were arrested in their homes" and subsequently "killed while trying to escape."[35] Finding an intentional deprivation of life "as a result of the deliberate action of the military police" against the fifteen, and that Suriname had "failed to submit any evidence proving that these persons were shot while trying to escape," the Committee found a violation of Covenant article 6(I) protecting the right to life. It went on to urge Suriname "to take effective steps (i) to investigate the killings of December 1982; (ii) to bring to justice any persons found to be responsible for the deaths of the victims; (iii) to pay compensation to the surviving families; and (iv) to ensure that the right to life is duly protected in Suriname."[36]

So, as with torture, international law probably requires that a state responsible for extra-legal execution must establish the facts, bring the perpetrators to justice, and provide compensation for the next of kin of the victims.

State Responsibility for Disappearances To the extent that the practice of disappearance may amount to torture or arbitrary deprivation of life, the consequence of establishing state responsibility for such acts would be the same as if the government had committed acts of torture or inflicted extra-legal executions. The practice of the Human Rights Committee and the Inter-American Commission on Human Rights bears out this expectation.

In the *Bleier* and *Quinteros* cases, the Committee held that Uruguay should take effective steps: (*a*) to establish what had happened to the victims; (*b*) to bring to justice those found to be responsible for the death (in the case of Bleier), disappearance, or ill-treatment; (*c*) to pay compensation for the wrongs suffered; and (*d*) to ensure that similar violations do not occur in the future.[37] Apparently mindful of the peculiarly mystifying nature of disappearances, the Committee stressed in the *Quinteros* case that "the author has *the right to know* what happened to her daughter"[38] (emphasis added) and that the Uruguayan government "has a duty to conduct a full investigation into the matter."[39]

The Inter-American Commission on Human Rights follows its practice of calling for investigation of the facts and punishment of the responsible individuals in cases of torture and extra-legal executions.[40] In *Cyprus v. Turkey* the European Commission of Human Rights maintained its practice of refraining from specifying the legal consequences of what it found to be the "presumption of Turkish responsibility for the fate of persons shown to have been in Turkish custody" after the invasion of Cyprus and now missing.[41] As indicated earlier, it is suggested that the practice of the Human Rights Committee best reflects the legal consequences for the government of a state where detainees have been made to disappear.

Individual Responsibility for Torture, Extra-Legal Executions, and Disappearances

The Concept of Individual Responsibility

Traditionally, international law has been a body of rules binding upon states which are represented by their governments. States have thus been both the legislators and subjects of international law, its framers and its addressees. Where one state claimed that another had violated an international legal obligation, it looked to the offering *state* for redress, rather than to the individual agents whose behavior had engaged the state's responsibility.

This general rule has long known the occasional exception, whereby international law has concerned itself with the behavior of individuals. The classic example is that of piracy on the high seas, which, under customary international law, was a violation of international law that all states were expected to redress and over which any state could exercise jurisdiction. More recently the "corporate veil" of the state has been pierced for certain other acts, such as hostage-taking.[42] The hallmark of these exceptions is that they seem to permit, and in some cases require, states which find within their jurisdiction persons alleged to have committed the prohibited acts to bring such persons to justice, regardless of the nationality of the persons or of where the crime was committed. This is known as the principle of universality of jurisdiction and clearly represents an exceptional assertion of criminal jurisdiction. Where states are actually *required* to take action, the principle of universality of jurisdiction is coupled with the concept known by the Latin phrase *aut dedere, aut judicare* (either extradite or try). In other words, the state on whose territory the alleged offender is found must either try the person or extradite him or her to a country willing to exercise criminal jurisdiction. Piracy would be an example of a case where states are *permitted* but not *required* to exercise criminal jurisdiction on a universal basis (permissive universality of jurisdiction), while hostage-taking would be an example of a case where states are *required* either to exercise such jurisdiction or to extradite to a country willing to do so (compulsory universal jurisdiction). These examples are of acts committed by private individuals or groups, not by state officials (unless acting as individuals). But the scope of what will now be called "crimes under international law" is not limited to private acts.

The category of crimes under international law committed *by public officials* emerged with the post–World War II trials in Nuremberg of persons accused of "crimes against peace," "war crimes," and "crimes against humanity."[43] The General Assembly of the United Nations later unanimously confirmed the principles of international law recognized by the Charter and the Judgment of the Nuremberg Tribunal.[44] Crimes against peace and war crimes are, by definition, matters of interstate relations, committed by public officials. The category "crimes against humanity" was framed to be applicable only "in execution of or in connection with" a crime against peace or a war crime.[45] Thus, even though crimes against humanity could be inflicted by government officials upon the government's own subjects, the crimes had to be committed "in connection with" international warfare.

Because the war crimes tribunals were ad hoc bodies set up to judge a specific set of war crimes, they had no need to deal with the issue of jurisdiction. The Geneva Conventions, however, which encompass a codification of war crimes, do make it clear that such crimes are to be prosecuted on the basis of universality of jurisdiction. They provide that perpetrators of "grave breaches" (effectively war crimes) shall be prosecuted by parties to the Conventions "regardless of their nationality," unless they are handed over to another party that "has made out a *prima facie* case" for jurisdiction.[46] Furthermore, the Geneva Conventions by now cover a range of behavior that would bring many, if not all, crimes against humanity within their ambit.[47]

Genocide, the most notorious crime against humanity committed during World War II, was made the subject of a special convention: the Convention on the Prevention and Punishment of the Crime of Genocide (1948).[48] This Convention does not require that genocide be committed in connection with a crime against peace or a war crime: it may be committed within the frontiers of a state and in the absence of international armed conflict. It is not, therefore, a "crime against humanity" as defined above. The Convention specifies that the offense is a "crime under international law" (article 1), and it is reasonable to see this term as the generic one for crimes for which international law may require individuals to be prosecuted. "Crimes against humanity" would then form a specific category of "crimes under international law," namely, that comprising acts committed in connection with war crimes or crimes against peace.[49] The Genocide Convention does not refer specifically to universality of jurisdiction. It requires trial "by a competent tribunal of the State in the territory of which the act was committed, or by such international penal tribunal as may have jurisdiction" over the offense. While the absence of reference to other bases of jurisdiction is regrettable (not even the nationality principle is mentioned), it should not be assumed that the Convention purported to exclude other bases of jurisdiction, including universality, at least on a permissive basis. Universality was certainly the most convincing claim to jurisdiction that could be made by the court in Jerusalem that tried Adolf Eichmann.[50]

Thus, in the case of war crimes, universality of jurisdiction, coupled with the obligation to try or extradite, is compulsory. It is also suggested that universality of jurisdiction is at least permissive in the case of crimes against peace and crimes against humanity. The same permissive application of universal jurisdiction may apply not only to genocide, but to other crimes under international law not committed in connection with crimes against peace or crimes against humanity.

Where then do individuals accused of torture or extra-legal execution or causing people to disappear stand? Do they commit "crimes under international law" as described above? Since most developments have related specifically to torture, the position of the alleged torturer will first be considered.

Individual Responsibility for Criminal Violations of Human Rights

Individual Responsibility for Torture It was earlier noted that torture is considered a grave breach of the Geneva Conventions insofar as they apply to international armed conflict. As has just been seen, grave breaches (war crimes) are breaches that *oblige* states parties to exercise criminal jurisdiction on the basis of the principle of universality of jurisdiction; in other words, alleged torturers of persons in the hands of a party to an international armed conflict may be tried anywhere or extradited for trial. More problematical is the case of the torturer who commits the act either during a noninternational armed conflict or in peacetime. Two recent cases go some way to elucidating the matter.

The first is that of Captain *Astiz*.[51] During the hostilities in the South Atlantic in 1982, Argentine naval captain Alfredo Astiz became a prisoner of war of the British. He was captured on the island of South Georgia and taken to the United Kingdom. Interest in this prisoner of war was occasioned by the fact that nongovernmental organizations had declared themselves to be in possession of numerous statements by survivors of a secret detention camp in the Naval School of Mechanics in Buenos Aires.[52] These statements asserted that Astiz was involved in the arrest, kidnapping, torture, and illegal execution of political opponents of the military government of Argentina. Specifically, he was suspected of involvement in the disappearance in Argentina of two French nuns and with the arrest and killing (again in Argentina) of a young woman of dual Argentine and Swedish nationality. These allegations led the French and Swedish governments to request the British authorities to have questions put to Astiz once his identity had been established. The questions were eventually put, but Astiz, shielded by the provision of the Geneva Conventions that requires a prisoner of war to give name, rank, and serial number only, refused to answer them. Astiz was subsequently repatriated to Argentina.

The case presents several problems of jurisdiction, since it concerns allegations of torture committed in Argentina, made against an Argentine national on behalf of victims who included French and Swedish nationals; a potential opportunity for prosecution of the charges arose because Astiz was captured by the British, in the course of an international armed conflict which had no connection with the acts of which he was accused. The question is, which of the several nations concerned had jurisdiction?

It is beyond doubt that Astiz could have been brought to trial in Argentina, had the Argentine authorities chosen to press charges, but they had not done so.[53] There remained, therefore, the more complicated question as to whether any other state might exercise jurisdiction—in effect Sweden or France, whose nationals were the alleged victims, or Britain, in whose custody Astiz was being held. The answer to this question is further complicated by the fact that Astiz was being held as a prisoner of war. The distinction between compulsory jurisdiction and permissive jurisdiction arises at this point: none of the three states mentioned had a clearly defined obligation to exercise jurisdiction in this case. It remains to investigate whether any might have done so on the basis of a permissive rule of jurisdiction. Neither Sweden nor France formally requested extradition of Astiz from the United Kingdom, but it might be inferred that their request to pose questions to him (and British acquiescence, which included transporting Astiz eight thousand miles to the United Kingdom for the purpose) took place in contemplation of the possibility of extradition. It is possible only to speculate on why extradition was not sought. One explanation might be that the governments concerned felt they had no case for jurisdiction, but there are others. First, Astiz' special status as a prisoner of war may have been relevant: it may have been felt that the problem of extradition should be left open, in order not to create a precedent whose long-term implications could be far-reaching and ultimately inimical to the humanitarian aims of the regime of prisoner-of-war protection.[54] Second, the evidence available against Astiz in the particular cases concerned may have seemed inadequate, especially since he availed himself of his right not to answer questions put to him.[55] Third, given the conflict between Britain and Argentina, Sweden and France may have wished to avoid embarrassing the United

Kingdom government by confronting it with a juridically controversial interpretation of the Third Geneva Convention (which is silent on the issue of the extradition of prisoners of war) that, if pursued, might have jeopardized Argentina's future compliance with the Conventions. Several explanations of the failure to pursue extradition are therefore available, none of which affects the issue of jurisdiction. In any event, since France and Sweden did not request extradition, their claim to jurisdiction is moot.

The possibility of such a claim by Britain was suggested at the time by a British scholar who advocated that "thought should be given to prosecuting the same Captain Astiz in this country [i.e., the United Kingdom] for breach of a crime under international law, namely torture."[56] In response, the International Commission of Jurists pointed out that domestic legislation would have been required for the British courts to be able to take jurisdiction over an act of torture committed outside the United Kingdom.[57] Indeed, the enactment of such legislation would probably be required in many countries. Even without this obstacle the United Kingdom would doubtless have had the misgivings referred to above regarding both Astiz' prisoner-of-war status and a desire not to provoke Argentina into noncompliance with the Geneva Conventions. Once again, therefore, no action was taken and the issue of jurisdiction remained untested.

Insofar as steps interpretable as preliminary to extradition were taken, the case provides some evidence that states whose nationals have been the victims of torture or disappearance could have a claim to exercise jurisdiction. It gives no indication one way or the other, however, as to whether a state totally unconcerned with the alleged practices might do so.

Meanwhile, a second recent case is pertinent to the question of whether it is already established that, under customary international law, alleged torturers may be tried on the basis of a permissive rule of universal jurisdiction. In *Filártiga v. Peña-Irala* the plaintiffs alleged that seventeen-year-old Joelito Filártiga was kidnapped and tortured to death on 29 March 1976 by defendant Americo Norberto Peña-Irala (Peña), the then Inspector General of Police in Asunción, the capital of Paraguay.[58] The Filártigas claimed that Dr. Joel Filártiga was a longstanding opponent of the government of President Alfredo Stroessner of Paraguay and that his son, Joelito, was tortured and killed in retaliation for his father's political activities and beliefs. In 1979 they brought a claim in tort (violation of noncontractual civil obligation) against Peña (who was at that time in the United States of America) in a United States federal district court, under an old, rarely-invoked provision (28 U.S.C. section 1350, the Alien Tort Statute) endowing the relevant courts with jurisdiction over "any civil action by an alien for a tort only, committed in violation of the law of nations or a treaty of the United States."[59] The district court dismissed the complaint "for want of federal jurisdiction." The court of appeals, however, reversed the district court judgment and held that

> deliberate torture perpetrated under color of official authority violates universally accepted norms of the international law of human rights, regardless of the nationality of the parties. Thus whenever an alleged torturer is found and served with process by an alien within our borders, section 1350 provides federal jurisdiction.

Following this decision, the district court awarded the plaintiffs damages totaling over ten million dollars.[60]

The judgment delivered for the court of appeals by Judge Irving R. Kaufman has elicited a plethora of scholarly reaction, most of which greeted the decision with acclaim,[61] though the occasional voice of doubt has also been heard.[62] The judgment is important in three respects. First, the court, relying on the human rights and humanitarian law instruments described earlier in this text, found that torture is prohibited by modern customary international law. Second, although it did not deal with the question of when a prohibition under customary international law imposes liability of the individual violator, the court did find that an individual could be responsible. Third, the court exercised jurisdiction, at least in a civil case, despite the fact that the torture occurred outside the United States and was inflicted on a foreign national by a foreign national. In support of its decision it cited article 7 of the Declaration Against Torture, which provides that states are to ensure that acts of torture are offenses under its criminal law. It also noted that it is possible for civil jurisdiction to occur outside the *lex loci delicti*,[63] especially where the act complained of would be unlawful in the place where it took place (this was the case in Paraguay and probably would be everywhere). It did not deal, however, with the intractable question of when an international law prohibition, even one that requires penal action by states to repress violations, becomes one that requires or permits universality of criminal jurisdiction.

It is worth quoting an extract of the concluding passage of the

Filártiga judgment because, while its language is limited to the issue of civil liability, it uses terminology resonant of international criminal liability:

> In the modern age, humanitarian and practical considerations have combined to lead the nations of the world to recognize that respect for fundamental human rights is in their individual and collective interest. Among the rights universally proclaimed by all nations, as we have noted, is the right to be free of physical torture. Indeed, for purposes of civil liability, the torturer has become—like the pirate and slave trader before him—*hostis humani generis*, an enemy of all mankind.

Although this language tends to suggest that for the purposes of international law the torturer is no different from the pirate or slave trader (i.e., is liable to universal jurisdiction), it must be remembered that the *Filártiga* case was one of civil, not criminal, law. There is no reason to conclude that criminal liability would not also be the case, but as yet there is no state practice to endorse the point.[64] Indeed, the chances of establishing such a practice will be rare. Evidence is hard to come by in torture cases, especially in cases heard outside the country where the torture took place, and other rules of international law (such as the Geneva Conventions in the *Astiz* case, or rules of diplomatic immunity) may inhibit the processes of justice.

The problem of having to look to customary international law to determine whether or not universal criminal jurisdiction may be applied to torturers may of course be bypassed by international legislation. The UN Convention Against Torture is an example of such legislation.[65] The Convention requires that torture be made a criminal offense (article 4). It is an offense that may be committed "by a public official or other person acting in an official capacity" (article 1). Such a person commits the offense by direct infliction, by instigation, by consent, or by acquiescence.[66] Attempts, complicity, and other participation are also to be penalized (article 4(1)).

States parties are required to establish criminal jurisdiction over cases of torture committed within their jurisdiction (territorial principle), by their nationals (nationality principle), or where their nationals are victims (passive personality principle) (article 5(1)). Jurisdiction is also to be taken in the absence of any such link (the universality principle) (article 5(2)). There is also an *obligation* either to extradite an alleged torturer or to try him or her on the basis of universality of jurisdiction alone (articles 5(2) and 7). This had been one of the most controversial issues before the working group of the Commission on Human Rights, which drafted the bulk of the text, but it was resolved at the group's last session in 1984.[67] This outcome is significant not only in terms of the actual provisions of the Convention, but also as an indication of the customary international law regarding the individual responsibility of torturers: while states parties will, of course, be *obliged* to try alleged torturers on the basis of universality of jurisdiction (unless they extradite them), it is now hard to imagine a convincing objection to any state's unilateral choice to exercise jurisdiction on a universal basis.[68]

Another innovation of the Convention refers to the same issue. It borrows from the Nuremberg Principles the rejection of the defense *respondeat superior:* "an order from a superior officer or a public authority may not be invoked as a justification of torture" (article 2(3)).

Individual Responsibility for Extra-Legal Executions There is no doubt that extra-legal execution of persons in the hands of a party to an international armed conflict, in violation of the Geneva Conventions of 12 August 1949, opens the perpetrators (like torturers) to trial or extradition wherever they may be, since these are grave breaches of the Conventions.[69] It is likely that, when committed in connection with an international armed conflict, such killings by a state of its own nationals, or others within its normal jurisdiction, are crimes against humanity. If so, they would be susceptible to adjudication by a subsequent international penal tribunal and would probably be amenable to universal jurisdiction. The same also applies to acts of genocide, which, since the adoption of and widespread adherence to the Genocide Convention, appears to have become a crime under international law, whether or not committed in connection with an international armed conflict. Further, while this Convention *requires* jurisdiction only by the state in which the genocide was committed, and also envisages a future international penal jurisdiction, it is reasonably certain that international law *permits* the exercise of jurisdiction on a universal basis.

The issue becomes less clear when the killings do not amount to war crimes, crimes against humanity, or acts of genocide. The discussion of the *Astiz* case is of interest to the issue of individual responsibility for extra-legal executions as well as for torture, since Captain Astiz was accused of both. The judgment in the *Filártiga* case, however, was so heavily couched in the language of the prohibition of torture that, even though the victim allegedly died under torture, it is difficult to analyze the case in terms of extra-legal execution. This does not mean that the perpetrator of an extra-legal execution is any less amenable to universal jurisdiction than a torturer, merely that the issue remains less tested. It would be strange, however, if the exercise of universal jurisdiction in respect of extra-legal executions was conditional upon whether or not the killing had occurred pursuant to torture.

One development may be interpreted as suggesting that international law accepts that extra-legal executions committed against *groups* of people are crimes under international law. In 1954, the International Law Commission, at the request of the General Assembly, adopted a draft Code of Offences against the Peace and Security of Mankind.[70] The text of the draft Code was primarily concerned with elaborating the rules flowing from the Charter and Judgment of the Nuremberg Tribunal. One provision went clearly beyond these: article 2, paragraph 11, included among offenses against the peace and security of mankind

> [i]nhuman acts such as murder, extermination, enslavement, deportation and persecutions, committed against any civilian population on social, political, racial, religious or cultural grounds by the authorities of a State or by private individuals acting at the instigation or with the toleration of such authorities.

Except for the inclusion of inhuman acts committed on *cultural* grounds, the text essentially followed the enumeration of crimes against humanity given in the Charter of the Nuremberg Tribunal. It differed radically, however, in one respect: the acts did not have to be committed in connection with crimes against peace or with war crimes. An earlier version of the draft Code had, in fact, required the list of "inhuman acts" to have been "committed in execution of or in connexion with other offences defined in this article [of the Code]."[71] The Commission acknowledged that it had "decided to enlarge the scope of the paragraph so as to make the punishment of the acts enumerated in the paragraph independent of whether or not they are committed in connexion with other offences defined in the draft Code."[72] It did not give reasons for the change and the disconnection was effected by the closest of votes.[73] Also, as with the Convention Against Torture, the draft Code excluded the defense of *respondeat superior.*

The General Assembly never took action on the draft, seemingly because it was unable to agree upon a definition of "aggression," the prototypical crime against peace.[74] The draft Code raised its head once more after the General Assembly had finally agreed on a definition of "aggression,"[75] and in 1981 the Assembly returned the matter to the International Law Commission, which was asked to resume its work on the draft.[76]

It may also be possible to consider extra-legal executions as a form of torture. If this were so, it would follow that the legal consequences for their perpetrators would be the same as for torturers. There is already authoritative support for this approach from the Sixth UN Congress on the Prevention of Crime and the Treatment of Offenders. In preambular paragraph 7 of its Resolution 5 on extra-legal executions, referred to earlier, it expressed the view that such executions "also violate the Declaration on the Protection of All Persons from Being Subjected to Torture or Cruel, Inhuman or Degrading Treatment or Punishment."

Individual Responsibility for Disappearances In international armed conflict, causing disappearances ("unlawful deportation or transfer or unlawful confinement") of persons in the hands of a party to the conflict is a grave breach involving liability to trial anywhere or to extradition. In other circumstances, to the extent that the practice of disappearance falls within the categories of torture or extra-legal executions, the legal implications for the individual perpetrator of disappearances are the same. That is to say, general international law probably permits, though may not require, a state to exercise criminal jurisdiction over an alleged perpetrator, regardless of the latter's nationality or the place where the offense was committed. If disappearances may be considered torture, as defined in the Convention Against Torture, which *requires* universality of jurisdiction over alleged torturers, then at least individuals who are responsible for disappearances and are in the territory of a party to the Convention are subject to criminal proceedings.

At the time of writing, it is difficult to proceed beyond such speculation. The only relevant case to have arisen at the international level, that of Captain Astiz of Argentina, was resolved inconclusively because of his prisoner-of-war status. Also, it is in the nature of the practice of disappearance (indeed, it may be assumed to be one of its purposes) that, there will rarely be sufficient evidence to attach responsibility for specific disappearances to particular individuals.

Conclusion

Torture, extra-legal execution, and causing people to disappear are serious violations of international law. It is logical that the legal consequences of each be similar. This is certainly so when they are inflicted during international armed conflict, on persons in the hands of a party to the conflict. It may well be so in peacetime.

Nevertheless, it is an area of law that is worth clarifying, in respect of extra-legal executions and disappearances. As far as issues relating to state responsibility are concerned, this could probably be done by "soft-law" means, such as General Assembly resolutions. As noted at the beginning of the essay, the General Assembly annually adopts resolutions about these practices. These resolutions could usefully call on the states concerned to take the measures in question. It would not be worth initiating a treaty-drafting process to confirm the already fairly evident obligation that states are expected to investigate the practices, seek to bring the perpetrators to justice, and compensate the victims or, as the case may be, their families. Without making specific reference to the particular category of crime that is the subject of this essay, the Seventh UN Congress on the Prevention of Crime and the Treatment of Offenders drafted and the General Assembly adopted, in 1985, the Declaration of Basic Principles of Justice for Victims of Crime and Abuse of Power, article 11 of which reads as follows:

> Where public officials or other agents acting in an official or quasi-official capacity have violated national criminal laws, the victims should receive restitution from the State whose officials or agents were responsible for the harm inflicted. In cases where the Government under whose authority the victimizing act or omission occurred is no longer in existence, the State or Government successor in title should provide restitution to the victims.[77]

Since extra-legal execution and causing people to disappear are, like torture, crimes within the meaning of this paragraph in most, if not all, countries, the Assembly could be understood already to have pronounced itself on the matter, as far as the issue of compensation (as is clearly meant by the misused word "restitution") is concerned. But it is better that these things be explicit and indeed repeated.

In the area of individual responsibility, however, this "soft-law" approach would probably not be the best means to secure the obligation to submit perpetrators to the threat of universal criminal jurisdiction, especially on a compulsory basis. Here there is no viable alternative to the treaty-based obligation. This does not necessarily mean that there has to be a new treaty, like the Convention Against Torture, for the phenomena of disappearances and extra-legal executions. As has been seen, there is a strong body of authoritative opinion suggesting that causing disappearance is a form of torture. A General Assembly resolution or declaration formally proclaiming this to be the case could attain the same objective.[78] The effect would be to provide a persuasive source of interpretation that would almost certainly be taken up by international and national bodies and courts applying the Convention. All the legal consequences of torture would be the same for disappearances, since they would be one and the same thing. It would also obviate the invidious problem that would be posed by a new treaty:[79] to contrive a legal definition of disappearance. We may not be able to specify what amounts to refusal to acknowledge detention or the length of time that has to elapse, but we know a disappearance when we see it.

The strategy for extra-legal executions is more difficult. The earlier-mentioned Resolution 5 of the Sixth UN Congress on the Prevention of Crime and the Treatment of Offenders appears to be consistent with a similar strategy: extra-legal executions violate the Declaration Against Torture. It may, indeed, be worth trying to promote the idea. Yet, one is left with the feeling that the phenomenon is not comfortably defined by the language used to define torture.[80]

An alternative approach might be one that falls somewhere between a new treaty and the use of mere "soft-law" attempts to secure a broad interpretation of the Convention Against Torture. This would involve initiating at the UN the drafting of a protocol to the Convention specifying that, where extra-legal executions occur in a state party to the Convention and protocol, the provisions of the Convention would apply to extra-legal executions as if they were acts of torture.

Even this strategy would have to be initiated with caution. While it may be possible to define extra-legal executions in such a way as to be clearly distinguishable from "legitimate" uses of force as a measure of law enforcement or in the conduct of armed conflict, applying the distinction in practice poses more problems. Some governments may be reluctant to see the codification process advanced. To attempt the exercise and to fail (thus risking retrogression) would be decidedly less desirable than to allow the process of clarification to evolve piecemeal.

Perhaps a more promising approach lies in the fact that the issue of extra-legal executions will be on the agenda of the meeting of the Committee on Crime Prevention and Control in 1988. The UN Secretary-General has been asked by the Economic and Social Council (Resolution

1986/10 VI of 21 May 1986) to prepare a report on "extra-legal, arbitrary and summary executions" for submission to the Committee. The Committee's consideration of the topic could lead it to adopt standards that would spell out the legal consequences of extra-legal executions in the same terms as those applicable to torture. Such standards could, through ECOSOC or through the Eighth UN Congress on the Prevention of Crime and the Treatment of Offenders, be forwarded for adoption or endorsement by the General Assembly. Once achieved there would be a better platform from which to pursue treaty-based codification.

NOTES

1. Manuel López-Rey, *Crime and Human Rights*. 42 FEDERAL PROBATION 10–15, 13 (March 1978).

2. *Id.* at 11.

3. GA Res. 3452(XXX) of 9 Dec. 1975.

4. UN Department of Economic and Social Affairs, Fifth United Nations Congress on the Prevention of Crime and the Treatment of Offenders, Geneva, 1–12 September 1975—Report prepared by the Secretariat, UN Doc. A/CONF.56/10, UN Sales No. E.76.IV.2, at 39–40 (1976).

5. UN Department of International Economic and Social Affairs, Sixth United Nations Congress on the Prevention of Crime and the Treatment of Offenders, Caracas, Venezuela, 25 August–5 September 1980—Report prepared by the Secretariat, UN Doc. A/CONF.87/14/Rev.1, UN Sales No. E.81.IV.4, at 8–9 (1981).

6. GA Res. 37/182 of 17 Dec. 1982.

7. GA Res. 33/173 of 20 Dec. 1978.

8. The scope and nature of the practices may be discerned from the following works. *On torture:* AMNESTY INTERNATIONAL, REPORT ON TORTURE (London: Duckworth, rev. ed. 1975); AMNESTY INTERNATIONAL, TORTURE IN THE EIGHTIES, (London: 1984); Matthew Lippmann, *The Protection of Universal Human Rights: The Problem of Torture,* UNIVERSAL HUMAN RIGHTS 25 (No. 4, 1979); *see also* the first three reports of the UN Commission on Human Rights Special Rapporteur on Torture, UN Docs. E/CN.4/1986/15, E/CN.4/1987/13 and E/CN.4/1988/17 and Add.1. *On extra-legal executions:* AMNESTY INTERNATIONAL, POLITICAL KILLINGS BY GOVERNMENTS (London: 1983); Edy Kaufman & Patricia Weiss-Fagan, *Extrajudicial Executions: An Insight into the Global Dimensions of a Human Rights Problem,* 3 HUM. RTS. Q. 81–100 (No. 1, 1981); *see also* the first six reports of the UN Commission on Human Rights Special Rapporteur on Summary or Arbitrary Executions, UN Docs. E/CN.4/1983/16 and Add.1 and Add.1/Corr.1; E/CN.4/1984/29; E/CN.4/1985/17; E/CN.4/1986/21; E/CN.4/1987/20; and E/CN.4/1988/22 and Add.1. On *"disappearances":* AMNESTY INTERNATIONAL USA, "DISAPPEARANCES"—A WORKBOOK, (New York: 1981); JAN EGELAND, HUMANITARIAN INITIATIVE AGAINST POLITICAL "DISAPPEARANCES," (Geneva: Henry Dunant Institute, 1982); Richard Reoch, *"Disappearances" and the International Protection of Human Rights,* YEARBOOK OF WORLD AFFAIRS 166–81 (London, 1982); Maureen R. Berman & Roger S.

Clark, *State Terrorism: Disappearances,* 13 Rutgers L.J. 531–77 (1982); Jerome J. Shestack, *The Case of the Disappeared,* 8 Human Rights (No. 4, 1980), *reprinted by* the International League for Human Rights (New York); *see also* the first eight reports of the Commission on Human Rights Working Group on Enforced or Involuntary Disappearances, UN Docs. E/CN.4/1435 and Add.1; E/CN.4/1492 and Add.1; E/CN.4/1983/14; E/CN.4/1984/21 and Adds.1 and 2; E/CN.4/1985/15 and Add.1; E/CN.4/1986/18 and Add.1; E/CN.4/1987/15 and Add.1; and E/CN.4/1988/19.

9. According to article 1 of the Convention,

> 1. For the purposes of this Convention, the term 'torture' means any act by which severe pain or suffering, whether physical or mental, is intentionally inflicted on a person for such purposes as obtaining from him or a third person information or a confession, punishing him for an act he or a third person has committed or is suspected of having committed, or intimidating or coercing him or a third person, or for any reason based on discrimination of any kind, when such pain or suffering is inflicted by or at the instigation of or with the consent of acquiescence of a public official or other person acting in an official capacity. It does not include pain or suffering arising only from, inherent in or incidental to lawful sanctions.
>
> 2. This article is without prejudice to any international instrument or national legislation which does or may contain provisions of wider application. (GA Res. 39/46 of 10 Dec. 1984.)

10. GA Res. 217A(III) of 10 Dec. 1948.

11. Case Concerning United States Diplomatic and Consular Staff in Tehran (U.S. v. Iran), [1980] I.C.J. 3.

12. GA Res. 2200A(XXI) of 16 Dec. 1976.

13. Council of Europe, Convention for the Protection of Human Rights and Fundamental Freedoms [hereinafter European Convention on Human Rights], done at Rome, 4 Nov. 1950, arts. 3 and 2, respectively, read with art. 15; Organization of American States, American Convention on Human Rights ("Pact of San José, Costa Rica"), 22 Nov. 1969, arts. 5 and 4, respectively, read with art. 27.

14. It is worth noting that the General Assembly, when adopting by consensus the Convention Against Torture, expressed itself to be desirous of achieving "a more effective implementation of *the existing prohibition under international and national law of the practice of torture* and other cruel, inhuman or degrading treatment or punishment" (emphasis added). *See* GA Res. 34/46 of 10 Dec. 1984, preambular para. 5.

15. Reservations to the Convention on Genocide Case, [1980] I.C.J. 15.

16. European Convention on Human Rights, art. 5; American Convention on Human Rights, art. 7.

17. *Supra* note 5, preambular para. 6.

18. Quinteros v. Uruguay Comm. No. 107/1981, Report of the Human Rights Committee, 38 UN GAOR Supp. (No. 40), UN Doc. A/38/40, Annex XXII (1983).

19. *Quoted in* Organization of American States, Inter-American Commission on Human Rights, Report on the Situation of Human Rights in Argentina, OAS Doc. OEA/SER.L/V/II.49, doc. 19, corr.1 (1980) at 53.

20. Resolution II; *quoted in* Jan Egeland, Humanitarian Initiative

AGAINST POLITICAL "DISAPPEARANCES" 57 (Geneva: Henry Dunant Institute, 1982). The Conference is composed of the International Committee of the Red Cross, The League of Red Cross Societies, the national Red Cross and Red Crescent Societies, and states parties to the Geneva Conventions of 12 August 1949; 83 governments of the latter states were represented.

21. Geneva Convention for the Amelioration of the Condition of the Wounded and Sick in Armed Forces in the Field (Geneva Convention I), art. 50; Geneva Convention for the Amelioration of the Condition of Wounded, Sick and Shipwrecked Members of Armed Forces at Sea (Geneva Convention II), art. 51; Geneva Convention Relative to the Treatment of Prisoners of War (Geneva Convention III), art. 130; and Geneva Convention Relative to the Protection of Civilian Persons in Time of War (Geneva Convention IV), art. 147. All the above articles apply to international armed conflict; article 3 common to the four conventions applies to noninternational armed conflict.

22. *See* Brownlie, *Principles of Public International Law* 433, 509 (Oxford: Clarendon Press, 3d ed. 1979).

23. Draft Articles on State Responsibility, art. 19, [1976] 2 Y.B. INT'L L. COMM., UN Doc. No. A/CN.4/SER.A/1976/Add.1 (Part 2), Ch. III B. The International Law Commission is a body of 34 lawyers appointed by the General Assembly to assist it in its task of "encouraging the progressive development of international law and its codification." (UN CHARTER, art. 13(1)(a).) A number of treaties have been adopted by the diplomatic conferences convened by the General Assembly on the basis of texts drafted by the Commission.

24. *See, e.g., id.,* Commentary to art. 19, para. 34.

25. The Commission has, however, begun considering draft articles prepared by its Special Rapporteur on state responsibility, Mr. Willem Riphagen, that would specify the legal consequences for states that commit internationally wrongful acts: Report of the International Law Commission, 39 UN GAOR Supp. (No. 10), UN Doc. Ch. VII (1984). According to part II, draft art. 14(2), in addition to the legal consequences for other internationally wrongful acts (draft art. 14(1)),

> An international crime committed by a State entails an obligation for every other State:
> (a) not to recognize as legal the situation created by such crime; and
> (b) not to render aid or assistance to the State which has committed such crime in maintaining the situation created by such crime; and
> (c) to join other States in affording mutual assistance in carrying out the obligations under sub-paragraphs (a) and (b). (*Id.*, para. 349, note 299.)

26. *See,* for example, International Covenant on Civil and Political Rights, art. 2(3)(a).

27. Rosalyn Higgins, *Damages for Violations of One's Human Rights,* in EXPLORATIONS IN ETHICS AND INTERNATIONAL RELATIONS 45, 46 (Simms ed.; 1981).

28. European Convention on Human Rights, art. 50 ("just satisfaction"); American Convention on Human Rights, art. 63 ("fair compensation").

29. Art. 9 ("unlawful arrest or detention") and art. 14 (punishment as a result of "miscarriage of justice").

30. Estrella v. Uruguay, Comm. No. 74/1980, Report of the Human Rights Committee, 38 UN GAOR Supp. (No. 40), UN Doc. Annex XII, para. 11 (1983).

31. For example, Res. No. 48/82, case 6586 (Haiti), 9 Mar. 1982, OAS, Annual Report of the Inter-American Commission on Human Rights 1982–1983, OAS Doc. OEA/SER.L/V/II/61, doc. 22, rev.1, 27 Sept. 1983) at 93. The findings of the Commission relate not only to torture, but also to arbitrary arrest and absence of due process. Since torture may be said to be the most grave of the violations, it may be assumed that the Commission's recommendations would have been the same, had the other violations not been present.

32. However, the Commission will be influenced, especially in considering friendly settlements under article 28(b) of the European Convention, by government actions to change potentially offending laws and practices.

33. Thus, in the *Northern Ireland* case, where the complainant government indicated that it was not seeking compensation for any individual person, the European Court of Human Rights considered that it was not necessary to apply article 50 (on just satisfaction): Ireland v. United Kingdom, European Court of Human Rights, Series A, No. 25, 94–95, paras. 245–46.

34. Report of the Human Rights Committee, 37 UN GAOR Supp. (No. 40), UN Doc. Annex V, general comment 7(16), para. 1 (1982) (emphasis added).

35. Baboeram et al. v. Suriname, Comm. Nos. 146/1983 and 148–154/1983, Report of the Human Rights Committee, 40 UN GAOR Supp. (No. 40), UN Doc. Annex X, para. 13.2 (1985).

36. *Id.*, para. 16. To similar effect, *see* Dermit v. Uruguay, Comm. No. 84/1981, Report of the Human Rights Committee, 38 UN GAOR Supp. (No. 40), UN Doc. Annex IX (1983).

37. Bleier v. Uruguay, Comm. No. 30./1978, Report of the Human Rights Committee, 37 UN GAOR Supp. (No. 40), UN Doc. A/37/40, Annex X, para. 14 (1982); Quinteros v. Uruguay, Comm. No. 107/1981, Report of the Human Rights Committee, 38 UN GAOR Supp. (No. 40), UN Doc. A/38/40, Annex XXII, para. 16 (1983).

38. Quinteros v. Uruguay, para. 14.

39. *Id.*, para. 15.

40. For example, Res. No. 17/82, case 7821 (Guatemala), 9 Mar. 1982, OAS, Annual Report of the Inter-American Commission on Human Rights 1981–1982, OAS Doc. OEA/SER.L/V/II.57, doc. 6, rev.1, at 87.

41. Cyprus v. Turkey (1976), 4 European Human Rights Reports 482, para. 351.

42. International Convention Against the Taking of Hostages, GA Res. 34/146 of 17 Dec. 1979.

43. The four Allied Powers that occupied Germany established an international military tribunal in Nuremberg composed of judges from each of them (France, U.S.S.R., United Kingdom, and United States) to judge the leading figures of Nazi Germany. The tribunal's mandate was contained in the Charter of the International Military Tribunal annexed to the Agreement for the Establishment of an International Military Tribunal, concluded at London, 8 Aug. 1945. UN Treaty Series No. 5, at 251. The judgment of the tribunal (1946) is reproduced in 41 Am. J. Int'l L. 172 (No. 1, 1947).

44. GA Res. 95(I) of 11 Dec. 1946.

45. Under article 6 of the Charter of the Nuremberg Tribunal, crimes against humanity are defined as: "murder, extermination, enslavement, deportation, and other inhumane acts committed against any civilian population, before or during the war, or persecutions on political, racial or religious grounds *in*

execution of or in connection with any crime within the jurisdiction of the Tribunal, whether or not in violation of the domestic law of the country where perpetrated" (emphasis added). The other crimes "within the jurisdiction of the Tribunal" were "crimes against peace" and "war crimes." "Crimes against peace" covers acts relating to the launching of a war of aggression (*jus ad bellum*); "war crimes" covers violations of the rules governing the *conduct* of warfare (*jus in bello*).

46. Geneva Convention I, art. 49; Geneva Convention II, art. 50; Geneva Convention III, art. 129; Geneva Convention IV, art. 146.

47. For example, article 147 of Geneva Convention IV on the treatment of civilian populations provides:

> Grave breaches to which the preceding Article relates shall be those involving any of the following acts, if committed against persons or property protected by the present Convention: wilful killing, torture or inhuman treatment, including biological experiments, wilfully causing great suffering or serious injury to body or health, unlawful deportation or transfer or unlawful confinement of a protected person, compelling a protected person to serve in the forces of a hostile Power, or wilfully depriving a protected person of the rights of fair and regular trial prescribed in the present Convention, taking of hostages and extensive destruction and appropriation of property, not justified by military necessity and carried out unlawfully and wantonly.

48. GA Res. 260A(III) of 9 Dec. 1948. UN Treaty Series No. 78, at 279.

49. However, it should be noted that the International Convention on the Suppression and Punishment of the Crime of *Apartheid* (GA Res. 3068(XXVIII) of 30 Nov. 1973) states the practice of *apartheid* to be a "crime against humanity" (art. I). This could be taken as suggesting that the term is no longer restricted to acts committed in connection with international hostilities. It might more satisfactorily be explained by the practice of UN organs, especially the General Assembly, to treat the situation in South Africa as one concerning the maintenance of international peace and security. Terminological inconsistencies abound in this area, however; for example, there have been moves to declare the perpetration of "disappearances" as a crime against humanity; *see, e.g.*, the 1983 OAS General Assembly Res. AG/RES.666(XIII–0183).

50. Attorney-General of the Government of Israel v. Eichmann, District Court of Jerusalem, 36 INT'L L. REP. 5 (1961).

51. *See* Michael A. Meyer, *Liability for Prisoners of War for Offences Committed Prior to Capture: The Astiz Affair* (pt. 4), 32 INT'L & COMP. L.Q. 948–80 (1983).

52. *Id.* at 952 and International Commission of Jurists *infra* note 57.

53. Complex trial proceedings against Astiz (in respect of the young woman of dual Argentine and Swedish nationality, Dagmar Hagelin) were initiated by the new civilian government in 1985, but the Federal Court of Appeals decided on 5 Dec. 1986 that the case should be dropped on the grounds that the six-year statute of limitations for the crime of illegal detention had expired: AMNESTY INTERNATIONAL, REPORT OF THE TRIAL OF THE FORMER JUNTA MEMBERS—ARGENTINA 1985 (London: 1987), at 23.

54. Article 99 (first paragraph) of the Geneva Convention II states: "No prisoner of war may be tried or sentenced for an act which is not forbidden by the

law of the Detaining Power or by International Law, in force at the time the said act was committed." This language is not restricted to trial for acts committed in connection with the armed conflict which led to the capture of a particular prisoner of war.

55. According to article 17 of Geneva Convention III, a prisoner of war, if questioned, is required to give only name, rank, date of birth, and serial number.

56. Dr. Malcolm N. Shaw, letter to The Times (London), 8 June 1982.

57. *The Case of Captain Astiz,* 28 The Review 3 (June 1982).

58. 630 F.2d. p. 876 (2d Cir. 1980).

59. Alien Tort Statute, 28 U.S.C., sec. 1350 (originally the Judiciary Act of 1789, ch. 20, sec. 9(b), 1 Stat. 67, 77 (1789)).

60. 577 F.Supp. 860 (E.D.N.Y. 1984); *summarized in* 78 Am. J. Int'l L. 677 (1984).

61. *E.g.,* Blum and Steinhardt, *Federal Jurisdiction over International Human Rights Claims: The Alien Tort Claims Act after* Filártiga v. Peña-Irala, 22 Harv. Int'l L.J. 53 (1981); Jordan J. Paust, Book Review, *Human Rights: From Jurisprudential Enquiry to Effective Litigation,* 56 N.Y.U. L. Rev. 227–57 (No. 1, 1981).

62. Farooq Hassan, *A Conflict of Philosophies: The Filártiga Jurisprudence* (pt. 2), 42 Int'l & Comp. L.Q. 250–58 (1983); William T. D'Zurilla, *Individual Responsibility for Torture under International Law,* 56 Tulane L. Rev. 186–226 (No. 1, 1981).

63. That is, outside the place where the acts of torture were committed.

64. It should be noted that in a later U.S. case before another circuit court of appeals, *Tel Oren v. Libyan Arab Republic,* the court doubted whether, in the absence of specific legislation, new offences against the law of nations (in this case, terrorism) committed outside the United States, were justiciable under section 1350 of the Alien Tort Statute: 726 F.2d 774 (D.C.Cir. 1984).

65. GA Res. 39/46 of 10 Dec. 1984, Annex.

66. It is worth noting the more complete language of the Convention. Article 1 of the Declaration Against Torture refers to acts "inflicted by or at the instigation of a public official," whereas the analogous article 1 of the Convention refers to such acts "inflicted by or at the instigation of *or with the consent or acquiescence of* a public official." The addition of the emphasized words is clearly aimed at those practices where the authorities turn a blind eye to atrocities committed against opponents of the government.

67. UN Doc. E/CN.4/1984/72. Apart from the (unstated) concern of some countries not to have their torturers tried abroad, the main argument against universal jurisdiction was that it would be very difficult for a court outside the jurisdiction where the torture took place to secure the necessary evidence and documentation. This was countered by the assertion that nothing in the draft convention would require a state to proceed in the absence of all the elements required by its legal system for a successful prosecution. The burden of the argument of those in favor of the principle of universality of jurisdiction was that there should be "no safe haven for torturers."

68. D'Zurilla, *supra* note 62, based much of his case against the *Filártiga* decision on the absence of agreement in the working group on the issue of universal jurisdiction.

69. Convention I, art. 49; Convention II, art. 50; Convention III, art. 129; Convention IV, art. 146.

70. [1954] 2 Y.B. INT'L L. COMM., UN Doc. A/2693, para. 54.

71. *Id.* para. 50: Commentary to article 2(1).

72. *Id.*

73. 6 for, 5 against, 1 abstaining; *id.* vol. I, 267th meeting, para. 59 (the preceding debate is found at paras. 40–57).

74. Benjamin B. Ferencz, *The Draft Code of Offences Against the Peace and Security of Mankind,* 75 AM. J. INT'L L. 674–79, 674–75 (No. 3, 1981).

75. *Id.* at 675.

76. GA Res. 36/106 of 10 Dec. 1981.

77. GA Res. 40/34 of 29 Nov. 1985.

78. In 1985, the UN Sub-Commission on Prevention of Discrimination and Protection of Minorities submitted to the UN Commission on Human Rights a draft Declaration Against Unacknowledged Detention of Persons, Whatever Their Condition, for possible adoption by the General Assembly: Sub-Commission Res. 1985/26, 29 Aug. 1985 (UN Doc. E/CN.4/1986/5; E/CN.4/Sub.2/1985/57, ch. XVIII A). The Commission in 1986 asked the Sub-Commission to reconsider the draft: Commission decision 1986/106, 13 Mar. 1986 (UN Doc. E/1986/22; E/CN.4/1986/65, ch. II B). A new draft could reflect the notion discussed here.

79. Such a draft has been proposed to the UN Working Group on Enforced or Involuntary Disappearances by FEDEFAM, the Latin American Federation of Associations of Relatives of Disappeared Detainees: UN Doc. E/CN.4/1985/15, Annex III.

80. *Supra* note 9.

9

After the Elections: Compensating Victims of Human Rights Abuses

ELLEN L. LUTZ

In the past decade the world has witnessed the toppling of a number of regimes with deplorable human rights records. While the freeing of political prisoners and the trials, or amnesties, of former government officials responsible for torture, political killings, and other serious violations of human rights attract significant national and international attention, little is reported concerning measures to assist or compensate individual victims of persecution. As the preceding article by Rodley discusses, there is consensus in international law that former victims of certain serious violations of human rights are entitled to compensation.[1] Yet international law is silent regarding the mechanics of implementing a fair compensation program. Countries seeking to repair the social damage caused by a sustained period of human rights abuses are provided with no guidelines for determining who is entitled to compensation, establishing the legal basis for claims, setting time limits for the filing of claims, or establishing procedures that at once are sensitive to former victims' needs and provide some measure of protection against false claims.

Some might argue that it is unnecessary for international law to delve into such details, as the mechanics of a compensation scheme most appropriately fall within the province of domestic law. This argument ignores the fact that the suffering produced by a state's failure to fulfill its international human rights obligations often extends beyond the occurrence of the violation. For example, it is now well documented that former victims of torture and other traumatic abuses of human rights, in addition to sustaining physical injuries, almost invariably suffer long-term psychological sequelae that frequently interfere with their day-to-day activities.[2] Families of victims of disappearance or political killing suffer both the loss of affection and support of their loved ones and the emotional distress produced by the events that led to that loss.[3] Under these circumstances the installation of a government that no longer violates human rights does not, in itself, end past abuses. Just as it is within the province of international law to proscribe human rights abuses, it is appropriate for international law to be concerned with the needs of former victims who suffer as a result of past violations of human rights.

In addition, established domestic systems of tort or criminal law on which states are likely to rely or draw for guidance in establishing new procedures for making claims are frequently inadequate for addressing cases where the state has engaged in criminal violations of human rights. For example, relatively short statute of limitations periods commonly imposed for intentional injury or wrongful death to ensure the availability of evidence or to protect defendants from stale claims may be unfair where the government has suppressed evidence or prevented, through law or intimidation, a claimant from seeking redress. Short statute of limitations periods also do not take into account the fact that the normal psychological response to severe human rights abuses may prevent a former victim from seeking redress for a much longer period of time than that prescribed by the statute. Neutral, internationally applicable standards that take into consideration the gravity of the acts committed as well as the health and justice-related needs of former victims need to be created.

Indeed, when one considers the usual political circumstances that surround the replacement of a regime that has engaged in human rights abuses, the need for international guidelines for redressing past abuses becomes imperative. Governments that sanction torture, political killing, and other serious human rights abuses also frequently tolerate or engage in corruption, misuse or theft of government funds, and other power-consolidating tactics that benefit those controlling the government at the expense of the populace. Moreover, a disproportionate number of the countries where human rights abuses occur are developing countries burdened with high levels of poverty and other social problems. Thus a government that inherits a legacy of past violations of human rights is likely also to inherit a host of other political, economic, and social problems that quickly assume overriding national importance.

A new government faced with severe economic problems may consider an expensive compensation program to be of considerably lower national priority than the revitalization of the economy or the repayment of foreign debt. Where individuals responsible for past violations of human rights (e.g., military officers) retain politically powerful positions, establishing mechanisms for compensating former victims may involve serious political risks. Society at large may have little sympathy for former victims of persecution either because they are members of racial, religious, or national minorities, or because they hold unpopular political beliefs. Under these circumstances there may be little public support for compensating former victims for past human rights abuses. And government officials may react indignantly to being called upon to pay for acts that they did not participate in or strongly opposed.

Governments are not alone in approaching compensation programs with hesitation. Former victims are likely to be suspicious of government-proposed compensatory schemes, especially when they perceive that the government does not represent their interests. They may also suspect that the government is trying to buy its way out of its culpability by paying "blood money." This suspicion is likely to be intensified when the government does not forcefully investigate human rights claims or fails to impose strong punitive sanctions on those responsible for violations. In addition, former victims may feel stigmatized by their need to seek redress and may fear that the procedures for claiming compensation will be degrading or will require them to relive painful past experiences.

International organizations can help to alleviate some of these problems by drafting guidelines for redressing past abuses of human rights. This process would serve as a reminder to the international community that the right to compensation for human rights abuses is itself an important human right. Governments, in turn, might be convinced to place higher priority on compensation programs, even when those programs compete for limited resources with other important economic or social concerns. The existence of international guidelines could also make it easier for states to implement compensation programs. During the chaotic early months when a new government must cope with a variety of other complex concerns, fashioning a program to redress past human rights abuses would not have to be added to the list. That government could simply adopt an internationally accepted plan. And, to the extent paying compensation is politically unpopular, international law responsibilities provide a justification for doing so.

In this article I begin by discussing the legal foundation for the right to compensation. I then discuss some of the key issues that need to be addressed by international organizations drafting guidelines for the redress of past human rights abuses. The focus of my remarks is on the needs of individuals. In particular I am concerned with defining procedures that will help to improve individuals' physical and mental health, restore their sense of social, emotional, and financial well-being, and satisfy their need for justice. While I do not ignore various competing governmental interests, I consider these helpful in establishing the perimeters rather than the foundation of a just compensation program.

The Legal Foundation for a Right to Compensation

International human rights law is created in the same way as other bodies of international law: by treaty and through the emergence of customary international law. Like other types of international law, international human rights law principally creates obligations between states; what is unique about this body of law is that those duties are imposed to protect the rights of individuals. The extent to which individuals may participate in the process of enforcing their rights under international human rights law depends upon the source of those rights.

An individual may make a claim founded upon a treaty-based right to redress for human rights abuses if the state in which that person resides has ratified the relevant treaty. Certain treaties, like the American and the European Human Rights Conventions, give individuals the right to file petitions with Commissions charged with investigating and arbitrating cases involving allegations of human rights abuses. Where a satisfactory resolution cannot be negotiated, those Commissions have the discretion to bring complaints before Human Rights Courts that, in turn, are empowered to investigate claims and order appropriate remedies. States that have ratified these treaties have an obligation under international law to comply with the orders of the Human Rights Courts.

Similarly, other treaties, such as the Optional Protocol to the International Covenant on Civil and Political Rights, permit individuals to file complaints before international investigatory bodies that have independent authority to recommend that governments found to have violated human rights pay compensation to victims. When a state becomes party to such a treaty it accepts the duty to cooperate with the investigatory body and, arguably, is bound to comply with its recommendations regarding compensation. Still other treaties, such as the United Nations Convention Against Torture and Other Cruel, Inhuman or Degrading Treatment or Punishment, impose specific duties on states to provide redress to former victims. Failure to establish effective domestic procedures to redress abuses of human rights would place a state that has ratified such a treaty in violation of its international law obligations.

In addition, it is within the power of all states to incorporate rights guaranteed by international human rights treaties into domestic law. This may involve nothing more than an acknowledgment that certain treaty-based rights are self-executing and thus give rights to individuals in domestic law. Or it may require the drafting of legislation that grants rights to individuals to seek redress under national law. To the extent that a state admits that certain treaty-based rights give rise to enforceable domestic rights, individuals may seek redress for violations of those rights.

Certain categories of human rights abuses are prohibited not only by treaty but by customary international law. Norms of customary international law arise out of state practice, combined with a general recognition among states that those norms are binding on all states. If a state gives effect to customary international law in domestic law, either directly or implicitly by acknowledging that the conduct involved constitutes a constitutional violation, a civil wrong (e.g., a tort), or a crime for which a domestic remedy is available, individuals who have suffered violations of that law are entitled to redress. Moreover, a state's failure to establish domestic procedures enabling individuals to seek redress for customary international human rights law violations may, in itself, indicate that the state is in violation of its customary international law obligations.[4] Thus, once a human rights norm is incorporated into customary international law, individuals, in theory if not always in practice, have a right to seek redress for violations.

Human Rights Violations for Which Former Victims May Claim a Right to Compensation

It is natural to be hesitant about propounding a list of human rights abuses for which individuals are entitled to seek compensation for fear of being underinclusive or lending support to repressive regimes that might otherwise design new forms of mistreatment not included on the list. Thus, this analysis is presented with the caveat that the rights discussed herein do not represent a comprehensive list of the rights for which individuals are entitled to seek compensation.

As Rodley discusses in the preceding article, the right to compensation for torture is specifically guaranteed in two international treaties—the United Nations Convention Against Torture and Other Cruel, Inhuman or Degrading Treatment or Punishment, and the Inter-American Convention to Prevent and Punish Torture—and is underscored by more general language in several others.[5] The right to seek compensation for disappearance and extra-judicial execution may also be derived from these treaties.[6] The Human Rights Committee established under the International Covenant on Civil and Political Rights, which is empowered by the Optional Protocol of that Covenant to receive individual complaints of human rights abuses, has demanded that compensation be paid to former victims or survivors of victims of torture, disappearance, and summary execution. The Inter-American Court of Human Rights is currently considering its first contested case, involving allegations of disappearance in Honduras, but under article 63(1) of the American Convention on Human Rights has authority to rule that fair compensation be paid to parties injured as a result of any violation of that treaty.

Compensation may also be due for a number of other violations of rights protected by the Civil and Political Covenant. The Human Rights Committee has demanded that compensation be paid to former victims of prolonged imprisonment who suffered egregious violations of certain due process rights including the rights to habeas corpus, access to counsel of their choice, fair trial within a reasonable time, and medical care.

As previously discussed, individuals are entitled to seek redress for violations of customary international law. The Restatement (Revised) Foreign Relations Law of the United States, Section 702, considers that a state violates customary international law if,

> as a matter of state policy, it practices, encourages or condones:
>
> (a) genocide,
> (b) slavery or slave trade,
> (c) the murder or causing the disappearance of individuals,
> (d) torture or other cruel, inhuman or degrading treatment or punishment,

(e) prolonged arbitrary detention,
(f) systematic racial discrimination, or
(g) consistent patterns of gross violations of internationally protected human rights.

To the extent that compensation offers appropriate redress for these abuses, or for other unlisted conduct that may come to be prohibited by customary international law, individuals have a right to receive it.

Model Compensation Guidelines

To date international human rights law has not adequately addressed the problem of providing redress to former victims. What is needed are guidelines that set forth the circumstances under which compensation should be paid. Those guidelines need to address the following questions:

1. Who is entitled to compensation?
2. For what categories of loss or damage should compensation be paid?
3. From whom may compensation be sought?
4. When may a person seek compensation?

The guidelines should also suggest procedural mechanisms for applying for compensation, investigating claims, and awarding payments or equivalent services.

Before making some preliminary suggestions regarding the proper scope and content of such guidelines, it is worth examining what is meant by "compensation." As the term is used here it is intended in its broadest meaning: that which is necessary to extinguish, as far as possible, all the consequences of the illegal act and reestablish the situation which in all probability would have existed if that act had not been committed. What is actually required will vary from case to case and from society to society. It is not necessary that compensation always take a monetary form, and indeed there are many circumstances under which monetary payments would be less appropriate than alternative forms of compensation. For example, where human rights abuses have produced physical injury or mental or emotional disturbance, the provision of medical, psychiatric, or psychological treatment might be the most appropriate form of compensation. Where violations have resulted in loss of employment or property, direct or comparable replacement of those losses might be the best response.

One might argue that it is impossible to restore former victims of atrocious violations of human rights to the positions they were in beforehand and that therefore creating a system to compensate them is fundamentally misguided. Under this view, one could still advocate that former victims be given necessary medical or psychological care, pensions, and other benefits to assist them in meeting their individual needs, not as compensation for their suffering but because their conditions entitle them to the aid and comfort that such services or benefits provide.

Indeed, such aid and comfort is sometimes available to former victims even when their own governments take no action. Other governments may offer assistance to former victims of human rights abuses who seek refuge within their borders, and some governments direct a portion of their foreign assistance to programs that directly benefit persons injured as a result of human rights violations. Nongovernmental organizations, both within and outside the countries where abuses take place, provide services to former victims, and increasingly intergovernmental organizations are taking the initiative to fund projects to assist former victims.[7] None of the recommendations proposed for the model compensation guidelines are intended to undermine these important humanitarian assistance efforts.

But while these programs may respond to the physical, psychological, social, and financial needs of former victims, they are inadequate to address the social justice needs of either the individual or the society involved. The model compensation guidelines proposed here are intended not only to help meet the particular needs of individuals, but to serve the larger interests of justice by giving a society that once tolerated or sanctioned human rights abuses an opportunity to come to terms with the past, accept responsibility for the acts committed, and participate in the process of making amends. Such atonement is the best and perhaps only way to compensate former victims for the intangible losses produced by flagrant violations of human rights such as humiliation and utter disrespect for the inherent worth and dignity of the person.

Finally, one might argue that the restoration of justice is impossible if those responsible for committing human rights abuses are not held publicly accountable for their acts and appropriately punished. Certainly one would be quick to question the good faith of a society that offers compensation to former victims but fails to bring their persecutors to justice. But public condemnation and punishment for criminal conduct is legally and analytically distinct from redress for individual injury. While the focus of this article is on the need for and the mechanics of effecting individual remedies, nothing suggested here is intended to undermine the importance of trying and punishing those responsible for human rights abuses.

Who Can Seek Redress?

When an individual has been subjected to and has survived serious violations of human rights, that person clearly should be entitled to seek redress. In addition, when a person is physically or mentally incapacitated as a result of human rights abuses or otherwise is incapable of making a claim, an attorney or close family member should be entitled to seek redress on his or her behalf. In such cases compensation is owed directly to the former victim rather than to the intervening third party.[8]

Potential difficulties arise when the former victim is deceased or when third parties seek to make claims on their own behalf that are based on the persecution of another. Such claims fall into three categories: (1) claims brought on behalf of the deceased for injuries incurred prior to death; (2) claims for wrongful death; and (3) claims brought by close relatives for their own injuries suffered as a consequence of the injury or death of a loved one.

The model compensation guidelines should permit recovery under each of these categories. Permitting recovery for injuries incurred by the deceased prior to his or her death at once recognizes the magnitude of the atrocities suffered by the deceased and has the potential to deter human rights violators from killing their victims to escape liability. International tribunals are already beginning to recognize that survivors have the capacity to bring such actions. For example, the Human Rights Committee has on several occasions demanded that compensation be paid to survivors of deceased victims of torture or disappearance for their mistreatment prior to death.[9] And a United States court deciding a case under customary international human rights law similarly awarded compensation for injuries incurred prior to death.[10]

International tribunals have long awarded claims brought by individuals for wrongful death.[11] Claims for wrongful death are usually measured in terms of the loss of financial support that survivors must endure as a result of the death. In addition, international tribunals have recognized that survivors suffer more than loss of income when a family member dies as a result of violations of international law. In *Janes v.*

United States, the Mexico–United States Claims Commission awarded damages to the wife and children of a man killed in Mexico for both "material losses" and "in satisfaction for damages of the stamp of indignity, grief or other similar wrongs."[12] While it is difficult to assign a measure of damages to suffering such as grief, loss of affection and companionship, loss of consortium, and so forth, these are the normal and foreseeable consequences of human rights violations that result in death, and survivors of victims should be entitled to compensation for such suffering.

In addition, family members of persons subjected to torture, incommunicado detention, disappearance, and other serious violations of human rights frequently suffer profound distress and anxiety for the safety and well-being of their loved ones. Such stress often produces temporary or permanent debilitating problems such as inability to concentrate, inability to work, or physical illness.[13] Because such stress is a foreseeable consequence of the illegal act, those family members should be entitled to compensation for their suffering.

The Measure of Damages

A just system of compensation must contemplate the submission of two classes of claims. The first is for reparation of that which was actually lost. Former victims of human rights abuses or their survivors should be entitled to seek indemnification for loss of life, physical or psychological injury or illness, loss of liberty, loss or damage to property, loss of opportunity, and other injuries proximately caused by their persecution. The Federal Republic of Germany, in fashioning a reparations program appropriate to the circumstances of Nazi persecution, offered indemnification for the following categories of suffering: loss of life; bodily injury or injury to health; deprivation or restrictions on liberty; loss or damage to property; loss of capital resources; loss through the payment of discriminatory levies, fines, penalties and costs; and damage to the career and to "economic advancement."[14]

The second class of claims is based on the nature or gravity of the violation. The acts for which compensation may be sought are not accidents, nor are they the result of negligence; they are deliberate, intentional acts calculated to inflict pain and suffering. Moreover, they are perpetrated under color of law by government officials or agents with the forbearance if not under the orders of those in control of the government.

More than mere restitution is required to make amends for acts of this magnitude. To this end, the compensation guidelines should recognize the right of former victims to seek exemplary damages in addition to actual damages.

From Whom Can Compensation Be Sought?

Former victims of human rights violations ought to be entitled to redress from all those who caused their suffering, but ultimate responsibility for ensuring that former victims receive adequate compensation should lie with the state. There are several reasons for this. First, former victims of human rights abuses often do not know the identities of those who perpetrated the abuses against them, and lack of written records or the unwillingness of those involved to admit their participation or implicate others may preclude discovery of their identities. This is especially likely where the abuses were committed by government-tolerated but autonomous paramilitary or civilian vigilante groups.

Second, to the extent the identity of the persecutors is known, individuals may be fearful of publicly (or even privately) naming those who harmed them for fear of retribution. Such fear may be well-founded in states where the government is unable to control paramilitary or civilian vigilante groups, or where former perpetrators of human rights abuses retain sufficient power that the government fears offending them.

Third, responsibility often lies with a number of individuals in a hierarchically organized chain of command. Each of these individuals, from the most senior government official to the person who actually committed the human rights abuses, should be held liable. The state involved is in the best position to insist that all those individuals share fully in the assumption of responsibility for their conduct.

Finally, damages must be measured according to the needs of the former victim, not the financial resources of the perpetrators. It would be unjust for former victims of wealthy rights abusers to receive damages but for former victims of poor ones to do without. Only the state involved is in a position to establish a compensation program that guarantees that all those subjected to human rights abuses will be treated equally according to need.

The fact that those running a government were not in power when the human rights abuses occurred does not lessen that government's obligation to ensure adequate compensation for former victims. An internal change of government does not have any bearing on a state's international law obligations. These obligations require states to protect human rights and to provide redress when abuses of power result in human rights violations. That duty passes to the new government just as do all other bilateral and multilateral legal obligations. Of course it is entirely appropriate for a new government to indemnify itself by fining or confiscating the wealth and property of the individuals who were previously involved in persecution to help fund the compensation program.

Even states faced with severe economic problems must honor their duty to provide redress to former victims of human rights abuses. A state's shortage of hard currency may, as a practical matter, delay some portion of compensation payments, but it should not be an excuse for failure to review claims or award appropriate damages. The very process by which a state acknowledges that a former victim is legally entitled to compensation is likely to help restore that person's sense that justice is being done and may have a positive impact on his or her mental health. Of course, verbal promises to pay compensation are not sufficient over the long run, and states must act in good faith to ensure that there is money in the coffers to pay those awards.

The fact that the state bears ultimate responsibility for ensuring that individuals receive compensation should not undermine an individual's right to bring ordinary civil actions against private individuals who shared responsibility for their suffering. For example, in the Federal Republic of Germany the existence of the Federal Indemnification Law did not bar individuals from bringing civil actions in West German courts against wealthy industrialists who profited during the National Socialist regime from the use of slave labor. On the other hand, lack of political enthusiasm for these private actions may explain why so many were dismissed on legal technicalities.[15]

Ideally claims should be brought before an appropriate forum in the country where the human rights violations occurred. When large numbers of former victims reside abroad, the government should make it possible for them to file their claims at consular or private agencies located in the countries where they now live. This method was successfully adopted by West Germany and made possible the filing of claims by many more former victims of Nazi atrocities than would have been possible had they been required to travel to West Germany to file such claims.

Finally, the model compensation guidelines should acknowledge the transitory tort character of human rights abuses and urge states to permit former victims to bring actions in their tribunals against both individuals and foreign states responsible for human rights abuses provided jurisdiction can be obtained and no adequate relief is available in the state where the human rights violations occurred. For example, in *Filártiga v. Peña-Irala,* a U.S. court recognized that while torture is a violation of customary international law, it is also a tort for which individuals are entitled to seek relief.[16] Applying the long-established legal principle that a tortfeasor's liability for wrongdoing follows him or her across national boundaries, the court provided redress to the torture victim's relatives even though the torture occurred in Paraguay. In that case no relief was available to the plaintiffs in Paraguay, and the court had personal jurisdiction over the defendant, who was illegally residing in New York.

When May an Individual Seek Compensation?

Under international law there is no statute of limitations for bringing criminal charges against individuals who committed war crimes or crimes against humanity. Since the human rights violations for which individuals may seek compensation have much in common with crimes against humanity, it is tempting to argue that similarly there should be no statutory time bar to individual claims for compensation. But political and economic realities and problems of proof make it unlikely that most governments would tolerate a compensation program that permitted new claims to be filed decades after the violations occurred. Countries prepared to offer redress for abuses of human rights are also likely to be eager to put the past behind them and turn their attention to current concerns. They may be wary of supporters of the repressive regime who may still be powerful enough to destabilize the new government should it be too forceful in addressing past human rights abuses. And the new government will likely want to estimate the financial burden a compensation program would place on the national economy. Thus, governments replacing regimes that engaged in gross violations of human rights would undoubtedly advocate a short, finite statutory period for the filing of claims.

On the other hand, former victims are not likely to focus immediately on seeking compensation, especially in the years just following their persecution. Their primary concern during that period will be to rebuild their lives. Once physical health needs are addressed it may take years for a former victim to recognize that he or she has unresolved mental health problems or is unable to work at his or her previous occupational level. In addition, in the early post-repression period former victims are likely to focus much of their political energy on demanding that the perpetrators of human rights abuses be tried and punished. Demands for individual compensation may appear selfish or petty in comparison to the larger social goal of bringing their persecutors to justice. Former victims may also feel that while their own suffering was great, that of others was greater and that it would be wrong for them to make demands on limited resources when others need them more.

In addition, it is normal for former victims to feel that their acceptance of compensation would absolve their persecutors of responsibility for the terrible deeds they committed, or simply to feel that since no amount of money could ever compensate them for their extreme suffering, no compensation should be accepted at all. They may also feel that their suffering has given them a moral advantage over those who committed the atrocities and those who closed their eyes to the situation or refused to act to end the abuses. They may fear that they will lose their high moral ground by accepting compensation.

The passage of time combined with the establishment of a compensation program that is humanely administered and offers fair and adequate compensation may help to diminish the resistance former victims feel, especially when compensation is needed for health reasons or to maintain a decent standard of living. Thus, from the former victims' perspective, an open-ended or very long period for filing claims is best.

The solution is for the model compensation guidelines to propose an extended but finite statutory period for filing claims. This period should be measured not from the date when the claim arose but from the date on which it first became possible to file a claim. This obviously will not be until the repressive government has been replaced and the judicial or administrative machinery for filing claims is in place. In addition, the legal principle of tolling the statute of limitations should be recognized where it would be unjust to enforce it, such as where the government deliberately has withheld evidence necessary to prove a former victim's claim.

Procedural Considerations

Procedures for receiving and investigating claims for compensation must balance a government's need for assurance that only legitimate claims are paid against the victims' need to have their claims handled sensitively and in a manner consistent with the interests of justice. In many respects the claims procedures set up under the Federal Indemnification Law in the Federal Republic of Germany provide an excellent model. The German government created a system of indemnification agencies that are empowered to receive and investigate claims and award appropriate compensation. The indemnification agencies are required to act on each claim as quickly as possible, and priority is to be given to claims filed by persons "who are more than sixty years of age or indigent or whose earning power has been reduced by illness, infirmity, or physical defects by more than 50 percent."[17]

The claims application requires victims of National Socialist (NS) persecution to set forth the following:

1. personal data and particulars of the claimant's economic circumstances,
2. a statement of the facts justifying the claim,
3. particulars of the evidence available,
4. particulars of the kind and extent of the claim, and
5. a statement as to whether and, if so, where the claimant has previously made an application or filed a claim.

In addition, claimants are to declare all other indemnification or restitution they have sought or received.[18]

The German indemnification law makes it relatively easy for former victims to obtain sympathetic assistance and legal representation to prepare and defend their claims. Private restitution agencies are given permission to represent claimants residing abroad free of charge. In addition, anyone living abroad who formerly was an attorney in Germany but lost that status as a result of NS persecution is permitted to represent claimants before the indemnification agencies. Unless an application is determined to be "obviously unfounded," applicants are charged no fees.

In drafting the indemnification law the German government recognized that in many circumstances evidence of persecution is difficult or impossible to obtain. Thus it provided:

> If, owing to the position in which the claimant has been placed by NS terror acts, any fact cannot be fully proved, the indemnification agencies, after considering all circumstances, may consider that fact as established in favour of the claimant. The same procedure shall be adopted if documentary evidence has been lost, if witnesses have died or cannot be traced or if the taking of the evidence of the claimant or of a witness should meet with difficulties incommensurate to the importance of the evidence.[19]

It also created a system of indemnification courts to which adverse decisions of the indemnification agencies could be appealed.

It is impractical to assume that every country that violates human rights will set up claims procedures as elaborate or as expensive to operate as those established in West Germany. The German procedures were formulated to cope with claims derived from one of the most massive campaigns of crimes against humanity ever perpetrated. Other countries faced with responsibility for redressing claims for human rights abuses may conclude that existing judicial or administrative agencies are competent to sensitively administer claims. But no matter what court or agency is charged with doing so, the procedures involved must meet certain minimum requirements.

First, they must respect the claimant's right to privacy. While absolute confidentiality may be impossible, claims should be handled discreetly. The claimant's permission should be sought prior to any investigation into areas such as health or family life that the society traditionally considers within the realm of personal privacy.

Second, claims procedures should be as simple and nonconfrontational as possible. To the extent hearings are required they should be conducted in a manner that displays utmost sensitivity to the claimant. Adversarial proceedings should be avoided, and if oral testimony is deemed necessary it should be taken in the least threatening environment possible. This is especially important where former victims are experiencing post-traumatic stress disorder or related mental health problems as a result of their persecution. Such persons may be psychologically incapable of describing the events they experienced or may do so with such a loss of affect that their stories appear unbelievable.

Third, claims procedures should respect any cultural or linguistic differences between those who suffered persecution and the larger society. For example, where victims are from a minority linguistic group, all application forms, instruction sheets, interviews, and hearings should be in their language. The services of attorneys or nongovernmental social service organizations of the former victims' ethnic group should be made available to assist claimants.

Fourth, there should be a fair degree of latitude in evidence requirements. If records or other proof of persecution are unavailable, the burden of proof should be on the government to rebut otherwise credible claims, and in the absence of proof to the contrary the claimant should be given the benefit of the doubt.

Fifth, claimants should be entitled to appoint legal representatives to act on their behalf in pursuing their claims. This is particularly important since former victims may be unwilling to interact directly with the government that formerly persecuted them.

Sixth, no person should be deprived of the right to file a claim owing to an inability to pay. Required documentation such as birth or death certificates, titles to property, employment records, and so on should be made available to claimants free of charge. Attorneys fees and costs of pursuing a claim should be reimbursed if the claimant is successful, and, of course, there should be no fee for filing a claim.

Seventh, procedures should be established for appealing denials of claims to ensure that administrative or judicial error or prejudice does not bar otherwise legitimate claims.

Conclusion

There is a certain irony in proposing the drafting of international model compensation guidelines. Obviously the primary goal of all those concerned with human rights is preventing rights abuses. Thus, while one recognizes that the guidelines may be a useful tool in ensuring the protection of former victims' right to compensation, one simultaneously hopes the guidelines will never be needed.

Utilitarians might argue that the existence of guidelines would have the preventive effect of diminishing human rights abuses because governments would see that the cost of violating human rights is more burdensome than whatever the rights abuses were supposed to accomplish. The rationale offered in this article is more humble. In this imperfect world where human rights abuses nip unyieldingly at the heels of human sensibilities, it is right and just that compensation be offered to former victims. The model compensation guidelines are proposed here as a step toward ensuring that those who have suffered human rights abuses are provided with the means to help restore their dignity and their physical, mental, and financial well-being.

NOTES

1. N. Rodley, *The International Legal Consequences of Torture, Extra-Legal Execution, and "Disappearance,"* 167 (this volume).

2. *See, e.g.*, L. EITINGER & A. STROM, MORTALITY AND MORBIDITY AFTER EXCESSIVE STRESS (New York: Humanities Press, 1973); F. Allodi, G. Randall, et al., *Physical and Psychiatric Effects of Torture: Two Medical Studies*, in THE BREAKING OF BODIES AND MINDS: TORTURE, PSYCHIATRIC ABUSE AND THE HEALTH

PROFESSIONS 58 (E. Stover & E. Nightingale eds.; New York: W. H. Freeman and Co., 1985); R. Mollica, *The Trauma Story: Psychiatric Care of Refugee Survivors of Violence and Torture,* in POST-TRAUMATIC THERAPY AND VICTIMS OF VIOLENCE 295 (F. M. Ochberg ed.; New York: Bruner/Mazel, Inc., 1988).

3. *See* AMNESTY INTERNATIONAL USA, "DISAPPEARANCES"—A WORKBOOK 109–18 (New York: Amnesty International, 1981).

4. *Restatement (Revised) Foreign Relations Law of the United States,* Sec. 703. Comment C.

5. Rodley, *supra* note 1, at 174.

6. *Id.*

7. For example, the United Nations Voluntary Fund for Victims of Torture, established pursuant to General Assembly Resolution 36/151 of 16 Dec. 1981, provides financial assistance to private organizations that assist victims of torture.

8. This approach has been adopted by the Human Rights Committee, which has stated:

> [N]ormally the communication should be submitted by the alleged victim himself or by his representative (for example, the alleged victim's lawyer), but the Committee may accept to consider a communication submitted on behalf of an alleged victim when it appears that he is unable to submit the communication himself. The Committee regards a close family connection as a sufficient link to justify an author acting on behalf of an alleged victim. On the other hand, it has declined to consider communications where the authors have failed to establish any link between themselves and the alleged victims.

Report of the Human Rights Committee 99, 33 UN GAOR Supp. (No. 40), UN Doc. A/33/40 (1978).

9. *See, e.g.,* Bleier v. Uruguay, Comm. No. 30/1978, Report of the Human Rights Committee, 37 UN GAOR Supp. (No. 40), UN Doc. A/37/40, Annex X (1982); Quinteros v. Uruguay, Comm. No. 107/1981, Report of the Human Rights Committee, 38 UN GAOR Supp. (No. 40), UN Doc. A/38/40, Annex XXII (1983).

10. Filártiga v. Peña-Irala, 630 F.2d 876 (2d Cir. 1980). *See also* Von Dardel v. U.S.S.R., 623 F. Supp. 246 (D.C.D.C. 1976) (in action for damages for kidnapping and mistreatment of Swedish diplomat Raoul Wallenberg, death not determined but default judgment entered for violations of international norms relating to diplomatic immunity and human rights).

11. *See* F. V. Garcia-Amador, L. B. Sohn and R. R. Baxter, RECENT CODIFICATION OF THE LAW OF STATE RESPONSIBILITY FOR INJURIES TO ALIENS, Dobbs Ferry, N.Y.: Oceana Pubs. 85–133 (1974).

12. Laura M.B. Janes et al. v. The United Mexican States, General Claims Commission (U.S. and Mexico) Opinions 108, 118 (1927).

13. Diagnostic and Statistical Manual III (Revised), (DSM III (R)), American Psychiatric Association (1987).

14. Bundesentschaedigungsgesetz (BEG), 29 June 1956.

15. B. Ferencz, *Less Than Slaves: Jewish Forced Labor and the Quest for Compensation* (Cambridge: Harv. U. Press, 1979).

16. *See* discussion of Filártiga v. Peña-Irala in Rodley, *supra* note 1, at 180–81.

17. BEG para. 179(2).

18. BEG para. 190.

19. BEG para. 176(2).

PART V

THE FRANK NEWMAN FILE

10

Creative and Dynamic Strategies for Using United Nations Institutions and Procedures: The Frank Newman File

THEO VAN BOVEN

> Freedom is not a gift received from the State or a leader, but a possession to be won everyday by the effort of each and the union of all.
>
> *Albert Camus*

Those colleagues, friends, and students who have had the privilege and the pleasure of receiving regularly Frank Newman's mailings of circular letters, notes, draft statements, draft publications, newspaper clippings, and other materials have often found enclosed, as a special gesture of cheer, some cartoons related to human rights. Humor, intellectual creativity, and a deep sense of commitment to the cause of human rights are characteristics that pervade Frank Newman's life and work. At the same time, in the long series of communications that Frank Newman has been conveying over the years to his friends and disciples, one finds some remarkable quotations, such as the one from the great French writer Albert Camus which I found appropriate as a *leitmotiv* for this article.

It is not my intention in this paper to recall the years of personal association and the precious experiences I shared with Frank Newman, but rather to provide some insight into how Frank Newman perceived the potentials of the United Nations institutions and mechanisms in the area of human rights and tried to use them creatively. I base my comments largely on materials that I recently rediscovered in a file containing a mixture of Frank Newman's communications during the period of August 1973 to July 1975. Newman acted in those years as a lawyer and counsel for a number of nongovernmental organizations and as a teacher and educator of students. He was at that time a relative newcomer in the UN human rights circuit. I happened to be an official at the Netherlands Ministry of Foreign Affairs; I was also a member of the UN Commission on Human Rights and later a member of the Sub-Commission on Prevention of Discrimination and Protection of Minorities, both UN policy organs in the field of human rights. The rediscovered 1973–75 file includes such materials as draft publications for comments, copies of letters to UN officials, and briefings and advisory notes addressed to "colleagues," "concerned colleagues," "selected colleagues," "several colleagues," "friends and others," "a few people in Washington," and to some officeholders in nongovernmental organizations, such as the International Student Movement for the United Nations, Amnesty International, the International Commission of Jurists, and the International League for the Rights of Man. A few letters are also exclusively addressed to me.

In order to fully appreciate Frank Newman's efforts in the years 1973–75 to make UN institutions and mechanisms more effective, one should recall some features of the UN human rights program in those days. In the late sixties and early seventies, there had emerged new procedures to identify situations that appeared to reveal consistent patterns of gross violations of human rights, as well as procedures to deal with communications (or complaints) concerning violations of human rights. A military dictatorship in Greece, which had attracted a great deal of attention on the part of the international human rights community, fell in those years in the shambles of its own incompetence. Frank Newman was one of the human rights advocates who had moved the Greek case to international human rights forums. Another military dictatorship affecting a truly democratic nation, this time in Chile, seized power and caused widespread human suffering in that country. Frank Newman visited Chile as early as 1973 on a nongovernmental inquiry mission. After his return he lobbied hard in many quarters to get the Chilean case on the

UN agenda. He did so primarily for the sake of human rights in Chile and for the victims of repression, but he was also interested in setting a precedent in the UN and getting the UN more actively involved in other situations of serious human rights concern.

The Frank Newman file of 1973–75 bears out his skills as a lawyer, his faith in the United Nations as a potentially important means for human rights action, his desire to challenge the odds of political realities, his capacity to distinguish short-term interests and long-term strategies and perspectives, and, related to this, his ability to predict and project policy lines and policy goals for the future.

The UN Setting in the Early Seventies

It was significant that in the years immediately following the completion in 1966 of the International Bill of Human Rights (consisting of the Universal Declaration of Human Rights, the International Covenant on Economic, Social and Cultural Rights, the International Covenant on Civil and Political Rights, and the Optional Protocol to the latter) and pending the entry into force of the International Covenants, which only occurred in 1976, the UN developed some far-reaching procedures and mechanisms for dealing with violations of human rights. The UN policy organs involved in human rights matters, in particular the Commission on Human Rights and its Sub-Commission, the Economic and Social Council, and the General Assembly, chose not to wait for the entry into force of the International Covenants, whose effects would at any rate be of a gradual and long-term nature.

In view of the broad concern with practices of colonialism and neo-colonialism and with patterns of racial discrimination and apartheid, these UN policy organs relied on the inherent powers of the UN Charter in the field of human rights. Consequently the Commission on Human Rights was authorized by Resolution 1235 (XLII) of 6 June 1967 of the Economic and Social Council (ECOSOC) to give annual consideration to the item entitled "Question of the violation of human rights and fundamental freedoms, including policies of racial discrimination and segregation and of apartheid, in all countries, with particular reference to colonial and other dependent countries and territories." The origin, the title, and the wording of ECOSOC Resolution 1235 made it clear that the resolution was aimed mainly at serious human rights violations in colonial and racist contexts. Nevertheless, its scope and target would not necessarily and *a priori* exclude violations of human rights in other contexts and situations ("in all countries"). When, in 1968, the Commission on Human Rights received the recommendation of its Sub-Commission to look not only into the human rights situation in southern Africa but also into the situations in Greece and Haiti, the Commission was unwilling and unprepared to deal with the two latter situations. Resolution 1235 remained for the time being, and into the early seventies, a tool only in the anticolonial and antiracist contexts. As we will see later, Frank Newman was nevertheless keenly aware of the broader possibilities of the resolution.

Human rights activists in the early seventies gave greater credit to a procedure adopted on 27 May 1970 by ECOSOC Resolution 1503 (XLVIII) for dealing with communications relating to violations of human rights and fundamental freedoms. It provided for a selection and thorough examination, in successive stages, of complaints and situations "which appear to reveal a consistent pattern of gross and reliably attested violations of human rights." Resolution 1503 put an end to a rule, which had prevailed since its adoption in 1947 by the Commission and ECOSOC, that the UN had no power to take any action in regard to the many thousands of complaints addressed to it each year by private persons, nongovernmental organizations, and other groups.[1] This is not the place to describe in detail the elements of this new device, which became generally known as "the 1503 procedure." The point to be emphasized here is the confidentiality requirement: all actions envisaged in the implementation of the resolution (including documents and proceedings) were to remain confidential until such time as the Commission decided to make recommendations to ECOSOC. The operation of the 1503 procedure is therefore (at least officially) not subject to public scrutiny and control. It soon turned out that the great hopes and expectations initially vested in the 1503 procedure did not materialize. The procedure was applied ineffectively, and it excluded the authors of communications from any information about decisions regarding their complaints, caused excessive delays, and, more dramatically, provided abusive governments a comfortable shield behind which to hide. Newman was one of those activists and lobbyists who made vigorous efforts, behind the scenes, in private interventions, and by public action, to make the procedure more effective. As one of the early critics of the application of the 1503 procedure, he put forward suggestions to improve it.[2]

The Confidential 1503 Procedure: A Maelstrom Becoming a Morass

Although the 1503 procedure was adopted in 1970, it was not until 1974 that particular situations selected under the procedure by the Sub-Commission as "appearing to reveal a consistent pattern of gross and reliably attested violations of human rights" began to reach the Commission for further consideration. According to disclosures in the press—journalists generally being more eager for confidential than public information—eight situations were referred to the Commission on Human Rights concerning the following countries: Brazil, Burundi, Guyana, Indonesia, Iran, Portugal, Tanzania, and the United Kingdom (in relation to Northern Ireland).[3] The Commission, faced at its 1974 session with a variety of more or less serious human rights cases, proved to be simply unable to handle the matter; lack of experience, lack of guidance, lack of time, lack of political will, and lack of a majority opinion prevented any action. The eight cases were left pending for another year, and a working group was established by the Commission to meet one week prior to its 1975 session in order to examine the materials relating to these cases and to prepare the ground for the Commission.

Frank Newman was an impatient actor on the sidelines. The Greek case, for which he acted as counsel, never did reach the Commission under the 1503 procedure because it was effectively blocked at the level of the Sub-Commission. On the other hand, the Northern Ireland (Belfast) case, in which Newman was also involved, did reach the Commission, though the Commission chose in 1975 to drop this case and leave the matter to the European Commission for Human Rights. In the meantime Frank Newman became increasingly dissatisfied with 1503. Already in 1973 he had written a paper with the suggestive title, "The New UN Procedures for Human Rights Complaints: Reform, Status Quo, or Chamber of Horrors?"[4] As a good American lawyer he tested the 1503 procedure on the basis of the principles of due process, natural justice, equality of arms, and *audi alteram partem,* and concluded that the procedure, though deficient in its application, deserved a fair chance in the light of a broad and liberal interpretation of its rules instead of being applied with excessive secrecy and bureaucracy. Newman pleaded in particular for a fair degree of information and participation for the authors of communications (the petitioners), and made corresponding recommendations. Under the practice of 1503 the petitioners are totally excluded from the procedure. They receive officially no information whatsoever, even when their case has been declared admissible and further action has been taken; they are not informed of the contents of any government reply, nor are they allowed to participate orally or in writing during the procedure.

In spite of efforts by Frank Newman and others, the position of the authors of communications under the 1503 procedure has remained unchanged: they merely serve as sources of information and they are not persons with standing before a legal or quasi-legal tribunal. In this respect the 1503 procedure differs considerably from the communications procedure instituted under the Optional Protocol to the International Covenant on Civil and Political Rights.[5]

Apart from Newman's views and proposals regarding the position of the authors of communications, a host of other ideas concerning the 1503 procedure were recurring themes in his briefings and submissions. He felt, and quite rightly so, that the Sub-Commission was not doing its job properly when it considered communications without taking into account, as paragraph 5 of Resolution 1503 prescribes, "other relevant information." As a result, the Sub-Commission may refer a situation to the Commission without a great deal of pertinent, and often more recent, information available in UN files and in reports of other organizations. Consequently, it is more likely that the Commission will drop the case because the information it is given is considered too sketchy, unsubstantiated, or outdated. Time and again Newman drew attention to a neat distinction made by Resolution 1503 between a "communication" and a "situation." According to the terms of 1503, the Sub-Commission initially considers *communications* as received from petitioners, but after taking into account any replies of governments *and other relevant information* the Sub-Commission then determines whether to refer to the Commission on Human Rights *particular situations* that appear to reveal a consistent pattern of gross and reliably attested violations of human rights requiring consideration by the Commission. As Newman wrote in a statement of 12 August 1974 to the Sub-Commission:[6]

> that difference between "situation" and "communication" becomes crucial when we re-read paragraph 5 of resolution 1503, particularly the words that request the Sub-Commission to consider "the communications brought before it—and any replies of Governments—and other relevant information." Is it not the phrase "other relevant information" that, when advisable, permits the Sub-Commission (1)

> to determine the true seriousness of a situation, (2) to treat related communications as evidencing a single situation, (3) to bring outdated communications up to date, (4) to aid the Commission generally regarding its own duties under paragraph 6 of resolution 1503?

These points raised by Frank Newman were absolutely correct, but unfortunately the potentialities of the phrase "and other relevant information" have hardly been utilized in the many years of operation of the 1503 procedure.

Under paragraph 6 of Resolution 1503 the Commission on Human Rights may carry out a thorough study of a particular situation or it may order an investigation by an ad hoc committee. In view of the Commission's obvious absence of experience and lack of determination to deal with situations referred to it in the initial years, Frank Newman gave a great deal of thought to the type of action the Commission could undertake by way of "a thorough study," a course of action which is less formal and therefore more realistic and likely to be undertaken than an investigation by an ad hoc committee. Newman suggested in a statement of 4 February 1974[7] to the Commission that "a thorough study" could be carried on in the following manner: by an ad hoc working group of experts (following the existing example of the *Ad Hoc* Working Group of Experts on Southern Africa), by a nongovernmental organization commissioned to undertake the task (on the basis of paragraph 32 of ECOSOC Resolution 1296 (XLIV) pertaining to the consultative arrangements of NGOs), by the Secretariat, or by special rapporteurs or consultants. Newman wrote: "it appears that many different kinds of studying might be appropriate when information available to the Commission appears to reveal consistent patterns of gross violations of human rights. Experiments will be necessary; and experience will be the best guide." In later years, the Commission did, more occasionally than as a general rule, follow under the 1503 procedure the types of "thorough study" modalities proposed by Frank Newman in 1974. With regard to the situations in Uganda and Haiti, special rapporteurs were appointed under Resolution 1503. Similarly, with respect to the situations in Paraguay, Uruguay, and Ethiopia, the UN Secretary-General was requested to appoint a representative to carry out "a thorough study."[8] This is not the occasion to examine how effectively and credibly those thorough studies were carried out. It is merely submitted here that Frank Newman indicated a method of proceeding which the Commission did follow in a number of instances.

Most strikingly, Frank Newman's skepticism regarding the effectiveness of the 1503 procedure grew rapidly. Failures could be registered in abundance,[9] and successes, if there were any, remained invisible. In one of his informal briefings of early 1974, Newman had already written, "my hunch is that the resolution 1503 procedures may well become a morass, not merely a maelstrom." Six years later, in February 1980, in an opening statement before the Commission on Human Rights, the Director of the UN Division of Human Rights questioned the value of the 1503 procedure in the following terms:

> Is it satisfactory to place so much emphasis on the consideration of situations in confidential procedures, thereby shutting out the international community and oppressed peoples? Are certain procedures in danger of becoming, in effect, screens of confidentiality to present cases discussed thereunder from being aired in public? While there is probably no alternative to trying to cooperate with the governments concerned, should we allow this to result in the passage of several years while the victims continue to suffer and nothing meaningful is really done? How can we deal with governments which do not act in good faith or abuse the procedures of the Commission by pretending to cooperate while in fact violations of human rights continue to take place?[10]

It is no surprise that governments, in particular those who have much to hide and who fear the effects of public criticism, soon considered the confidential 1503 procedure as a shield to avoid becoming the subject of public procedures.[11] Frank Newman was one of the first human rights activists to warn against the tendency of abusive governments to play the confidential 1503 procedure against the public 1235 procedure. That is the subject of the next section.

Don't Downgrade Public Procedures

As early as 1973, the Greek military government had discovered the convenience of the confidential 1503 procedure. In an official letter to the UN Secretary-General, dated 12 August 1973, the Greek Permanent Representative wrote, *inter alia,* that all communications must be considered in clearly defined stages, that all communications were to be considered in private meetings, and that all actions envisaged by the Sub-Commission or the Commission on Human Rights *were to be confidential* (italics in original). Commenting on references to the human rights situation in Greece by a few delegates in the Commission on Human Rights, the Greek Ambassador wrote to the Secretary-General: "this delegation is certain that, in your wisdom and acumen, you will take the necessary steps to put an end to the prejudiced and discriminatory attitude adopted towards Greece by the Commission on Human Rights, whose very reason for being is the elimination of all discrimination."[12] The points made by Greece in 1973 became in later years the main procedural argument advanced by many abusive governments and their friends in their efforts to prevent public discussion of human rights violations relating to their countries. This line of reasoning was used in varying degrees of consistency and persistency, and in some instances with success, by representatives of repressive regimes such as Afghanistan, Argentina, Paraguay, and Uruguay.

Frank Newman was one of the first human rights actors, if not the very first, to refute the argument that the confidential 1503 procedure would overtake public procedures. In a written statement dated 1 February 1974, submitted to the Commission on Human Rights on behalf of four leading nongovernmental human rights organizations, Newman wrote:

> We and other non-governmental organizations have hailed Council resolution 1503 (XLVIII) as a significant contribution to United Nations procedures. By no means, however, did it supersede or downgrade the Commission's powers under Council resolution 1235 (XLII), also a significant contribution. Textually that is shown by paragraph 6(a) of resolution 1503 (XLVIII), which specifically refers to resolution 1235 (XLII). More importantly, the 'thorough study' that is contemplated by paragraph 3 of resolution 1235 (XLII) may in many situations be appropriate even when those situations have not been referred by the Sub-Commission pursuant to paragraph 5 of resolution 1503 (XLVIII).

And Newman continued in the same statement:

> To illustrate: Is it not clear that the Commission occasionally might disagree with the Sub-Commission and decide to make a thorough study even though the Sub-Commission thought no action was appropriate? It would be bizarre were the Commission's powers regarding the 'Question of the violation of human rights—in all countries' restricted to those situations, if any, that the Sub-Commission has decided to refer. A contrary view would drastically limit paragraphs 2 and 3 of Council resolution 1235 (XLII).[13]

In the above statement, Newman addressed particularly the Greek argument of the "clearly defined stages," which would make the Commission on Human Rights powerless in regard to situations not referred to it by the Sub-Commission. The issue would soon pose itself not necessarily in the relationship between Commission and Sub-Commission but in terms of public versus private procedures. It was therefore of critical importance that the Commission and the Sub-Commission chose to act publicly in the case of Chile, without reference to or reliance on resolution 1503.[14]

The Commission decided at its 1974 session to send a telegram to the Chilean authorities,[15] and the Sub-Commission acted with respect to the Chilean situation under the topic "human rights of persons subjected to detention or imprisonment." Undoubtedly, the widespread public concern about the repressive situation in Chile and the serious nature of the human rights violations occurring in that country, as well as the political consensus that was emerging across the various groupings in the UN, made it imperative to resort to public and visible action. Frank Newman wrote early in January 1975 in some of his "musings" to me: "How inexcusable would it be were there a useless quarrel relating to the Sub-Commission's resolution 1503 referral! Chile must not be treated as a 1503 matter. Juridically it should be handled under resolution 1235. Existing information available to the Commission justifies a swift study now." It was this course of action that the Commission did follow in 1975 by its decision to set up an ad hoc working group of experts on Chile. The decision reconfirmed the independent meaning of Resolution 1235 as complementary to and not superseded by Resolution 1503; it gave renewed content to the "thorough study" concept in paragraph 3 of Resolution 1235; and it set an important precedent for similar Commission actions that would follow in the future. Quite rightly and prophetically Newman termed the actions by UN organs in Chile as "precedent-shattering."

The actions by the Commission and the Sub-Commission as well as by the General Assembly in the years 1974 and 1975 concerning the human rights situation in Chile were indeed of great significance from the legal and practical points of view and paved the way for similar public actions by UN organs regarding other situations revealing consistent patterns of gross violations of human rights.

As a matter of fact, the case of Chile was not the first to trigger investigatory procedures in the UN human rights sphere. The situations in southern Africa and in the territories occupied by Israel in the Middle East were already the object of investigation by UN fact-finding groups. Nevertheless, those who took a restrictive view of the competence of the

UN to make a thorough study of concrete human rights situations distinguished those situations as ones affecting international peace and security. Such was the consistent position of the socialist countries of Eastern Europe: only gross and systematic human rights violations amounting to a threat to international peace were a matter of legitimate concern to the international community.

The Chilean situation after the coup d'état in September 1973 had definite international ramifications—foreign forces having collaborated in the preparation and the staging of the military takeover—but the UN made no pronouncement that that situation constituted a threat to international peace. It is therefore no surprise that even though the USSR had good political reasons to mobilize international public opinion against the military junta in Chile (and its supporters in the United States) and wished also to use the UN as a platform for that purpose, it was initially most reluctant to accept the establishment of fact-finding machinery on the human rights situation in that country. It pleaded for an outright condemnation of the Chilean junta without prior investigation. Only after lengthy and tedious negotiations did the USSR join the consensus. How could the Chile enquiry be made compatible with the strictly constructionist position of the USSR on the competence of the UN to deal with violations of human rights? Not long after the UN had ordered the Chile enquiry, the answer was given by a learned Soviet lawyer in an article outlining the traditional USSR position but also upholding the legality of the Chile enquiry. He wrote:

> Special agencies may be formed by the United Nations Organization to investigate violations of human rights by fascist and militarist dictatorships. The legality of formation of such agencies rests on the fact that the policy pursued by military-fascist dictatorships negates the aims and principles of the UN Charter and is accompanied by mass and systematic violations of elementary human rights and freedoms. This is why the 31st session of the Commission on Human Rights, held in February–March 1975, formed an ad hoc working group of five members to investigate the situation in the field of human rights existing in Chile.[16]

Obviously, as soon as one concedes that gross and systematic violations of human rights committed by military-fascist dictatorships are a legitimate concern and a proper subject of enquiry by the UN, irrespective of whether international peace and security are at stake and whether a colonial or neocolonial situation prevails, then the door swings open to a good number of "Chile-like" situations. That is what actually happened. Since the establishment in 1975 of the Chile enquiry, numerous other countries have become subjects of UN study and investigation, notably Afghanistan, Bolivia, Cyprus, El Salvador, Equatorial Guinea, Guatemala, Iran, Kampuchea, Malawi, Mauritania, Nicaragua, and Poland.[17] Special rapporteurs, experts, and envoys have been appointed to carry out these studies and investigations, and the situations have been the subject of public discussion and decision-making by UN organs, particularly the Commission and Sub-Commission, the Economic and Social Council, and the General Assembly. The breakthrough in the Chile case was an important factor in this broadening of UN interest in particular situations involving consistent patterns of gross violations of human rights. Frank Newman predicted this development, and he was among the first human rights actors to be fully aware of the importance and the potentialities of the Chile case. In fact, already at the session of the Commission of Human Rights of February–March 1974 Newman (on behalf of some prominent human rights NGOs), as well as government delegates from Italy, the Netherlands, and Pakistan, pleaded for a UN enquiry into Chile.[18] In 1974 the minds of the majority were not yet ready, but the ground was prepared for 1975 and the years to follow.

The Thematic Approach: Breaking New Ground

Some significant events occurred at the 27th session of the Sub-Commission on Prevention of Discrimination and Protection of Minorities in August–September 1974. The preceding section discussed public action on the human rights situation in Chile, with its effects on subsequent decision-making in the General Assembly and the Commission on Human Rights. No less important at the same session were actions by the Sub-Commission on two other issues: first, setting up a working group on slavery, the slave trade, the traffic in persons, and the exploitation of the prostitution of others; and, second, establishing a special procedure concerning the human rights of persons subjected to any form of detention or imprisonment, in particular practices of torture and other forms of cruel, inhuman, or degrading treatment or punishment.

These procedures were important not only because they contributed to raising public awareness in the international community of those widespread evil practices, but also because they looked to nongovernmental organizations as one source of pertinent and reliable information.

Frank Newman insistently drew the attention of his colleagues in the world of nongovernmental organizations to the possibilities of these new public procedures. He termed them "the Sub-Commission's potentially most creative items," and he pleaded with his colleagues to nurture them with solid information. "Critics often forget that individuals, not nations, are those who keep wheels turning," wrote Newman as encouragement to his colleagues. Aware of the bureaucratic pitfalls and hurdles in the UN Secretariat, Newman advised his colleagues, when making submissions to the UN, to refer to resolution numbers pertaining to these new procedures in order to avoid confusion with the 1503 procedure and to preclude the likelihood of disappearance of the submissions in procedural and bureaucratic mills. He also made suggestions as to the desirable content and format of submissions.

Again, Frank Newman proved to be forward-looking and capable of devising dynamic and creative directions for the future. The approach of focusing on widespread practices of an evil nature which require the urgent, consistent, and public attention of the international community has gained increasing momentum through UN techniques and strategies for dealing with consistent patterns of gross violations of human rights.[19] In 1980, the Commission on Human Rights established a working group to deal with questions relating to enforced or involuntary disappearances. In 1982 the Commission appointed a special rapporteur on summary and arbitrary executions, and in 1985 the Commission appointed a special rapporteur in order to respond effectively to credible and reliable information regarding torture. A working group on the rights of indigenous populations has functioned in the framework of the Sub-Commission since 1982. These new mechanisms, which aim to protect the integrity and inviolability of the human person, combine in practice some significant features. First, they avoid an unduly selective and political approach because they focus primarily on practices and not on countries, although it remains important for the sake of accountability that countries be named. Second, they pertain to those basic human rights which are considered peremptory norms of international law. Third, they utilize reliable information from all relevant governmental and nongovernmental sources, and therefore constitute a bridge between human rights realities experienced by victims as well as their relatives and official international institutions. Fourth, their mandates are being carried out by persons who serve in their private and expert capacity, which is conducive to the objectivity and impartiality of human rights implementation. Fifth, their mandates have allowed urgent actions vis-à-vis the authorities of the countries concerned, an innovation in UN human rights procedures which may save the lives of human beings. Sixth, as part of these special thematic procedures, fact-finding missions to a considerable number of countries have been carried out, thus enriching the practice and the experience of enquiries *in situ* and enabling the UN to relate more directly with national and local societies and with concerned peoples and persons.

Concluding Remarks

It would overstate the role of Frank Newman to give him sole credit for some of the positive developments in UN dealings with human rights that have occurred since 1973. Nobody can claim such credit, and Frank Newman would be the last to do so. Nonetheless, it is striking to note that the three trends which are borne out in Newman's correspondence, notes, and submissions of the years 1973–75 have been confirmed and strengthened in UN practice since 1975. First, the 1503 procedure has in my judgment proved to be not much more than a "paper tiger" and a suitable alibi for the UN and its member states. It has raised false hopes and betrayed many people. Second, the Chile case was a precedent and has indeed been followed by many other situations that were the subject of public scrutiny and investigation by working groups and rapporteurs. In some instances these country investigations served the cause of human rights; in other instances they were not carried out with due consideration for the cause of human rights and were deemed a failure.[20] Third, in more recent years the subject-oriented or thematic approach has been adopted with regard to such grave practices as disappearances, executions, and torture. Good reasons exist to believe that this thematic approach holds fine prospects for the future and constitutes a promising trend.

In going through the Frank Newman file of the years 1973–75, we have found some convincing evidence that Frank Newman is—in addition to a distinguished professor, lawyer, and educator, as he is generally known—a forward-looking politician and a prophet.

NOTES

1. *See* Jakob Th. Möller, *Petitioning the United Nations,* in 1 UNIVERSAL HUMAN RIGHTS 57–72 (No. 4, 1979).

2. Frank C. Newman, *The New UN Procedures for Human Rights Com-*

plaints: Reform, Status Quo, or Chamber of Horrors, in HEARINGS ON THE INTERNATIONAL PROTECTION OF HUMAN RIGHTS BEFORE THE SUBCOMMITTEE ON INTERNATIONAL ORGANIZATIONS AND MOVEMENTS OF THE HOUSE COMMITTEE ON FOREIGN AFFAIRS 715–22 (1973). *Also partly reprinted in* LILLICH AND NEWMAN, INTERNATIONAL HUMAN RIGHTS: PROBLEMS OF LAW AND POLICY 371–72 (Boston and Toronto: 1979).

3. *See* LILLICH AND NEWMAN, *supra* note 2, at 363.

4. *See supra* note 2.

5. *See,* for the basic differences between the two procedures, the report of the UN Secretary-General containing an analysis of coexisting UN procedures for dealing with communications concerning violations of human rights, UN Doc. E/CN.4/1317 (1979), in particular paras. 28–29.

6. UN Doc. E/CN.4/Sub.2/R.13. This written statement was formally submitted by the International Student Movement for the United Nations, Amnesty International, and the International League for the Rights of Man, under the rules governing the consultative status of NGOs with the ECOSOC and its sub-organs. The actual author is not mentioned on the document, but it is no secret that many NGO submissions of those days were written by Frank Newman. It should also be noted that this document was distributed by the UN Secretariat in the R (restricted) series, which meant that it was made available only to those having access to the confidential documents in connection with the 1503 procedure. A commentary in the Review of the International Commission of Jurists stated in this regard: "The almost obsessive concern for secrecy on this subject extends even to discussion of these procedural matters. . . . It is difficult to see why the publication of an NGO statement on a purely procedural matter should be treated as confidential. . . ." (Review of the International Commission of Jurists, Dec. 1974, at 31.)

7. UN Doc. E/CN.4/NGO/178. Statement written by Frank Newman and submitted by the International Student Movement for the United Nations, Amnesty International, International Commission of Jurists, and the International League for the Rights of Man.

8. *See* Marc J. Bossuyt, *The Development of Special Procedures of the United Nations Commission on Human Rights,* in 6 HUMAN RIGHTS LAW JOURNAL 179–210 (1985). An account of cases dealt with under the confidential 1503 procedure is given by Bossuyt on pp. 181–85.

9. *E.g.,* in The Times (London), articles appeared under the titles *UN Lethargy on Human Rights is Criticized* (21 Sept. 1973) and *Selective Silence on Human Rights* (27 Feb. 1975), *reprinted in* LILLICH AND NEWMAN, *supra* note 2, at 359–61 and 365–66.

10. THEO VAN BOVEN, PEOPLE MATTER, VIEWS ON INTERNATIONAL HUMAN RIGHTS POLICY 65 (Amsterdam: Meulenhoff Publishers, 1982).

11. Notorious in this regard was the position of Argentina during the period of the military dictatorship. *See in particular* the letter dated 8 Dec. 1980 from the Permanent Representative of Argentina in Geneva to the Chairman of the Working Group on Enforced or Involuntary Disappearances, in the First Report of the Working Group, UN Doc. E/CN.4/1435, Annex IX.

12. UN Doc. E/5412.

13. UN Doc. E/CN.4/NGO/177, submitted by the International Student Movement for the United Nations, Amnesty International, International Commission of Jurists, and the International League for the Rights of Man. It is

interesting to note that the arguments put forward by Newman vis-à-vis the Greek position were later also utilized against the reasoning of other governments. Thus, the special rapporteur on the situation of human rights to Chile wrote in his 1979 report to the UN General Assembly: "the procedure established under resolution 1503 of the Economic and Social Council is complementary to other pre-existing, or subsequent, procedures established by the United Nations. . . . The fact that the procedure established under resolution 1503 complements rather than superseded other procedures, is also borne out by the way in which the Chilean situation itself was handled in the past." (UN Doc. A/34/583, para. 11.)

14. It should not be overlooked that ECOSOC Resolution 1503 does not apply to matters taken up by the General Assembly. Therefore, the General Assembly was under no constraints of a confidentiality rule when it adopted on 6 Nov. 1974 its first resolution on the human rights situation in Chile (Res. 3219 (XXXIX)), which endorsed the recommendation made by the Sub-Commission that the Commission on Human Rights at its thirty-first session study the reported violations of human rights in Chile.

15. The text of this telegram is *reprinted in* LILLICH AND NEWMAN, *supra* note 2, at 293–94.

16. V. Kartashkin, *Human Rights and Peaceful Coexistence*, in 9 HUMAN RIGHTS JOURNAL 5, 14 (1976).

17. *See* more detail in Bossuyt, *supra* note 8.

18. In a written statement (UN Doc. E/NGO/14) to the 1974 spring session of ECOSOC submitted by the International Student Movement for the United Nations and the International League for the Rights of Man, Newman summarized and analyzed the action taken by the Commission on Human Rights as regards a Member State (Chile). He recalled in particular the sending of the telegram by the Commission and the reply of the government concerned. This reply stated *inter alia:* "the government cannot put an end to violations which it has not committed. . . ." (UN Doc. E/CN.4/1153.) Newman urged ECOSOC that a report be prepared setting forth the true facts.

19. *See also* Bossuyt, *supra* note 8, in particular at 194–99 where he deals with the "thematic" approach.

20. *See* AMERICA'S WATCH, ASIA WATCH, HELSINKI WATCH: FOUR FAILURES, A REPORT ON THE UN SPECIAL RAPPORTEURS ON HUMAN RIGHTS IN CHILE, GUATEMALA, IRAN AND POLAND (New York/Washington, D.C., January 1986).

APPENDIX: CITATIONS OF MAJOR INTERNATIONAL HUMAN RIGHTS INSTRUMENTS (IN CHRONOLOGICAL ORDER)

American Declaration of the Rights and Duties of Man, *signed* 2 May 1948, OAS Off. Rec. OEA/Ser.L/V/II.23, doc. 21, rev. 6

Convention on the Prevention and Punishment of the Crime of Genocide, *opened for signature* 9 Dec. 1948, *entered into force* 12 Jan. 1951, 78 U.N.T.S. 277

Universal Declaration of Human Rights, *signed* 10 Dec. 1948, GA Res. 217A (III), UN Doc. A/810, at 71 (1948)

Geneva Conventions of 1949: Geneva Convention for the Amelioration of the Condition of the Wounded and Sick in Armed Forces in the Field, *opened for signature* 12 Aug. 1949, *entered into force* 21 Oct. 1950, 75 U.N.T.S. 31; Geneva Convention for the Amelioration of the Condition of Wounded, Sick and Shipwrecked Members of Armed Forces at Sea, *opened for signature* 12 Aug. 1949, *entered into force* 21 Oct. 1950, 75

U.N.T.S. 85; Geneva Convention Relative to the Treatment of Prisoners of War, *opened for signature* 12 Aug. 1949, *entered into force* 21 Oct. 1950, 75 U.N.T.S. 135; Geneva Convention Relative to the Protection of Civilian Persons in Time of War, *opened for signature* 12 Aug. 1948, *entered into force* 21 Oct. 1950, 75 U.N.T.S. 287

Declaration on the Granting of Independence to Colonial Countries and Peoples, *adopted* 14 Dec. 1960, GA Res. 1514 (XV), 15 UN GAOR Supp. (No. 16) at 66, UN Doc. A/4684 (1960)

International Convention on the Elimination of All Forms of Racial Discrimination, *adopted* 21 Dec. 1965, *entered into force* 4 Jan. 1969, 660 U.N.T.S. 195

International Covenant on Economic, Social and Cultural Rights, *adopted* 16 Dec. 1966, *entered into force* 3 Jan. 1976, 999 U.N.T.S. 3 (1966)

International Covenant on Civil and Political Rights, *adopted* 16 Dec. 1966, *entered into force* 23 Mar. 1976, 999 U.N.T.S. 171 (1966)

International Convention on the Suppression and Punishment of the Crime of Apartheid, *adopted* 30 Nov. 1973, *entered into force* 18 July 1976, GA Res. 3068 (XXVIII), 28 UN GAOR Supp. (No. 30) at 166, UN Doc. A/9030 (1974)

Protocol II Additional to the Geneva Conventions of 12 Aug. 1949, and Relating to the Protection of Victims of Non-International Armed Conflicts *opened for signature* 12 Dec. 1977, *entered into force* 7 Dec. 1978, UN Doc. A/32/144 (1977), 16 INT'L LEGAL MATERIALS 1442 (1977)

Convention on the Elimination of All Forms of Discrimination Against Women, *adopted* 18 Dec. 1979, *entered into force* 3 Sept. 1981, GA Res. 34/180, 34 UN GAOR Supp. (No. 46) at 193, UN Doc. A/34/46 (1979)

European Convention for the Protection of Human Rights and Fundamental Freedoms, *signed* 4 Nov. 1940, *entered into force* 3 Sept. 1953, 312 U.N.T.S. 222

American Convention on Human Rights, *signed* 22 Nov. 1969, *entered into force* 18 July 1978, O.A.S.T.S. No. 36, at 1, OAS Off Rec. OEA/Ser.L/V/II.23, doc. 21, rev. 6

African Charter on Human and People's Rights, *adopted* 27 June 1981, OAU Doc. CAB/LEG/67/3 Rev. 5, *entered into force* 21 Oct. 1986

Convention against Torture and Other Cruel, Inhuman or Degrading Treatment or Punishment, *adopted* 10 Dec. 1984, *entered into force* 28 June 1987, GA Res. 39/46, 39 UN GAOR Supp. (No. 51) at 197, UN Doc. A/39/51 (1984)

CONTRIBUTORS

Kathryn J. Burke received her law degree from the University of California, Berkeley (Boalt Hall School of Law) in 1976. While in law school she worked as an intern at the International Commission of Jurists and as a research assistant to Frank Newman. She later worked as Newman's staff attorney when he actively served on the California Supreme Court. She has taught international human rights law to undergraduates and law students at several San Francisco Bay Area schools and currently works as the supervising research attorney for a California superior court.

Antonio Cassese is a professor of international law and relations at the University of Florence and the European University Institute. He formerly served as Director of the Post-Graduate Institute of International Affairs in Florence and as a visiting Fellow at All Souls College, Oxford. He has been a member of the Italian Government's delegation to various United Nations bodies including the General Assembly and the Commission on Human Rights, and he is currently Chairman of the Council of Europe Steering Committee for Human Rights.

Sandra Coliver, a lawyer in private practice, co-chairs the international human rights committees of the bar associations of San Francisco and California. She has taught courses on international law and human rights, authored several *amicus curiae* briefs on human rights issues, and represented Human Rights Advocates and other NGOs at the United Nations Commission on Human Rights and its Sub-Commission on Prevention of Discrimination and Protection of Minorities. She received her law degree from the University of California, Berkeley at a time when Frank Newman was an active member of the California Supreme Court but benefited from his teaching thereafter in the course of working with him on United Nations and other projects.

HURST HANNUM received his law degree from the University of California, Berkeley. Since 1980 he has been the Executive Director of the Procedural Aspects of International Law (PAIL) Institute in Washington, D.C. He has served as counsel in cases brought before the European and Inter-American Commissions on Human Rights and the United Nations and is author or editor of *Guide to International Human Rights Practice*, Philadelphia: University of Pennsylvania Press (1984); *Materials on International Human Rights and U.S. Constitutional Law*, Washington, D.C.: PAIL Institute (1985); and *The Right to Leave and Return in International Law and Practice*, Dordrecht, The Netherlands: Martinus Nijhoff Publishers (1987). The chapter in the present book is drawn from a larger study, funded by the Ford Foundation, on *Autonomy, Sovereignty, and Self-Determination: The Accommodation of Conflicting Rights*, which will be published in 1989.

ELLEN L. LUTZ is an attorney in private practice in Los Angeles, California. A graduate of Boalt Hall School of Law of the University of California, Berkeley, she is a former staff member of Amnesty International U.S.A. and has served as an NGO representative to the United Nations Human Rights Commission and its Sub-Commission on the Prevention of Discrimination and Protection of Minorities. She is a regular consultant to the American Civil Liberties Union of Southern California on cases involving international human rights issues and is presently co-authoring (with Glenn R. Randall) a book for health professionals on the treatment and documentation of traumatic human rights abuses.

NIGEL S. RODLEY is head of Amnesty International's Legal and Intergovernmental Organizations office in London and a part-time lecturer in law at the London School of Economics and Political Science. He has represented Amnesty International at the United Nations Commission on Human Rights and other United Nations and inter-governmental meetings since the mid-1970s, after Frank Newman blazed the trail of enhancing the contribution of NGOs in the promotion and protection of human rights under international law. He is the author of *The Treatment of Prisoners Under International Law* (Oxford: Clarendon Press 1987).

Stephen Rosenbaum received his law degree and his Masters of Public Policy from the University of California, Berkeley. He is an attorney with California Rural Legal Assistance, specializing in immigrants' rights litigation, and a Lecturer at Boalt Hall School of Law where he teaches a course on poverty law. While in law school he interned with UNESCO's Division of Human Rights and Peace, and shortly after graduation he coauthored an article (with Kathryn J. Burke, Sandra Coliver, and Connie de la Vega) on the domestic application of international human rights law. He is a former board member of Human Rights Advocates.

Dinah L. Shelton is a Professor of Law at the University of Santa Clara (California) and received her law degree from the University of California, Berkeley. On leave from her teaching responsibilities, she is currently Director of the Office of Staff Attorneys for the United States Court of Appeals for the Ninth Circuit. She sits on the Executive Council of the International Institute of Human Rights in Strasbourg, France, and is Chair-elect of the International Law Section of the American Association of Law Schools. She is the coauthor (with Thomas Buergenthal and Robert Norris) of *Protecting Human Rights in the Americas* (Kehl: N. P. Engel, Publisher, 1982), which won the Inter-American Bar Association's 1982 Book Prize.

Theo van Boven is a professor of international law at the University of Limburg, Maastricht (The Netherlands). He served as The Netherlands representative to the United Nations Commission on Human Rights from 1970 to 1975 and was a member of the United Nations Sub-Commission on Prevention of Discrimination and Protection of Minorities from 1975 to 1977. In 1977 he was appointed Director of the United Nations Division of Human Rights and served in that capacity until 1982. In 1987 he was again appointed to serve on the Sub-Commission. Active in a number of NGOs, he presently serves as Moderator of the Commission of the Churches on International Affairs of the World Council of Churches and as Chairman of International Alert.

Jon M. van Dyke teaches international and constitutional law at the William S. Richardson School of Law of the University of Hawaii and is Director of the University of Hawaii Institute for Peace. He earned his B.A. at Yale University in 1964 and his J.D. at Harvard Law School in 1967. Before joining the faculty at the University of Hawaii in 1976, he taught at Catholic University Law School in Washington, D.C. (1967–69) and the Hastings College of Law of the University of California in San Francisco (1971–76). He began his work on human rights in 1968 when, under the direction of Frank Newman, he participated in a summer seminar on international human rights at the University of California, Berkeley. He has written on issues related to the laws of armed conflict, is litigating a case against former Philippine President Ferdinand Marcos to collect damages for the torture and murder of Philippine citizens, and is now working on the Pacific Human Rights Charter described in his contribution to this volume.

David Weissbrodt is Professor of Law at the University of Minnesota, where he teaches a seminar on international human rights law and supervises law students in various clinical projects on human rights. He received his law degree from the University of California, Berkeley, and after graduation received a Robbins Fellowship from the University of California Law School for work at the International Commission of Jurists in Geneva. He has represented and/or served as an officer of a number of international nongovernmental human rights organizations, and is Legal Counsel of the Minnesota Lawyers International Human Rights Committee. His scholarship includes articles on the work of these human rights organizations, on human rights treaties, international fact finding, and international trial observers.

INDEX